This book is due on the last date stamped below.
Failure to return books on the date due may result
in assessment of overdue fees.

FINES	.50 per day	

American River College
4700 College Oak Drive
Sacramento, California 95841

D1019094

South of Tradition

Trudíer Harrís-Lopez

The University of Georgia Press

Athens and London

South of Tradition

Essays on African American Literature

© 2002 by the University of Georgia Press
Athens, Georgia 30602
All rights reserved
Designed by April Leidig-Higgins
Set in Monotype Garamond by Bookcomp, Inc.
Printed and bound by Thomson-Shore
The paper in this book meets the guidelines for
permanence and durability of the Committee on
Production Guidelines for Book Longevity of the
Council on Library Resources.

Printed in the United States of America
06 05 04 03 02   C   5   4   3   2   1

Library of Congress Cataloging-in-Publication Data

Harris-Lopez, Trudier.
South of tradition : essays on African American
literature / Trudier Harris-Lopez.
        p. cm.
    Includes bibliographical references and index.
ISBN 0-8203-2433-7 (hardcover : alk. paper)
1. American literature—African American authors—
History and criticism.   2. African Americans in literature.
3. Southern States—In literature.   4. Race in literature.
I. Title.
PS153.N5 .H295 2002
810.9'896073—dc21   2002006738

British Library Cataloging-in-Publication Data available

Contents

Preface vii

ONE • Humor in Alice Walker's *The Color Purple* 1

TWO • Slanting the Truth: Homosexuality, Manhood, and Race in James Baldwin's *Giovanni's Room* 18

THREE • New Invisible Man: Revisiting a Nightmare in the 1990s (Brent Wade's *Company Man* and Ralph Ellison's *Invisible Man*) 31

FOUR • Zapping the Editor, Or, How to Tell Censors to Kiss Off without Really Trying: Zora Neale Hurston's Fights with Authority Figures in *Dust Tracks on a Road* 51

FIVE • Architecture as Destiny? Women and Survival Strategies in Ann Petry's *The Street* 68

SIX • Chocklit Geography: Raymond Andrews's Mythical South 91

SEVEN • The Necessary Binding: Prison Experiences in Three August Wilson Plays 121

EIGHT • Hands beyond the Grave: Henry Dumas's Influence on Toni Morrison 140

NINE • Salting the Land but Not the Imagination: William Melvin Kelley's *A Different Drummer* 149

TEN • Transformations of the Land in Randall Kenan's "The Foundations of the Earth" 160

ELEVEN · Expectations Too Great: The Failure of Racial
Calling in Ralph Ellison's *Juneteenth* 175

TWELVE · Ugly Legacies of the Harlem Renaissance and
Earlier: *Soul Food* and New Negroes 196

· Index 217

Preface

Attempting to account for how one comes to a particular scholarly project is perhaps comparable to viewing one of Jackson Pollock's paintings. You know there is a pattern there, but it reveals itself only upon intense reflection. The twelve essays included in this volume were written—and rewritten—over a fourteen-year period. They reflect a range of my thoughts on African American literature and culture. In some cases, I was inspired to develop an idea about a work because I had recently read or reread it, as happened when I read Brent Wade's *Company Man* shortly after it was published in 1992. In other instances, a request for a presentation prompted me to think in the direction specified by the institution requesting the lecture, or in accordance with some particular conference theme; an invitation from the Schomburg Library to participate in its conference on James Baldwin in 1989, for example, led me to focus on *Giovanni's Room* (1953) because I suspected that it would be one of the less-covered works at the conference. In still other cases, as with Randall Kenan, an author or work nagged at me for months or years until I finally developed the critical commentary specifically for this volume. After allowing many of the essays to languish for years, as with "Humor in Alice Walker's *The Color Purple*" and "New Invisible Man," I revised them as appropriate and decided to bring them together with the newly written ones to shape this collection.

As I contemplate the essays presented here, I am ever aware of my position as a southern African American scholar of African American literature. Therefore, though the essays were not written originally with any deliberate thematic continuity in mind, they do have several points of connection among them; these include focus on the South and southern African American folk and cultural traditions, reconceptualizations of and transcendence of Christianity, questions of sexual and racial identity, and issues of racial justice. I designed several of the essays deliberately to treat authors and works that are less well studied, such as Raymond Andrews, William Melvin Kelley, and Brent Wade, or less well studied works by authors who are well known, such as *Dust Tracks on a Road* (1942), Zora Neale Hurston's autobiography.

In all of my scholarly endeavors, I seek an unusual approach to whatever author or work I happen to be contemplating. I am always looking for an approach that will spark the "I hadn't thought about that" response in my readers. I am also inspired by the little people, so to speak, in texts (perhaps that is a result of having been influenced by Alice Childress), the less glamorous characters and concerns on which readers would not linger immediately. For example, Min, one of the "little people" in Ann Petry's *The Street* (1946), inspired me to consider how architecture influences character in that text. I am also at times drawn to the iconoclastic, to the slightly outrageous interpretation of a particular text simply because I do not want to bore myself or my readers.

The results of these self-imposed challenges as reflected in this volume have evolved into what I call "south of tradition." I intend the phrase to refer to geography when it is appropriate, as is the case with Raymond Andrews's creation of his southern territory in Georgia, but more specifically to refer to readings of texts that are not in keeping with expected responses to the works. A slant, an angle, or a jolt just below the line of what would be considered the norm for usual responses to African American literary production is where I find my point of departure for most of the essays here.

I invite my readers to take a journey along one scholar's divergent pathway from the mainstream of interpretations of these authors and texts. My journey begins with Alice Walker's *The Color Purple* (1982), a text that has plagued me perhaps as much as it has plagued its creator. The intense critical response I offered to that text when it was published led me to challenge myself to find something less negative to say about the novel. In the tradition of the blues and from the vantage point of my position as a scholar of African American folklore, I went looking in the text for the humor that would make the pain more bearable. Where was it? Had I simply read over it? Was I too focused on the physical and psychological violence to realize that, as Zora Neale Hurston avows, no one can experience oppression twenty-four hours a day? There has to be some form of relief. In 1987, 1988, and 2001, I found that relief in quiet ways that are now contained in chapter 1, "Humor in Alice Walker's *The Color Purple*." That multiyear experiment made the novel much more tolerable for me, and I can even laugh out loud now when I read sections of Celie's narration.

I initially developed chapters 2 and 4, on James Baldwin and Zora Neale Hurston, in response to requests for participation in special conferences. I presented an earlier version of the Baldwin chapter at the Schomburg Library in June 1989. Promises of publication of conference presentations led me not to seek publication elsewhere. I returned to the essay in the fall of 2000 when I was invited to organize a panel on James Baldwin for the "Looking Back with Pleasure" conference held at the University of Utah. A fresh look at the work led to its inclusion here. Similarly, I initially developed the piece on Hurston in response to a request to present a keynote address at the annual Hurston Festival in Eatonville, Florida, in January 1994. It was such a fun piece to write and deliver, but for some reason, I let it languish as well after the conference. It has now "zapped" its way into this volume.

I was so struck by the echoes of Ralph Ellison's *Invisible Man* (1952) in Brent Wade's *Company Man* that that connection alone was enough for me to contemplate the novel further (chapter 3). I was also interested in it because it had been published by Algonquin Press, which is based in Chapel Hill and whose founder is Louis D. Rubin Jr., one of my retired colleagues in English at the University of North Carolina at Chapel Hill, and I was delighted to see that Algonquin had published the first novel of a young black male writer. The press's excellent reputation in having introduced writers of the reputation of Jill McCorkle was sufficient for me to consider *Company Man* somewhat of a gem. The tie to Ellison, one of my all-time favorite writers to teach, made it all the more attractive for some kind of scholarly development. I completed the work in 1992 and have since had the pleasure of introducing Wade's novel in many lectures I have given around the country.

Ann Petry, Raymond Andrews, William Melvin Kelley, August Wilson, and Randall Kenan are the writers who have nagged at me over the years. Every time I tried to get them out of my mind, they came back demanding that I say something about their works. Petry's Min stayed with me after I directed a student's dissertation on Ann Petry and discussed my interest with Hazel Arnett Ervin, who was busily establishing herself as an expert on Petry. Hazel and I exchanged scholarship on Petry, and she invited me to include the essay on architecture in a volume of essays on Petry that she was editing. I decided instead to hold on to it after drafting it in 1994, and it is now chapter 5 in this volume. I presented a version of the work as a keynote address at the A.E.D.E.A.N. conference held in Leon, Spain, in December 1999 (caught the worst flu in the history of flues on that trip).

Raymond Andrews (chapter 6) was more demanding than Petry. I could not let go of that world in Northeast Georgia that so captured his imagination. His works brought together my interest in African American folklore with my tale-telling background in Tuscaloosa, Alabama. The voices of Andrews's narrators and characters, and the big grin that I always imagined on his face as he created them, led me to return to his works year after year from the late 1980s forward. My interest was heightened by a lecture trip he made to UNC at Chapel Hill as well as through his participation on a panel at the annual convention in Columbia, South Carolina, in 1991, of the College Language Association, which I attend with religious fervor. His hold on me moved from demand to insistent dedication after Andrews committed suicide in 1991 and after I read his lengthy, neatly typed suicide note in the Special Collections Library at Emory University. So I wrote about Andrews for the Yale University conference in honor of Cleanth Brooks (May 1995), for the St. George Tucker Society (June 1995), and for the conference "African American Literature and the South" held at the University of Alabama, Tuscaloosa, in 1997. I am still not totally satisfied that I have done justice to Andrews's creative genius, and the engaging human interest story always remains, but I am content to let go of the tiger's tail.

I was led to develop chapter 9, on William Melvin Kelley, because of a folkloristic, legendary quality in his *A Different Drummer* (1962) comparable to that I had observed in the works of Raymond Andrews. I had also written on Douglas Turner Ward's *Day of Absence* (1966) and was generally intrigued by the domestic arena of black-white relationships in the South. "The African," Tucker Caliban's ancestor in *A Different Drummer,* shares with Appalachee Red in Andrews's novel the folk mystique that captures the imagination and lingers in it. That lingering quality, combined with the facts that I had written about Kelley's novel *dem* (1964) in my book on domestic workers, and that so few other scholars had commented on any of his works, led me to develop this short piece for presentation at the Agricultural History Society Conference held in Chapel Hill in 1997. Beyond what I have presented here, I am still fascinated by the narrative posture Kelley takes in *A Different Drummer.* An elderly white man, well respected by the community, is assigned the role of narrative guru. What are the implications of Kelley having made this choice? How can Tucker Caliban ever be free if the very narrative about him comes from the imagination of one of his forces of oppression? Perhaps I will have to return to Kelley on another occasion.

Of the writers who nagged me over the years, August Wilson and Randall Kenan were the most aggravating. I became interested in prison experiences in Wilson's plays (chapter 7) after I completed an essay for a collection on Wilson. Why did so many of Wilson's characters have a prison background, especially since they were mostly conspicuously rehabilitated? Was this simply a comment on American society during the periods in which the plays were set, or did it have something to do with black men's conceptions of themselves as men? Well, nag, nag, nag. Over the years, I would say to myself, "Write the essay." Then, in 1995, I actually created a file and wrote a couple of paragraphs. Then I ignored the nagging until 2001. Finally, here's the essay.

I admit it. I have a love affair with Randall Kenan's works. From the time I read "Clarence and the Dead" shortly after Kenan's short-story collection appeared in 1992, I became a lifelong Kenan groupie. My focus on "The Foundations of the Earth" in chapter 10 comes from a particular set of circumstances. When I was coediting the contemporary section of *The Literature of the American South: A Norton Anthology* (1998) with Minrose Gwin (now of the University of New Mexico), we each came up with lists of works we thought should be included. I listed "Clarence and the Dead" for the Kenan selection, perhaps because I had written on it and really liked it. Minrose convinced me that we should include "The Foundations of the Earth." It has more layers of teachability, she asserted, and the issues it raises are more compelling. So, I agreed to leave my folkloristic appreciation of a story well told in the supernatural vein and descend into the miry clay of sticky social issues. Since I had agreed to the inclusion of "The Foundations of the Earth," I wanted to explore its various layers. I therefore challenged myself to write on the story. At the American Literature Association convention in San Diego in May 1998, I managed to put together a few pages of text. I occasionally looked at those pages after then, read over what I had written, and returned them to their file folder. Then, in 2001, I was able to complete the challenge. I figured I owed it to Kenan as well as to myself.

As my friend Eugene Redmond edited and published various volumes of Henry Dumas's works, I became more and more intrigued by and engaged with Dumas's writings. I taught "Ark of Bones" repeatedly and directed an undergraduate student's honors thesis on the nature of heroism in Dumas's works. Learning that Dumas was from Sweet Home, Arkansas, and bringing that knowledge to bear upon Toni Morrison's *Beloved* (1987; one of my all-time favorite novels) and its famous plantation of the same name, led me to contemplate the connections between the writer shot to death before the full realization of his potential and the Nobel Prize–winning writer who also served as the dead writer's editor and advocate. Dumas therefore joined Toni Cade Bambara in providing some of the percolation for Morrison's tremendous creativity and success. I had the opportunity to comment on that possibility when I was invited to lecture at one of the conferences sponsored by the American Literature Association in Cancún, Mexico, in December 1996. I realize that my discussion of the connections between these two writers in chapter 8 is but the tip of the iceberg that other scholars might be inclined to excavate more fully.

It was a daunting task to contemplate criticizing Ralph Ellison, African American literary icon, but it had to be done. When I was invited to join a panel to discuss the novel with other scholars at the St. George Tucker Society conference held in Nashville in August 2000, I hesitated because I was not certain about what I would say. I had made several starts and stops at reading *Juneteenth* (1999), but I had not been able to bring myself to finish the novel. Nonetheless, I accepted the invitation and figured that I would come up with some approach later (at least I would be forced to read the book). Chapter 11 is where my evaluation of the text led me. It is not exactly a happy place to find oneself, but it is an honest place. Since that presentation, I have had countless conversations with other African American scholars about *Juneteenth;* many of them simply dismiss it. I decided to assign it in a graduate seminar on African American writers and their critics in the spring semester of 2001 to see what my very astute doctoral students would say. They generally thought that it did not work and that it probably would not have been published if it had not carried the name "Ralph Ellison."

While the Ellison essay sapped more energy than it inspired, chapter 12 on ugly legacies from the Harlem Renaissance was energizing. The project began in 1997 when I presented a shorter version of it as a keynote address at Paine College in Augusta, Georgia, in connection with a conference on the Harlem Renaissance. I expanded the section on *Soul Food* for presentation at the College Language Association convention in New Orleans in April 2001, then produced the version contained here. Circumstances surrounding this essay are as much social as they are scholarly. In May 2000, at the annual gathering of the Wintergreen Women (a group of African American women scholars primarily from North Carolina and Virginia), a few of us began commenting on how, as more senior scholars, we were more inclined these days to attend conferences and chair sessions instead of giving papers. I insisted that we organize a panel for the annual College Language Association convention and that we focus on the idea of soul food. We would discuss it in terms of culture, cuisine, and commerce. In a well-attended, raucous, at times hilarious session in New Orleans, at which there was standing room only, we regaled our audience with presentations and discussions in what will assuredly be remembered as one of the legendary moments of those gatherings. Inspired in its final stages by fun and sisterhood, therefore, this essay is important to me not only for its serious critical perspective and arguments, but also for what it documents in contemporary social and literary history.

Together, these essays are little parts of my mind that I am sending happily on their way. I hope that readers will find them engaging, at times provocative, and always informative. I am also hopeful that this volume will spark further treatment of some writers and works discussed here and simply contribute to ongoing conversations about others.

As is the case with any volume, many people helped me to bring this one to its final form. I extend my thanks to colleagues around the country and abroad who invited me to discuss various of these topics, including Allen Tullos and Walter Reed of Emory University; Howard Dodson of the Schomburg Library; N. Y. Nathiri, Executive Director of The Association to Preserve the Eatonville Community, Inc.; Sponsors of the Zora Neale Hurston Festival; Blyden Jackson, now deceased, who was Professor of English at the University of

North Carolina at Chapel Hill; Viralene J. Coleman of the University of Arkansas at Pine Bluff; Hazel Arnett Ervin of Morehouse College; Karla F. C. Holloway of Duke University and Kristine Yohe of Northern Kentucky University for their careful and insightful readings of chapter 3; Michael Kreyling of Vanderbilt University and Elizabeth Fox Genovese and Sally Wolff-King of Emory University for their inspiring readings of chapter 6; Julius Y. Nyang'oro of the University of North Carolina at Chapel Hill; Candace Wade, formerly of Yale University; Alfred Bendixen, who organized the conference on American Literature held in Cancún, Mexico, in December 1996; Peter Coclanis, Chair of the History Department at the University of North Carolina at Chapel Hill; Marva Stewart of Paine College, Augusta, Georgia; María Frías, now of the University at La Coruna, Spain; Carmen Flys of the University of Alcalá de Henares, Madrid, Spain; Peter Banner Haley, who organized the panel on *Juneteenth* for the annual meeting of the St. George Tucker Society in Nashville, Tennessee, in 2000; and Wilfred Samuels of the University of Utah.

Finally, I honor the memory of my mother, Unareed Harris (26 April 1914–8 January 2001).

South of Tradition

One

Humor in Alice Walker's
The Color Purple

 Repeated teachings of Alice Walker's *The Color Purple* (1982) require constant vigilance in terms of what one offers students. Each return to the novel invites reevaluations and reexaminations of themes, approaches, structure, or whatever else may be highlighted upon additional readings. After the rash of controversy surrounding the novel in the three or four years following its publication and after the depressing responses many of my students had to it, I decided that, whenever I taught the novel again, I would focus on whatever humor I could find in it. In classes I have taught since then, I have asked my students what, if anything, they found lighthearted or humorous about the book. One woman commented: "The voice of Celie is fresh and new to me—it delights me as if she's real, almost from the first word, and I think of her as a funny character. I don't mean haw-haw funny, but smiley funny. She certainly does not live through humorous situations, but her comments on them often are."[1] While I did not share that student's overall, blanket evaluation of the humor, I did become more attuned to the lighter moments in the novel.

Obviously it is fairly easy in reading *The Color Purple* to concentrate on the brutality and violation of the human spirit that Celie endures rather than upon what repeated readings make clear: abused though she is, Celie has an understated but striking sense of humor. It is frequently manifested in a carefully controlled playfulness of narration as well as in the usual incongruities in situations that we identify with humor. While the question of how anyone so abused can find the wherewithal to see anything funny in her life is a sticking one, Celie nevertheless manages rather well. In her ability to keep on keeping on, to laugh instead of crying, she lives in a state of blues transcendence.

The type of humor Celie relies upon is in keeping with her personality; it is quiet and sometimes subtle. It is the kind of humor that evokes smiles and light laughter rather than guffaws or belly laughs, and it is the kind that depends upon what readers bring to the novel; it is, in other words, a participatory humor in which readers are invited, as Toni Morrison would assert, to fill in various "holes" and "spaces" in the text by supplying some of the interpretive details. Our knowledge of how people usually act and react in various situations enables us to supply the missing links for some of Celie's abbreviated humorous references. For example, we have been socialized to believe that men beat their wives, not vice versa. When we learn that Harpo's reaction to his inability to beat his wife is a logic that tells him to gain weight as a solution to his dilemma, we recognize the absurdity of such an endeavor. It is comparable to that of an African American folktale, "The Knee-High Man," in which a man barely eighteen inches high eats and eats in an effort to squeeze into his itsy bitsy body the same muscle power as that of a horse or a bull. He converses with both to uncover the secret of their size, but his increased eating only gives him stomachaches. An owl finally points out to him that, instead of being bigger in the body, he needs to be bigger in the brain. So does Harpo.

In addition to recognizing the absurdity of Harpo's desire to beat a woman who has been a good wife to him and an excellent mother to his children, Celie relates the incident in such a way that Harpo's actions take on the features of slapstick comedy. What Celie allows us to fill in in the abbreviated narrative privileges us to Harpo's plight and involves us in Celie's evaluation of it. Her detachment, which is a part of what makes the humor work narrationally, derives less from lack of concern than from conscious understatement. When Harpo decides he needs to underscore his manhood by making Sofia "mind" him, he is advised to beat her. Celie writes:

> Next time us see Harpo his face a mess of bruises. His lip cut. One of his eyes shut like a fist. He walk stiff and say his teef ache.
>
> I say, What happen to you, Harpo?
>
> He say, Oh, me and that mule. She fractious, you know. She went crazy in the field the other day. By time I got her to head for home I was all banged up. Then when I got home, I walked smack dab into the crib door. Hit my eye and scratch my chin. Then when that storm come up last night I shet the window down on my hand.
>
> Well, I say, After all that, I don't spect you had a chance to see if you could make Sofia mind.
>
> Nome, he say.
>
> But he keep trying. (43)

The straight-faced response from Celie is a form of signifying in African American culture, a way of laughing just beneath the surface reality; she is playing "straight woman" to Harpo's absurd representation of his comedic situation. Signifying enables individuals in a verbal exchange to comment upon a situation indirectly, to poke fun at what both participants know to be the truth, but which neither wishes to refer to directly or openly. For example, a woman is married to a construction worker who usually wears blue denim and a hard hat to a job he works between seven in the morning and five in the afternoon. The wife knows that her husband is having an affair, but neither he nor she is willing to confront that issue directly, so when she sees him getting dressed in a suit and tie, preparing to go out at nine in the evening, she can say to him, "Well, I see you're working late at the office tonight." The indirection boldly but quietly asserts, "Yes, I know, and you know that I know even if we don't say anything about it."

The incremental repetition Celie recounts Harpo using to cover his injuries—from mule to crib door to window slamming—undercuts notions of manhood and further blurs gender roles in the novel. It is usually women who make up excuses about how they have acquired the bruises their husbands have given them. Unlike Harpo, they usually let one lie do the trick. The fact that Harpo piles story upon story to gain credibility only highlights how "unmanly" he is and makes his desire to control the "manly" Sofia even more absurd. The surface level of conversation between Celie and Harpo (signifying) covers over the actual cause of his bruises (fighting), while the bruises reveal the desire to have strict gender segregation (being a man) by forcing Sofia into a weaker, submissive role. Superficially, Celie accepts Harpo's story that, with all these "accidents," he has not had a chance to make Sofia "mind." His cryptic "Nome" is a face-saving conversation ender, because he does not want the unstated conversation to replace the superficial one. Celie's "But he keep trying" is the signal to her audience that she has not been fooled by all those "accidents" Harpo has endured; it also signals that she knows that the audience has not been fooled either. The last line is the clincher to the laughter between Celie and her audience, who are united against the absurdity, the "Little Moron" quality, of Harpo's situation and explanation. Even many years later, when Celie returns for Sofia's mother's funeral, she and Harpo still will not confront husband beating *directly*, although the topic is clear to all listeners: "How you, Harpo? I ast. Still eating? He and Sofia laugh" (196). The humorous indirection of signifying still controls the unspeakable situation.

Signifying provides one frame of reference from which readers and students can gain some sense of the humor in *The Color Purple*. The implausibility of Harpo's misfortunes forms the level of the unreality, and Celie responds to this fiction by playing the game by the rules Harpo has defined. Yet she improves upon it, intensifies it to its natural absurdity and ends up quietly laughing *at* rather than *with* Harpo. In this signifying performance, which has humor as its basis, both players may know the rules, but the one in the compromised situation is usually the butt of the joke. Celie's nonparticipation in the fight between Harpo and Sofia gives her the vantage point for exploding the fiction and providing the laughter.

Celie pokes fun at Harpo by couching his story of his bruising adventures in the form of a tall tale. Exaggeration is the usual standard in that medium. Here, Harpo describes himself as the victim of successive forces of nature—a mule and a storm—when the one force Celie knows is responsible for his condition—hurricane Sofia—is the one that he does not acknowledge. Thus Harpo's desire to subdue Sofia is just as unnatural as the set of circumstances he recounts.

The humor surrounding Harpo's attempted beatings of Sofia continues in Harpo's eating binges. The knowledge of his desire to control Sofia lies at the base of all Celie's comments on Harpo at this point, so that there is a text and a subtext to all their conversations. How the subtext informs the text provides the frame for the ongoing joke about Harpo. Celie writes:

He still skinny, bout half Sofia size, but I see a little pot beginning under his overalls.

What you got to eat, Miss Celie? he say, going straight to the warmer and a piece of fried chicken, then on to the safe for a slice of blackberry pie. He stand by the table and munch, munch. You got any sweet milk? he ast . . .

He rummage through the drawer for a spoon to eat the clabber with. He see a slice of cornbread on the shelf back of the stove, he grab it and crumble it into the glass.

Us go back out on the porch and he put his foots up on the railing. Eat his clabber and cornbread with the glass near bout to his nose. Remind me of a hog at the troth.

Food tasting like food to you these days huh, I say, listening to him chew.

He don't say nothing. Eat. . . .

No matter what happening now. No matter who come. No matter what they say or do, Harpo eat through it. Food on his mind morning, noon and night. His belly grow and grow, but the rest of him don't. He begin to look like he big.

When it due? us ast.

Harpo don't say nothing. Reach for another piece of pie. (63, 64)

In the midst of being beaten and constantly placed under the thumb of the men, Celie can find time to laugh at Harpo's ridiculous desire to overpower his wife physically. The catalog of food, the awareness of his rationale for eating, and the simulation of pregnancy all come together to reduce Harpo to an object of laughter. Celie's stylistic ordering of the information about Harpo, as in the repetition of "no matter," "food on his mind," and "his belly grow and grow," simulates delivery that we identify with oral jokes and stories, thereby cementing her in that tradition of verbal play as well. In her selection and delivery of detail, Celie becomes a kind of "woman of words," a traditional role much respected among storytellers in African American culture. She shapes and orders the material in the way that Mildred does in her accounts of her troubles with white employers in Alice Childress's *Like One of the Family: Conversations from a Domestic's Life* (1956), which suggests that Celie is aware of the tradition into which her humorous narration falls as well as of the effect it will have upon her audience. Admittedly, in this instance Celie joins in the larger community laughter against Harpo, but it is laughter nonetheless.

Celie is a subtle raconteur who knows how to order details and who understands the impact of narrative presentation upon a prospective audience. Those skills are a significant part of the humor in which she participates as well as the humor she delivers. Consider, for example, her description of a fight between Harpo and Sofia; it shows her light-hearted approach in the selection and presentation of details for the most dramatic effect. She approaches Harpo and Sofia's house and, upon hearing something crash, proceeds even more slowly:

I open the door cautious, thinking bout robbers and murderers. Horsethieves and hants. But it Harpo and Sofia. They fighting like two mens. Every piece of furniture they got is turned over. Every plate look like it broke. The looking glass hang crooked, the curtains torn. The bed look like the stuffing pulled out. They don't notice. They fight. He try to slap her. What he do that for? She reach down and grab a piece of stove wood and whack him cross the eyes. He punch her in the stomach, she double over groaning but come up with both hands lock right under his privates. He roll on the floor. He grab her dress tail and pull. She stand there in her slip. She never blink a eye. He jump up to put a hammer lock under her chin, she throw him over her back. He fall *bam* up gainst the stove.

I don't know how long this been going on. I don't know when they spect to conclude. I ease on back out, wave to the children by the creek, walk back on up home. (44)

The *rhythm* of Celie's narration and the details she presents make for the lightness in the passage. How, we might ask, could anyone truly concerned about another woman's—or man's—welfare stand by for so long to note and recount so much? Celie's style of relation is that of a camera's eye, roaming over the details of an encounter and recording them meticulously for those who were not privileged to witness the incident for themselves. Clearly, Celie knows that Sofia is in no danger, that the tone of this fighting is significantly different from Albert beating her. For the few minutes she stands gawking at the match, therefore, she is entertained and engaged. "What he do that for?" positions her as observer and evaluator, as knowledgeable commentator about the abilities of the two combatants, so that their little war looks more like a page out of southwestern humor than a life-threatening encounter. Her use of "conclude" to mark termination of the fight is a word less geared connotatively toward destruction as a finale than toward mere ending. Her waving to the children is especially important in putting the finishing touch on the lighter tone for the overall occurrence.

And it is her control of the narrative that provides the *pace* for the delivery of the fight sequence as well as the joke about Harpo's eating binges. In the joking situation, Celie builds up bruising and eating scenes until the pot-gutted Harpo stands before her looking more like a replica of a pregnant woman than a masculine conqueror of females; he mirrors the stereotype of what he seeks to destroy. The humor throughout the situation is apparent, but there is also a kind of *aftershock* in the telling of the tale. The point is made, but the added, secondary punch line ("When it due, us ast") emphasizes it even more.

The aftershock is apparent also in the scene in which Celie and Shug collaborate on the drawing of their dream house once they arrive in Memphis. They take turns in adding unbelievably unlivable features to the round, concrete house. Celie tells us:

> I sit down on the bed and start to draw a kind of wood skirt around her concrete house. You can sit on this, I say, when you get tired of being in the house.
>
> Yeah, she say, and let's put awning over it. She took the pencil and put the wood skirt in the shade.
>
> Flower boxes go here, she say, drawing some.
>
> And geraniums in them, I say, drawing some.
>
> And a few stone elephants right here, she say.
>
> And a turtle or two right here.
>
> And how us know you live here too? she ast.
>
> *Ducks!* I say.
>
> By the time us finish our house look like it can swim or fly. (189)

The Memphis setting is certainly more conducive to lighthearted banter; humor here emphasizes the escape/entertainment function it has served throughout the ages. Celie has escaped from horrible Albert, and she is with someone who values her and her creativity, even when that creativity takes strange leaps of imagination. It is clear that this sharing is more of a pastime to Shug and Celie than it is contemplation of a house that anyone would live in. Thus, when Celie adds the punch line, the effect again is of a secondary evaluation of what has already been said, a reiteration of the climactic point in an argument.

"By the time us finish our house look like it can swim or fly." The incongruity between present and future, dream and reality, concrete and flying makes the humor effective.

There is also humor in the innocent way in which Celie relates things that we know are devastating. The incongruity in this instance exists between our knowledge of human behavior in reaction to certain situations and Celie tossing them off as if they were inconsequential. For example, the exchange between Celie and Nettie about Albert's bestowing of compliments upon Nettie moves away from Albert's sinister intentions to the context of the usual girlish exchange when youngsters contemplate the men who are attracted to them. Celie blunts the constant danger by focusing on Nettie's transfer of Albert's compliments to her.

> That's a real pretty dress you got on, he say to Nettie.
>
> She say, Thank you.
>
> Them shoes look just right.
>
> She say, Thank you.
>
> Your skin. Your hair. Your teefs. Everyday it something else to make miration over.
>
> First she smile a little. Then she frown. Then she don't look no special way at all. She just stick close to me. She tell me, Your skin. Your hair, Your teefs. He try to give her a compliment, she pass it on to me. After while I git to feeling pretty cute. (26)

The more plausible reactions would be that Celie would become even more frightened of Albert or that she would become ecstatic that someone finds her attractive. The toned down, middle ground response enables her to blunt the sinister with humor while politely, modestly accepting the compliments. We smile at her reaction for its appropriateness to a difficult situation; it emphasizes that humor can serve as a potential survival strategy and again places Celie in the realm of blues transcendence. It is noteworthy as well that Celie describes her response to Nettie's compliments as making her feel "cute" rather than "beautiful" or "good looking"; "cute" is more in keeping with several comments she makes about her perceived—and what she believes to be—unattractiveness. "Cute" is a word that can apply to looks as well as to behavior. Celie's use of the word therefore becomes a flexible observation that does not deviate too drastically from where Celie has placed herself before her audience.

Celie also develops humor that illustrates the clash between expectation and outcome even as it depends primarily upon what readers bring to the text. When Miss Eleanor Jane brings her son, Reynolds Stanley Earl, for Sofia to marvel over him after Sofia is finally released from jail, Sofia short-circuits her expectations by denying the historical role into which Miss Eleanor Jane stereotypically slots her. In most southern situations, so this logic goes, African American women would just naturally croon over white babies. When Sofia refuses to do so, Miss Eleanor Jane simply will not accept Sofia's reaction; she works to transform her, to force her back into the role of loving black mammy.

Ain't little Reynolds sweet? say Miss Eleanor Jane, to Sofia. Daddy just love him, she say. Love having a grandchild name for him and look so much like him, too.

Sofia don't say nothing, stand there ironing some of Susie Q and Henrietta's clothes.

And so smart, say Eleanor Jane. Daddy say he never saw a smarter baby. Stanley Earl's mama say he smarter than Stanley Earl was when he was this age.

Sofia still don't say nothing.

Finally Eleanor Jane notice. And you know how some white-folks is, won't let well enough alone. If they want to bad enough, they gon harass a blessing from you if it kill.

Sofia mighty quiet this morning, Miss Eleanor Jane say, like she just talking to Reynolds Stanley. He stare back at her out of his big stuck open eyes.

Don't you think he sweet? she ast again.

He sure fat, say Sofia, turning over the dress she ironing.

And he sweet, too, say Miss Eleanor Jane.

Just as plump as he can be, say Sofia. And tall.

But he sweet, too, say Eleanor Jane. And he smart. She haul off and kiss him up side the head. He rub his head, say Yee.

Ain't he the smartest baby you ever saw? she ast Sofia.

He got a nice size head on him, say Sofia. You know some peoples place a lot of weight on head size. Not a whole lot of hair on it either. He gon be cool this summer, for sure. She fold the piece she iron and put it on a chair.

Just a sweet, smart, cute, *innocent* little baby boy, say Miss Eleanor Jane. Don't you just love him? she ast Sofia point blank. (232)

Tired of trying to be congenial in the face of such mental denseness, Sofia finally "sighs," breaks the façade, and tells Miss Eleanor Jane, point blank, that she does *not* love the child.

While the charade is going on, however, it is the clash between expectation and outcome that shapes the quietly humorous response to a white woman desperate for a black woman to love her child and the black woman effortlessly refusing to do so. Reader awareness of the role reversal at work also informs the humor; usually—and as represented at significant points in the novel—it is a black person who seeks a favor from a white person, not vice versa. If Miss Eleanor Jane is so complete and superior, why in the world does she need Sofia to name and approve the special qualities of her son?

While the clash between Sofia and Miss Eleanor Jane informs one part of the humor, another part is contained in Celie's narration. Again, her positioning of the actors in the drama—Sofia ironing and unconcerned, Miss Eleanor Jane insistent and pleading—sets the stage for something not exactly going right. Also, before she begins recounting the conversation between the two women, Celie remarks that Reynolds Stanley Earl is "a little fat white something without much hair, look like he headed for the Navy," which defies notions of cuteness; her use of "something" instead of "baby" similarly distances readers from the child and makes them more susceptible to laughter at the expense of him and his mother. Celie therefore prepares the way for Sofia to comment on the child's hair, and that reiteration brings smiles. Celie's comments on white people "harassing" blessings from other folks and the baby's "stuck open eyes" serve to layer the surface action between Miss Eleanor Jane and Sofia. Everything Miss Eleanor Jane remarks upon, therefore, is undergirded by Celie providing a black perspective, so to speak, for interpretation.

A slightly different kind of humor emerges when Celie returns from Memphis to Georgia and now has knowledge, such as smoking pot, into which she can initiate others. In a short period of transformation, therefore, Celie has become a version of the city slicker who must explain things to the country bumpkins. In these scenes, she is a more active conversationalist than at any earlier point in the book, which suggests that she is moving comfortably into the realm of storyteller reflected in the overall narration of the book. This relaxed manner—and the reefer—enhances her receptivity to humorous responses to situations.

Reefer, say Harpo. What kind of a thing is that?

Something make you feel good, I say. Something make you see visions. Something make your love come down. But if you smoke it too much it make you feebleminded. Confuse. Always need to clutch hold of somebody. Grady grow it in the backyard, I say.

I never heard of such a thing, say Sofia. It grow in the ground?

Like a weed, I say. Grady got half a acre if he got a row.

How big it git? ast Harpo.

Big, I say. Way up over my head. And bushy.

And what part they smoke?

The leaf, I say.

And they smoke up all that? he ast.

I laugh. Naw, he sell most of it.

You ever taste it? he ast.

Yeah, I say. He make it up in cigarettes, sell 'em for a dime. It rot your breath, I say, but yall want to try one?

Not if it make us crazy, say Sofia. It hard enough to get by without being a fool. . . .

Do I look like a fool? I ast. I smoke when I want to talk to God. I smoke when I want to make love. Lately I feel like me and God make love just fine anyhow. Whether I smoke reefer or not.

Miss Celie! say Sofia. Shock.

Girl, I'm bless, I say to Sofia. God know what I mean. (197)

If we wanted to write confidence into the formula for Celie's humor later in the novel, then that would certainly be a factor. No longer fettered by the chains of male domination, she can express herself creatively and even appear teasingly blasphemous. Her superiority in knowledge and expansiveness in freedom of attitude give her an edge over Harpo and Sofia; that edge, combined with their reactions, translates into humor.

Most of the humor derives from general human situations. Walker recognizes the fine line that one must walk if one would make exploitative or handicapping situations humorous. Interestingly, Whoopi Goldberg, who played Celie in the movie version of the novel, manages to walk that fine line in one of her comic routines about a handicapped woman. The result, however, is one that warrants silent appreciation for the comedian's talent, not even the smiles that are permissible in Celie's world. Those general human situations, therefore, such as eating or dreaming or accepting compliments, seep in through the cracks of the destructive physical and psychological violence in the novel. We can laugh at Harpo because we know that, in physical combat, he is no real threat to Sofia. Under no circumstances, however, are we allowed to laugh at Albert beating Celie, or at the treatment Sofia receives at the hands of the mayor and his wife. The lines of acceptability are drawn almost instinctively, and we respond to them in just that manner.

We respond to the humor and perhaps are willing to accept it in a novel that raises many questions about credibility because it is such a relief from the oppressive tone of the story. It gives us reason to pause and contemplate what manner of woman Celie really is if she can find light moments in the midst of such abusive oppression. Certainly tragedy has its need, its desire, for comic relief, but is there another way in which we can account for the few humorous tidbits in the novel and perhaps bring another dimension to the teaching of the book? One way would be to think of the blues paradigm, where the shortest definition of the genre is "laughing to keep from crying." Shug sings the blues, but Celie, like Pecola Breedlove in Toni Morrison's *The Bluest Eye* (1970), lives the blues: the stifling of human potential, the mistreatment by a male companion/lover, the need to travel on to better opportunities—these experiences are the essence of the blues. From this perspective, the tone of many scenes could move from pain to tolerance to lightheartedness. The ability to laugh becomes equivalent to the ability to sing: it provides cathartic release, as in Langston Hughes's poem "The Weary Blues." In the poem, the piano player's creative ability enables him to endure the pain of being alone. He moves from declaring "ain't got nobody but ma self" to asserting that he will put his troubles "on the shelf." Although the blues keep him from being satisfied and make him wish that he were dead, he moves finally to a triumphant posture. After his cathartic singing, he is able to sleep "like a rock or a man that's dead" (33–34). No matter how frequently there is contemplation of suicide or a wish for death in the blues, they are ultimately life affirming. The recognition of the state can put one on the road to recovery, and the singing is the path to exorcism of the pain. Singing the blues does not solve problems, but it *does* boost the spirit sufficiently to continue to deal with the problems.

Celie's ability to tell her tale is comparable to the piano player's playing and singing, and to Shug's ability to sing, so that one way of viewing the novel is to think of it as a blues composition in the tradition of Ralph Ellison's *Invisible Man* (1952), in which the narrator, *through the act of telling his tale,* comes to understand what he did to be so black and blue. In his essays on the novel, Ellison has asserted that there is much he finds funny about his unnamed narrator. For those of us less able to see or to appreciate some of that humor, the interpretation of the blues might help—the philosophy of singing from pain to transcendence, from trouble to lightheartedness. Celie seems to manage both in singing/narrating her state of the blues and arriving at a reflective, lighthearted transcendence of it. The voice that Celie acquires in relating her tale is perhaps her ultimate triumph over the destructive forces that dominate her life for so long. She acquires the power to make Harpo look ridiculous, and she acquires the power to humanize Albert.

Moments throughout the text indicate Celie's ability, even under the most trying circumstances, to forget her situation long enough to share in laughter, to transcend the pain. The heart-wrenching scene in which she sees her daughter in the grocery store with Corrine is one such instance. Although she would probably rather grab her child and run, she nonetheless controls herself long enough to laugh with Corrine about the "*horse*pitality" (24) they have shared sitting in the wagon together. Similarly, when Sofia confronts Celie about advising Harpo to beat her and suggests that Celie should bash Albert's head open rather than thinking of heaven (47), the two of them can laugh together about the men who have made their lives difficult. A similar scene occurs later when all the women, in their private lesbian knowledge, laugh at the ridiculous suggestion that a woman cannot get a man "if peoples talk" (182). There is also a bit of humor in the way Celie transcends public opinion in the defiant act of spitting in the glass of water she hands to Albert's father (59), as well as in her transcendence of the negative connotations of the lower-class countryness of her speech by asserting that "only a fool would want you to talk in a way that feel peculiar to your mind" (194).[2]

Another way to account for the humor is to think, as I suggest with Toni Morrison's *Song of Solomon* (1977), of the overall African American worldview, one that emphasizes the synthesis of seeming dichotomies, the most prominent of which is the secular and the sacred. For example, black people who sing the blues call on God in their blues verses. John D. Hooker in "Hobo Blues" asserts of one trip to hop a freight train: "My mother followed me that morning, she followed me down to the yard. She said, Lord, my son is going away from here. He's hoboing somewhere. Take care of my child, take care of him." And he moans during the verse in the manner of the best black church sister at a revival meeting. The parenthetical phrases in Langston Hughes's "The Weary Blues," such as "O Blues," and "Sweet Blues," might just as well be "O Lord" or "Lord Have Mercy." Black people who go to church on Sunday do not feel any crisis of faith when they consult root doctors on Monday or carry rabbits' feet throughout the week. Those who sing spirituals can draw their images from the Bible as well as from the cotton fields and the auction block.

If we posit, then, in the traditional split of good and evil, that violence and brutality are "secular" and that laughter is "religious," that people in prison can sing gospel and people in churches can be backbiters and murderers, then it is not farfetched to expect laughter somewhere in the midst of all the pain Celie experiences. It is ultimately that feature of her personality that sides with life and transcendence, that enables her to go to heaven with Shug instead of remaining in hell with Albert.

It is interesting to note in this duality that most of the laughter Celie experiences in the book is with other women—Sofia, Shug, Jerene, and Darlene. If the women have the so-called "religious" and preferable quality that the men lack, it is appropriate then that the synthesis between their goodness and the men's evilness be manifested in the personality of Albert, who has been the most "secular" of the secular. Such a duality makes it less possible for absolute evil to reign in the book, for despite the fact that Albert beats Celie, Shug loves him. Because we appreciate what Shug does for Celie, we can perhaps begin to believe that there is something about Albert that we have missed, for how could anyone as good as Shug love the man if he is totally a brute? Perhaps a rereading of the evidence of the text would suggest early on that, in spite of his actions, Albert had the potential to be saved. Perhaps.

It is also that duality in the African American worldview—the belief that humor can lie at the heart of pain—that enables us to try to find something salvageable in a novel where psychological and physical brutality could be soul destroying; it gives us the potential for hope in spite of pain and horror. It is that duality, finally, that might allow us to explain how Celie rises from abuse and violation to health and affirmation.

(1987, 1988, 2001)

Notes

1. Quoted from a student enrolled in my African American literature survey course in the spring of 1986.

2. Celie's act of spitting in Albert's glass aligns Celie with African Americans who used that method historically as one way of defying white control over them, or so the folk tradition would have us believe. She thereby positions Albert's father in the same oppressive role as blacks historically positioned white people.

Works Cited

Childress, Alice. *Like One of the Family . . . Conversations from a Domestic's Life.* 1956. Reprint, Boston: Beacon Press, 1986.

Hooker, John D. "Hobo Blues."

Hughes, Langston. *Selected Poems of Langston Hughes.* 1959. Reprint, New York: Vintage, 1974.

Walker, Alice. *The Color Purple.* 1982. Reprint, New York: Washington Square Press, 1983.

Two : Slanting the Truth

Homosexuality, Manhood,
and Race in James Baldwin's
Giovanni's Room

 In James Baldwin's fiction, homosexuality can be a quagmire or a haven. For some characters, participation in homosexual acts is the pathway to acquiring a copyright on manhood; for others, it is the road to losing that status forever. For these latter characters, homosexuality is the grand fiction they use to delude themselves about their sexual and racial identities, a clouded mirror up to which they hold some standard of themselves and find themselves wanting. Torn between what they are and what they believe they ought to be, these males lead lives devoid of sexual health and frequently devoid of emotional and mental health. Before they can truly love someone else, they must rid themselves of their illusions; failing that, they slip even further into illusion. For characters who attempt to rid themselves of illusions, such as David, the white protagonist in *Giovanni's Room* (1956), the process of extrication frequently involves tragic consequences. David not only loses Giovanni, but Giovanni is near execution before David is willing to accept how much he has loved him.

Giovanni's Room, Baldwin's so-called raceless novel, provides fascinating conditions under which to consider Baldwin's depiction of male homosexuality with sexual as well as racial overtones. In anticipation of many of the black and white male homosexuals in Baldwin's fiction, David wages a battle with himself about what it means to be less than a man if one indulges in homosexual activity. Like almost all of the male characters for whom Baldwin shows tolerance or borders upon respecting, David is bisexual, which, paradoxically, seems a prerequisite for those males who would truly attempt to control their destinies as men. Such males are distinct from the cross-dressing, excessively foppish men Baldwin judges to be "fairies" throughout his fiction. Yet they seem to use bisexuality as the last refuge from the image they cannot accept of themselves, that is, as men who love men.

David's image of homosexuality as the "black cavern" of human existence could serve as a metaphor for the experiences of some of the other homosexual and/or bisexual men in Baldwin's fiction. I think particularly of Hall Montana in *Just above My Head* (1979) and his attempts to convince himself that his homosexual activities should be placed in a realm of existence outside his "normal" life, that he is superior to the men with whom he copulates. With few exceptions—perhaps Eric in *Another Country* (1962) is the healthiest one and Arthur Montana in his early, rather romanticized relationship in *Just above My Head* is the most naïve one—men who love men in Baldwin's fictional worlds are simultaneously embracing and rejecting of those relationships. Although they may find their most satisfying sexual encounters with men, they nonetheless conclude that homosexuality is a pit into which they have fallen and from which they may spend perhaps a lifetime extricating themselves. Almost invariably, they question their self-concepts, their sense of themselves as men. Consider, for instance, the occasion on which the youthful David and his friend Joey discover their affection for each other. In the pattern that Baldwin establishes throughout his fiction, the pleasure of sexual encounter gives way to the fear and shame of postcoital reflection. Tenderness descends into a black hole, for that color imagery is relevant here:

> *But Joey is a boy.* I saw suddenly the power in his thighs, in his arms, and in his loosely curled fists. The power and the promise and

the mystery of that body made me suddenly afraid. That body suddenly seemed the black opening of a cavern in which I would be tortured till madness came, in which I would lose my manhood. . . . A cavern opened in my mind, black, full of rumor, suggestion, of half-heard, half-forgotten, half-understood stories, full of dirty words. I thought I saw my future in that cavern. I was afraid. I could have cried, cried for shame and terror, cried for not understanding how this could have happened to me, how this could have happened *in* me. And I made my decision. I got out of bed and took a shower and was dressed and had breakfast ready when Joey woke up. (15; Baldwin's emphasis)

David's decision is to deny what he has just considered one of the most fulfilling experiences of his young life, a denial that leads him to antisocial behavior toward Joey. Joey becomes the living mirror of what David cannot accept in himself; consequently, he picks up with a "rougher, older" crowd and becomes very "nasty" to Joey. In his attempt to escape from the black cavern of unacceptability and lack of manliness, David begins a journey of self-hatred not unlike that Rufus Scott undergoes in *Another Country*. Both journeys involve meanness to those who care about them as well as meanness to their own spirits in their psychologically warping refusals to accept their own sexual reality.

Like Rufus, David, significantly nicknamed "Butch" for his football exploits, dreams a world in which his manhood—whatever that means—will not be challenged. He asserts at one point in his relationship with Giovanni: "I wanted to be inside again, with the light and safety, with my manhood unquestioned, watching my woman put my children to bed . . . it had almost been so once. I could make it so again, I could make it real" (137, 138). To contemplate situations in which his manhood could possibly be questioned is to envision himself as an outsider, a displaced person not unlike the "fairies" he will later despise for their desperate attempts to seek liaisons on the streets and in the cafés of Paris.

Although David labels his encounter with Joey as somewhat of an accident, he nonetheless finds other occasions before Giovanni to engage in homosexual activity. His response to such actions is consistently to minimize their meaning and to absolve himself of complicity by attempting to maintain his image of purity. His running away from himself is depicted geographically in his tour of military duty and psychologically in his refusal to see himself. He values "constant motion," but

> Even constant motion, of course, does not prevent [an] occasional mysterious drag, a drop, like an airplane hitting an air pocket. And there were a number of those, all drunken, all sordid, one very frightening such drop while I was in the Army which involved a fairy who was later court-martialed out. The panic his punishment caused in me was as close as I ever came to facing in myself the terrors I sometimes saw clouding another man's eyes. (31)

Despite his efforts to have us believe otherwise, David's "drops" on the vertical hierarchy of morality are really the substance of his life, not all the protected, sober spaces in between. Alcohol becomes a liberating narcotic for him, one that allows him to wallow in the quagmire, just as Sonny's use of heroin presumably increases his ability to play the piano in Baldwin's "Sonny's Blues." And when David is drunk, he reveals his true self. On one occasion in Paris, he "had been accused of causing a minor sensation by flirting with a soldier" (39). He avoids the bar in which the incident occurred and asserts that the patrons have been blind and the reports false: "My memory of that night was, happily, very dim, and I took the attitude that no matter how drunk I may have been, I could not possibly have done such a thing" (39). Self-delusion is the complement to the stripping away of subconscious inhibitions under the influence of alcohol.

Even when David knows that Hella, his girlfriend, is returning from Spain and that her return will cause a change in his relationship with Giovanni, he still tries to convince himself that his affair with a male is a one-time thing: "it would be something that had happened

to me once" (125). David believes that language and the presence
of women can change the reality of his sexual preference. Because
he excuses and denies rather than confronts his attraction to men,
the reality of that attraction—from his perspective—does not exist.
His lapses all can be explained in terms of alcohol or other external
circumstances; nothing must mar his image of himself.

To David, his extended affair with Giovanni is another one of those
"drops," or drunken lapses, that he can place safely back in the cavern
of his mind when necessary in the assertion of "pure" manhood. Indeed, Giovanni's room becomes an objective correlative for the cavern David has envisioned as his future if he had remained attached to
Joey or made some comparable attachment. His months with Giovanni provide the final escape into a blacker blackness that contains
the capacity not only to degrade, but also to purify. Giovanni's room
is the prison house of David's sexuality as well as the true reflection
of what he is: a man who loves men but cannot afford, for the sake
of his fragile masculine ego and his familial, societal ties, to admit
that truth.

Two small windows smeared over with white cleaning polish, air-
less, a smoldering enclosure for the funkiness of passion, Giovanni's
room is the mirror image of David's mind. It is a place where reality
can be shaped to suit the imagination ordering the chaos. The door
to the room is comparable to the window of language that David
uses to shut himself off from who he is. Once he and Giovanni close
the door on that dank, dark little enclosure, they join the many face-
less tourists strolling the streets of Paris. The interior/exterior of the
room compares favorably to the interior/exterior of David's mind;
he can shut away his troubling thoughts and emerge in the eyes of
Hella and the world as a clean, upright citizen with all the potential
of an American youth shaping his destiny in Europe.

David can name the room for what it is only after his manhood has
been sufficiently restored through sexual encounters with Hella. With
her, he refers to the room as "so stinking and dirty" (179); the disorder
Giovanni has created is a matter of "punishment and grief." Littered

with leather and cardboard boxes, "yellowing newspapers and empty bottles," and rotting food, the room becomes "frightening" to David. His observations of it extend his ambivalence about his sexual identity, as well as about morality and judgment:

> And I stared at the room with the same, nervous, calculating extension of the intelligence and of all one's forces which occurs when gauging a mortal and unavoidable danger: at the silent walls of the room with its distant, archaic lovers trapped in an interminable rose garden, and the staring windows, staring like two great eyes of ice and fire, and the ceiling which lowered like those clouds out of which fiends have sometimes spoken and which obscured but failed to soften its malevolence behind the yellow light which hung like a diseased and undefinable sex in its center. (115)

The images evoke the Garden of Eden gone sour, with the eye of God passing judgment and His mouth waiting to spew forth fire and brimstone upon sinners who dare to lurk overly long in the yellow glare of sex instead of escaping into the pure light of traditional manhood and acceptability. Yet in this confining, physically unattractive space, David spends what he will later realize are some of the happiest moments of his life.

Nonetheless, he tries to order the chaos of the room in the same way that he tries to transform his mental images of himself. He spends days while Giovanni is at work cleaning, straightening, and tossing the trash out of Giovanni's room, perhaps as Giovanni's wife back in Italy had done before the death of their child drove Giovanni out of the marriage. David can excuse the traditionally feminine role he plays by asserting that he "invents" in himself "a kind of pleasure in playing the housewife" (116).

David's ambivalence about that role—he ultimately concludes that "men never can be housewives"—is yet another mirror image of his ambivalence about his sexual encounters with Giovanni. He deludes himself into thinking that the giving of his body to men is somehow separable from the essence of himself. When Giovanni touches

David intimately, David sometime concludes that "it doesn't matter, it is only the body, it will soon be over" (116–17). This voluntary submission to displeasurable pleasure is a willed intrusion into other people's lives, one that David effects again and again. His assumed innocence is precisely his guilt, for he has neither the strength of will nor the desire to remove himself from the circumstances he superficially judges to be distasteful; the concomitant pleasure is exactly what he craves.

As Giovanni asserts on various occasions, David's lack of commitment to any human being is precisely his failing; it makes him a despicable user of everyone he encounters in the novel, male and female. And his lack of commitment to a sexual identity, especially the predominant homosexual one, ties David most closely to his American heritage and to the racial environment that informs that heritage.

Scholars have repeatedly made the obvious observation about *Giovanni's Room:* there are no black characters in the novel. And they have used this absence to conclude that the novel is raceless, thereby erroneously assuming that race is relevant and can be discussed only if black folks provide the primary focus. However, David's race, his whiteness, is at the center of the book, and I would argue that what is absent from the text—that is, blackness—is what he most fears.[1] His American heritage has taught him that the outsiders in his environment are black people. They are the ones to be despised; they are the ones to whom any white individual is unquestionably superior. As long as black people exist in their historical relation to white people in the United States, there can be no inferiority for white people. Black people are dirty and filthy, in addition to being black, which are the descriptions that Rufus Scott similarly applies to himself when he is wandering the streets just before his suicide.

In describing despicable actions, therefore, David, without specific references to black people, or any encounters with them, uses the terminology of the cultural myths attached to them to define what he envisions as being outside, filthy, and dirty if he were to give in to his homosexual proclivities. In a perversion of Charles Chesnutt's "Mars

Jeems's Nightmare," to be openly homosexual is, in David's mind, the ultimate transformation into the despised Other. In Chesnutt's story, an insensitive slaveholder is transformed into an enslaved person and forced to experience the punishment he usually dishes out to people of African descent.

The images David uses repeatedly are ones of darkness, blackness, dirt, and filth to convey his repulsion for the part of himself that gives in to homosexual activities and to the possibility of becoming the despised "nigger" in the minds of his family and friends. As the white master, however, he can place any of a number of other "niggers" into that role. Joey, his first lover, is probably Italian[2]—darker in color than the Anglicized wasp and certainly on a lower scale of social acceptability in the American society; David observes that he lives in a "better neighborhood" (11) than Joey does. It is easy, therefore, for David to join the mob of disapproval in being nasty to Joey after he has used Joey sexually. It brings to mind those white southern belles who lusted after black men and then yelled rape once the relationship was consummated.

David's psychological calisthenics in placing others in that "black cavern" he associates with homosexuality are another scapegoating ritual of transference: he ascribes what he considers slime and filth onto someone else, just as the "pure," socially elite white men of Ralph Ellison's *Invisible Man* (1952) ascribe lust to the black boys during the battle royal scene in that novel. David has the cultural imperative to be superior, and he has the skills of scapegoating from his culture to escape the pit he has created for others.

Those relegated to the black cavern of pariah status cannot control their destinies, therefore David resolves to control his at all costs; he sacrifices Giovanni without ultimate regret. Sure, he can spend an evening reflecting upon his relationship with Giovanni, and we can perhaps be drawn into sympathy with his feelings of guilt and seeming growth, but David, in the final analysis, places Giovanni in the realm of another of those episodes, those "drops," that he has successfully maneuvered his way through. David's culture has carefully outlined the parameters of his manhood; thus, there can be no equivocation about how he, a clean-cut, blond, former football star, should behave.

He is the master; others exist for his pleasure. The pattern David establishes with Joey becomes his modus operandi—he uses his male lovers and deserts them. Later, he adds a culturally based power/subjugation dimension to his relationships. Consider his interactions with Jacques, the older homosexual in Paris. David is aware that Jacques finds him attractive; he therefore uses that attraction to his own advantage. The interchange is no longer about feelings, but power. Feelings simply place Jacques in the position of the outsider, the one who can be used and manipulated by David, who does exactly that to acquire from Jacques some of the necessities of life, such as money. David becomes a coquette in teasingly accepting the money without granting the sexual favor, the kind of manipulation that characterizes many of his intimate exchanges.

He is willing to live with Giovanni as long as Hella is in Spain, willing to invent pleasure in being a "housewife," because there is no one around whose opinion is substantial enough to damage his image of himself; he views himself as infinitely superior to the other streetwalkers/bar prowlers. The power/subjugation may be subtle in David's relationship with Giovanni, but it is there nonetheless. In the classic pattern of the powerful subsisting on the powerless, David lives by the fruit of Giovanni's labors. Since David had been put out of his room, he can overlook the squalor of Giovanni's place, for, from this practical perspective, it is not that important. It is a place to stay, and love-struck Giovanni is only too happy to please his lord and master. David later observes of Giovanni: "he's got this *thing* about me, he thinks I'm God" (179; Baldwin's emphasis). By contrast, when Giovanni loses his job, it is not "convenient" for David to ask his father for money to assist them. He is playing house, playing with Giovanni's life, having a tryst, whereas Giovanni is clearly, seriously committed to the relationship; indeed, his very life does depend upon it.

For David, Giovanni becomes another of the outsiders who can be used sexually and discarded, not unlike the sheriff in Baldwin's

"Going to Meet the Man" who casually traipses over to the black side of town for that little spice of sexual adventure that making love with his wife will not provide. The master/slave, power/subjugation analogy is vivid in the final scene between David and Giovanni. Giovanni is pleading for his life and David's maturity; David is merely inconvenienced. He wants desperately to get away from the outburst of emotion that is so antithetical to those who control, rather than get controlled by, the situations in which they are involved.

Giovanni becomes, then, the black cavern, the "nigger" side of town, life on the other side of the tracks. He is just one of the many other outsiders, outcasts, displaced, despised persons roaming the streets of Paris whose destiny, like that of many blacks in the United States, could be so easily controlled by others. For David, whose manhood is equivalent to his superiority, which is equivalent to his Americanness, which is equivalent to his whiteness, life with Giovanni can exist only as one of those excusable "drops" into which men sometimes rather innocently fall, comparable to the last promiscuous sexual fling before one settles down to marriage and a family.

Leslie A. Fiedler suggests that Baldwin made David "a shade *too* pale-face, almost ladies-magazine-Saxon, gleaming blond" (147). I would maintain that he made him just blond enough for the cultural imperatives driving him to work themselves out in black and white, both literally and figuratively. It is the very exaggeration of whiteness that gives David his power, his sense of the absence of limitations on what he can do to others. In his whiteness is the center of his manhood, and that whiteness is the source of its perversity.

The dishonesty and deviousness David employs to protect his so-called manhood only reveal that status as a seriously flawed construct. Real men, if we would adhere to David's definition, use people with impunity. They are by nature exploitative and duplicitous; they particularly exploit and dehumanize women. A comparison of David's sexual conquest of Sue, a sometimes friend of his in Paris, and his timidity with Giovanni is striking. With Giovanni, he is initially coquettish and pretends that seduction is not the object of the game they are playing. With Sue, he assumes the role of the man-in-charge and quickly reduces her to the female organ that will give him practice for Hella's return; he does not respect her as human being or as woman.

To be a man, David asserts, entails possession of woman. He wants "his" woman in place, much as Hall Montana in *Just above My Head* compares himself to a lion with his lioness and cubs visibly present and dependent upon him. Like many of Baldwin's male characters, David deludes himself into thinking that women can uncover and understand their true selves only with the aid of men. With man as guide, woman can achieve whatever potential her man's warped notion of that status allows.

David's definition of manhood is also flawed from the standpoint of his treatment of other men. He is similarly dishonest with and uses them. He, like most of Baldwin's male homosexuals, is not only chauvinistic, but also homophobic. They hate the men who are the most striking examples of men who love men. That hatred becomes a way, indeed a reminder, for them to retain control of themselves or they will similarly be despised by others.

Manhood, then, is a notion much discussed and sought after in Baldwin's fiction, but seldom if ever achieved. Yet Baldwin manages to incorporate and adhere to many stereotypes of what men should be. Such stereotyping is perhaps in itself surprising. But what is infinitely more surprising is Baldwin's adherence to stereotypical conceptions of color in his novel. That a black novelist in the mid-1950s would accept the prevailing negative characteristics of blackness is not only noteworthy, but also potentially indicting. Baldwin had used images of dirt and dust to suggest a sinful state in *Go Tell It on the Mountain* (1953), but blackness had not been cast in the same role. In *Giovanni's Room,* blackness takes on all the traditional stereotypical connotations of ugliness and repulsiveness that have been historically attached to it on American soil. Blackness represents sin, guilt, and the potential for rejection in the novel, and no matter how desperately we want to read irony into David's portrait of himself and who and what he thinks he is, we cannot escape Baldwin's manipulation of that color imagery. Still, perhaps in Baldwin's sustained attempts to escape from the United States, from the threats to his own manhood, that symbolism is perversely appropriate. Perhaps, as he wrote about David, he was exorcising his own self-hatred, his own notion that somehow blackness was responsible for its own persecution.

With this tangled web of exploitation and uncertainty of identity, and with the negative use of blackness, it is surprising that some scholars have tried to read *Giovanni's Room* as a "coming out" narrative. Those who do so must gloss over much ugliness to arrive at that point. Not only is David unable to accept his sexual identity throughout the narrative, but also there is no affirming evidence to suggest that there has been any significant change in his attitude or behavior by the end of the narrative. His voice is still somehow above it all, and the potential remains that the memory of Giovanni's death will be readily erased with another of those attractive drops into exploitative homosexual activity. Baldwin tries to write David out of the corner in which he has placed him by adopting the images of salvation from the black churches in which Baldwin grew up, which makes them grossly inconsistent with David's cultural heritage as well as with his earlier conception of himself. In this incongruity of cultural representation, in this final way in which blackness enters the novel, David appropriates and exploits yet again. Neither he nor Baldwin encourages a healthy outlook for David's future as a heterosexual, homosexual, or bisexual human being who is confident in that identity and who is willing to accept the consequences of that choice.

(1989, 2000)

Notes

1. Toni Morrison has published commentary on colorphobia and stereotypes that pervade American literary texts when black characters are not present or when they are minimally so. See *Playing in the Dark: Whiteness and the Literary Imagination*. Authors Morrison treats in detail, however, are all white.

2. I hold this view in contrast to John S. Lash, who inexplicably asserts that Joey is "a Negro boy"; however, given the context in which I am reading the novel, that explanation might be perfectly logical.

Works Cited

Baldwin, James. *Giovanni's Room.* 1956. Reprint, New York: Laurel, 1980.

Chesnutt, Charles W. "Mars Jeems's Nightmare." In *The Conjure Woman.* 1899. Reprint, Ann Arbor: University of Michigan Press, 1969, 64–102.

Fiedler, Leslie A. "A Homosexual Dilemma." In *Critical Essays on James Baldwin,* ed. Fred L. Standley and Nancy V. Burt, 146–49. Boston: G. K. Hall, 1988.

Lash, John S. "Baldwin beside Himself: A Study in Modern Phallicism." In *James Baldwin: A Critical Evaluation,* ed. Therman B. O'Daniel, 47–55. Washington, D.C.: Howard University Press, 1981.

Morrison, Toni. *Playing in the Dark: Whiteness and the Literary Imagination.* Cambridge: Harvard University Press, 1992.

Three

New Invisible Man

Revisiting a Nightmare in the 1990s
(Brent Wade's *Company Man* and
Ralph Ellison's *Invisible Man*)

 In the 1990s, African American writers broke down more and more barriers to their creativity. This was especially true of depictions of insanity and homosexuality, against which there seemed to have been particular taboos historically. *Company Man* (1992), by Brent Wade, with its dual focus on mental instability and sexual "perversion," is a striking example of this trend. Responding to Ralph Ellison's *Invisible Man* (1952) and many other works that have deemed certain characters and themes to be taboo, Wade's novel stands in bas relief against a tradition of repression in African American literature. A brief review of that constricting literary history, and portraits of male and female characters who were so restricted, will illuminate the significance of the dialogue *Company Man* carries on with *Invisible Man*. Wade highlights—or at least sheds substantially different light on—what Ellison and other writers repress.

African American literature can be read as the study of censorship imposed from within the group in response to forces from without. Historically, there were certain unspoken taboos for black writers concerning which topics were appropriate for coverage and which were untouchable. In regard to black female characters, those taboos fit into several easily definable categories. First of all, black women in the literature were expected to have the shelter of the church, and they in turn were to work for the salvation of their sometimes heathen husbands. One epitome of the representation is Ellison's Mary Rambo; others are Baldwin's Elizabeth Grimes in *Go Tell It on the Mountain* (1953) and Lorraine Hansberry's Mama Lena Younger in *A Raisin in the Sun* (1959). By 1970, when Toni Morrison portrayed Pauline Breedlove in *The Bluest Eye*, the type had begun to fray. The general tenet of composition, however, was that long-suffering and self-sacrificing in the manner of Christ defined a role for black women (subservient to God, men, their children) that kept them "knuckled under" and safe. The alternative was to become scarlet women, like some of those lost souls in Jean Toomer's *Cane* (1923) and like the archetypal Esther, also in Baldwin's *Go Tell It on the Mountain.*

The year 1970 serves as a before-and-after dividing line for other sanctioned depictions of black female characters as well as for black male characters. Prior to 1970, black girls/women could not go crazy—whatever happened, they had to manage as best they could. Helga Crane (Nella Larsen, *Quicksand,* 1928) can think only of church, marriage, and children as alternatives to her identity crisis; she cannot conveniently slip into insanity. Lutie Johnson (Ann Petry, *The Street,* 1946) can go into a fit of murderous rage in response to her sexual exploitation, but insanity is not available to her as a permanent escape from her problems; she must return to contemplate her killing of Boots Smith and take moral if not civil responsibility for it. Kate Trueblood and her daughter Matty Lou, both impregnated by their husband/father in Ralph Ellison's *Invisible Man,* can have only prayer as consolation during their pregnancies; they cannot have abortions or be carted away to the local insane asylum. And even those black men institutionalized in Ellison's famous Golden Day are not insane.

With the arrival of Pecola Breedlove on the literary scene in Toni Morrison's *The Bluest Eye,* insanity becomes not only a viable, but also an acceptable option for a black female character. By 1973, Alice Walker could make Myrna in "Really, Doesn't Crime Pay?" a character who cultivated her nervous breakdowns. Prior to this point, the appellation "crazy nigger" almost never applied to black women.

Black men could fit the role, but it usually defined action against the grain of societal norms, not mental deterioration. For example, Bigger Thomas in Richard Wright's *Native Son* (1940) is a "crazy nigger," but he is not insane.

The injunctions against portrayals of certain types of characters continued in the unwritten rule that black women could not abandon their children and could not have abortions. Morrison again exploded that injunction with Cholly Breedlove's mother and father (*The Bluest Eye*), as well as with Eva Peace (*Sula,* 1974). Alice Walker made abortion an option in *Meridian* (1976) and *You Can't Keep a Good Woman Down* (1981), and Paule Marshall continued the trend in *Daughters* (1991).

The injunctions against depictions of male and female homosexuality have before-and-after 1970 manifestations as well. Certainly Baldwin's *Giovanni's Room* (1956) is a novel dealing with homosexuality, as is his *Another Country* (1962). However, the relationships depicted in the first novel are between nonblack males, and those foregrounded in the second are among Frenchmen, southern white males, and northern white males. It is only after his death that we are told that black Rufus Scott experimented briefly in a homosexual act with one of the white characters. That event, in contrast to his violent seduction of Leona near the beginning of the novel, is not dramatized in the text.

Restrictions on lesbianism have been especially intense. It was only in 1974 that Ann Allen Shockley published *Loving Her,* a novel depicting a relationship between black and white lesbians. She followed that with *Say Jesus and Come to Me* (1982), about a black woman preacher who capitalizes on the authority of her pulpit by seducing "sweet young things" (female) in her congregation until she enters a more viable relationship. While Shockley's works might have experienced an underground popularity, Walker's *The Color Purple* (1982) waded through the storm of public disagreement and made lesbianism a central focus of African American literature. It has been more acceptable, therefore, for writers after Walker not only to portray lesbianism, but also to portray close friendships between women without lesbian overtones. While Nella Larsen's *Passing* (1929) has been the subject of speculation about a possible lesbian relationship between Irene and Clare, as has Morrison's *Sula* with Nel and Sula (which is hard for me to see), no such arguments can be made about the close friendships between women in Paule Marshall's *Daughters,* Terry McMillan's *Waiting to Exhale* (1992), or Alice Walker's *Possessing the Secret of Joy* (1992).

The greatest injunction, however, was the one against depictions of incest. Immediately, we might think Ellison's *Invisible Man* is a violation of that injunction, for certainly Trueblood impregnates his wife and his daughter. But think about it a little longer; Ellison's treatment of the topic might more properly be called an instance "when incest is not incest." The narrator relates from his underground world, many years removed from his college days, the story of having met Jim Trueblood, who in turn related a story of having the "dream" that enabled him to have sex with his daughter. Through chronology, layers of narrative, multiple narrational viewpoints, Freudian symbolism, and general distancing, Ellison transforms the dramatic incident of incest into something so far removed from its victims and so compellingly artistic that we have difficulty truly seeing and identifying with their plight. On the other hand, Toni Morrison gives us no such reprieve in Cholly Breedlove's rape of his daughter in *The Bluest Eye,* and Alice Walker puts incest "in your face" in *The Color Purple*. Still, *The Bluest Eye* has only one poignant incestuous scene, while *The Color Purple* has several. Randall Kenan's "Cornsilk," on the other hand, from his 1992 collection, *Let the Dead Bury Their Dead,* has incest as its primary focus, with a brother-sister relationship that almost overwhelms the story, that becomes pornographic in its obsession. Marita Golden, in her 1992 *and do remember me,* similarly focuses on the theme, holding the lens in place so long that our eyes cannot stray from the horror it captures.

It is not hard to find reasons for the earlier self-imposed restrictions on the depictions of black characters. As Charles Chesnutt indicated in a journal entry in 1880, it was "the negro's part . . . to prepare himself for social recognition and equality," and it was "the province of literature to open the way for him to get it—to accustom the public mind to the idea; . . . to lead them on imperceptibly, unconsciously step by step to the desired state of feeling" about race relations (140). Understandably, then, a "best-foot-forward" literature emerged that dominated creativity for many decades. Critics within the race were ever vigilant that black writers focus on "nice colored people," and in the 1980s and 1990s, on "nice colored middle-class people." Many writers before 1970 felt that they needed to add their pens to the war against racism, and observers of their output encouraged them along that path.

And the rationale is understandable. African Americans in the late nineteenth and early twentieth centuries—and for many decades thereafter—were maligned from without. What did it behoove the writers to malign them from within? Since black women had been set outside the realms of protection, outside the caste of the cult of true womanhood, it could only do more damage to their reputations to depict them as being morally loose, or abandoning their children, or having questionable or unacceptable sexual habits. Such portrayals would only fuel the flames of criticism, as Alice Walker discovered when she depicted wife beating, incest, and lesbianism in *The Color Purple*. It is not at all surprising that so many of the injunctions focus on sexuality, for in the Victorian societal caste in which the literature sprouted its first roots, that philosophy was dominant.

In spite of his bow to an almost shattering of the statute against incest, Ralph Ellison was clearly writing *with* the grain of expectations about coverage in African American literature, and that adherence to unspoken rules is clearly one of the reasons his novel became so popular. *Invisible Man* invokes that culturally foreign word, "universal," in its placing of African American experience within the larger context of American experience. Call me a "thinker-tinker" in the tradition of Franklin and Emerson, the narrator says, and thereby establishes himself within the social norm instead of against it.

He may depict scenes in which he is clearly shut out of the American ideal of democracy, but he consistently "affirm[s] the principle on which the country was built" (433). He maneuvers the sexual waters of his environment so successfully that he may arguably be called asexual. Remember, his only real potential sexual encounter is with Sybil, the white woman from whom he hopes to extract information about the brotherhood, but instead of having sex with her, he romanticizes her presence, begins to feel maternal toward her, and ultimately does not expose the weapon that could despoil this already tainted and slightly less than fair maiden.

And remember at the end of the novel when the narrator discovers how treacherously his assumed friends have treated him, he goes into a fit, but an acceptable *temporary* fit. He can be crazy, but only for a few minutes and in the privacy of an unlit sewer under New York City. Even there, however, he quickly comes to his senses and realizes that the action of inertia is preferable to the vegetation of insanity.

In his final dream sequences, the Invisible Man returns to what nonblack Americans most fear about black males: their sexuality. He grants to his accusers the power to emasculate him, acting out in this symbolic sequence a destructive psychological parody of what has happened to him throughout the novel. From the moment he changed the word "responsibility" to "equality" in his battle royal speech, he had performed a castration on himself, handing over his manhood and sexuality to the "upstanding" white citizens of his community in exchange for the briefcase and the scholarship to the Tuskegee-like college. From that point until the end of the novel, those in power have nothing to fear from the narrator, for he has willingly acquiesced in his own psychological, sexual, and human demise. In the paradoxical reversal that guides the novel, however, this demise is precisely the kind of acceptable, "normal" behavior that presumably gets rewarded in the society of which he envisions himself to be a part. He can only forever be a good little boy, and be rewarded—or punished—accordingly; he can never be a black man.

That Ellison would write a novel in which a black man gives up his manhood as the price of entry into the possibility of fulfilling the American Dream—not even its *actuality,* but just the possibility of fulfillment—is itself a most negative commentary on the status of American society. That critics would for generations read the novel as one of the least grating statements of black people's relationship to American society is a telling commentary on the willful blindness that has guided such criticism.

Manhood, sexuality, and access to the American Dream: that is the triumvirate paradigm upon which Ellison builds his novel, and that is the triumvirate that guides the construction of Brent Wade's *Company Man*—with the question of identity obviously underlying all three concepts. Published by Algonquin Books in 1992, the novel rewrites the Invisible Man's nightmare in contemporary living color. "The end is in the beginning," the Invisible Man asserts early in his novel, and where he has ended is also where William—"Bill," "Billy"—Covington begins. One of those misguided consequences of civil rights access to higher education, Billy has completed the obligatory college course and landed a job as director of Marketing Communications at Varitech Industries, Inc., the type of company that epitomizes corporate America. He lives "in the heart of Roland Park, one of northern Baltimore's oldest and most fashionable neighborhoods" (3), drives a Jaguar XJ6, and is married to a woman who is the envy of most of his fellow businessmen, especially the white males. The end at which Billy's story begins is either a hospital for the criminally insane or a psychiatric recovery ward. To put it bluntly, this successful beyond reproach company man has tried to blow his brains out. Now, in a series of journal entries written for a boyhood friend, he recounts his rise through the ranks and his fall through his manhood, past his sexuality, into insanity, and finally into reflections upon the possibility for recovery.

The intertextual relationship of *Company Man* to *Invisible Man* raises questions about where Ellison's invention leaves off and Brent Wade's creativity begins. After all, for more than forty years, scholars antici- pated that Ellison would bring his hibernating narrator back into the fray of the world above ground (that expectation only ended with Ellison's death in 1994). In essence, Wade provides one scenario of what *might* have been possible if an Invisible Man–type character had indeed entered the corporate world into which Ellison's narrator so desperately sought admission. That scenario establishes an irrefutable kinship and debt to *Invisible Man,* but it also opens new territory by taking the literature into an arena it has not previously entered. And it introduces topics that would have been anathema to Ellison's reading audience. Wade's creativity lies in his ability simultaneously to look backward and forward, to owe Ellison but to expand the territory that Ellison had in some ways only begun to explore. That expansion dovetails with the literary taboos that informed Ellison's writing but explodes them in ways that would have sent the Invisible Man running for cover in a second life underground.

The taboos covered here end with impotency. But the end is again in the beginning because Billy Covington, like the Invisible Man, takes the knife to himself and hands his manhood/sexuality over to the powers that be in exchange for the key to the executive toilet. From the beginning, Covington is a man who recognizes that willful erasure of the individual racial identity is a necessary ingredient to his rise at Varitech:

> You must understand that I had spent my entire career avoiding situations where my race would put me at odds with my race, or my employer. And to a degree I had achieved that. The result was, however, that I had no real credibility as a black person at Varitech. I was not known by them, I had not associated with them, I had never gone out of my way to cultivate an awareness of myself as a black person. And the whites seemed to appreciate that. (Wade, 180)

This character sounds enough like the Invisible Man to be his twin brother. Billy's references to "them" echo the Invisible Man's reaction to lower-class blacks: "We were trying to lift them up and they, like Trueblood, did everything it seemed to pull us down" (Ellison, 37);

both view their own people with the eyes of the Other, which the Invisible Man refers to as that peculiar disposition not to see. The Invisible Man spends so much time constructing an image that he believes will be acceptable to whites—arriving for appointments on time, ensuring that his clothing and hair are not offensive, never talking loud—that he becomes a veritable walking refutation of all the stereotypes usually identified with black people.

Whatever is black in Billy gets equally suppressed in favor of an image, an image so thin that the veneer is like a coating of neutral nail polish. It consists of the material things—clothes, a car, and the possession of a wife—that define the toast tradition in which African Americans evince a respect for people, usually males, who have manipulated the economic system successfully enough to acquire outward signs of prosperity. A recurring theme in toasts, those long narrative folk poems such as "The Signifying Monkey" and "Stagolee," is an appreciation for acquiring the material aspects of American culture without being assimilated into the culture, and certainly without abiding by the society's rules; that part of his heritage is what Billy forgets.

Billy also performs repeated self-induced lobotomies by anesthetizing himself with alcohol. Bourbon and water dull the effect of his racial sellout and temporarily obliterate memories that would tie him to anything except the most palatable reconstructions of his notion of family. On a corporate trip to Atlanta, he consumes more alcohol than would probably be healthy for four people. The alcohol enables him to lie smoothly (a trait he thinks all good businessmen should have), and the quantities he consumes presumably mark him in yet another way as a masculine, company-oriented type. Recall that Bledsoe asserts that the Invisible Man should have lied to Mr. Norton instead of taking him to Trueblood's shack: " 'My God, boy! You're black and living in the South—did you forget how to lie?' " (Ellison, 107).

In executing his blueprint for corporate success in America, Billy is as deliberate as—and far more successful than—the Invisible Man ever could be. Remember that the Invisible Man initially views Bledsoe as the model of success. Bledsoe, records the Invisible Man,

> was the example of everything I hoped to be: Influential with wealthy men [read white] all over the country; consulted in matters concerning the race; a leader of his people; the possessor of not one but *two* Cadillacs, a good salary and a soft, good-looking and creamy-complexioned wife. (78)

Billy Covington acquires possessions in direct proportion to their ability to enhance his progression in the business world. He molds the role for his fair-skinned, green-eyed, black wife with a clear-sighted sense of her value as a commodity: "There was a certain coital snugness about it. I had a great salary, the patronage of the company president, a beautiful wife, a handsome old house, and a cardinal red xj6" (Wade, 17). He elaborates on the role his wife plays:

> Having a beautiful wife is an asset in the corporate world. For the rising young executives, it's quietly looked upon as one of the rewards of good cocksmanship. There's an attendant prestige for the man with a beautiful wife. Her beauty gets extrapolated somehow into a presumption of his good salesmanship, good marketing skills, or some larger savvy. (18)

We could argue how like chattel slavery this all sounds—twelve hundred dollars for Christian virtue, as William Wells Brown would say—but for the fact that Paula enjoys her role so thoroughly. Indeed, she goes on stage in a role as "black corporate wife" (19) that will shortly have her deciding when Billy should purchase the new upscale car to go along with his progress in the company. When he and Paula discover that they cannot have children, they spend the money saved for that expense on a Mercedes Benz. Later, when Billy gets a promotion, Paula recommends his moving up to a Jaguar (33).

Notice in the quotations, however, the description of his intact middle-class image as "coital snugness" and the possession of a beautiful wife as "good cocksmanship." And to culminate these references, he writes, "It was as if through Varitech our union had been consummated, as if Paula and I were now bound by something more expansive than a legal document and two yellow rings" (20). And he admits having fallen in love with her "commodities," that is, "her bearing" and "her presence" (19), before he fell in love with her; her traits are ones he has observed "in very attractive white women" (22). Sexual references are obviously so blatant in Billy's discussion because of their equation to manhood in business, but they also serve to show how far away from healthy, real sexuality the poor man actually is.

By comparison, consider the Invisible Man's asexuality. He moves through a rather long novel without any hint of involved sexual encounter. When he accidentally brushes against a white woman on the subway, he is careful to assume a posture of unintentionality. When he plans to seduce Sybil, he ends up only writing a cryptic note on her stomach: "SYBIL, YOU WERE RAPED / BY / SANTA CLAUS / SURPRISE" (Ellison, 395). He uses the veneer of dress and manners, and pretensions to ambitious job responsibilities, to cover up his sexual ineffectualness as assuredly as Billy uses material things and conversation to cover up the same problem.

Paula, Billy's promotions, and his xj6 become physical substitutes for his penis. Sexual activity is the equivalent of acting "niggerish," his light-skinned grandmother's word for Toni Morrison's idea of "the funk." A certain kind of black women, Morrison writes, those who aspire to middle-classness, will cultivate "thrift, patience, high morals, and good manners. In short," they determine "how to get rid of the funkiness. The dreadful funkiness of passion, the funkiness of nature, the funkiness of the wide range of human emotions" (68). Like Morrison's Geraldine in *The Bluest Eye,* Billy wants to rein in the potential riotous outbreak of sexual feelings and colored behavior. Sex must be confined to time and space—evenings, beginning in the television room and ending up in bed—that are distinct markers from the life he lives at work. In this setting, Billy and Paula can play at being liberated;

they indulge in an elaborate game of partial exposure of body parts from across the room until one of them becomes sexually aroused to the point of actually touching the other one. The one who touches first "loses," so to speak, but "wins" by initiating sexual intimacy. Think of the Harlem Renaissance in this connection. What happens sexually between Billy and Paula is comparable to whites coming into Harlem in the 1920s. Varitech Industries is downtown, and Billy's house is uptown, where all the jungle rhythms can be let loose because either no one is watching, or, as with the case in Harlem, no one who *matters* is watching.

"Niggerishness" and sexuality become conflated in Billy's mind, so that both are identified with "colored," black, unacceptable behavior, indeed with blackness itself. He indicates at one point that his consideration of seducing his secretary "was not the simple dumb niggerish lust of a morally stranded businessman" (Wade, 199), thereby making the exact equation that has lurked in the back of his mind throughout the text. The only way that Billy can make mad and passionate love to his wife is to mask the fact that he is involved in the act, to take on another personality, play another role. Knowing that his bosses would conceive only of the stereotypical "screw 'til you collapse" image of black sexuality, Billy breaks through his veneer to execute that stereotype. When he is no longer able to differentiate between mask and wearer, he becomes impotent. Even if his coworkers are not in his bedroom, he carries the monsters in his head. When he realizes he may yet be doing something of which they either do not approve or would want suppressed, his ability to play the role of sexual conquering black male stud disappears. His troubles at work, therefore, portend more and more directly his troubles in bed.

This duality, this Dr. Jekyll and Mr. Hyde keep-it-hidden-or-let-it-rip approach to sexuality, parallels the racially split personality into which Billy has blossomed and the control/containment mode that he believes is essential to corporate success. He believes he can make it by telling the right jokes, developing just the right touch of conversation with the secretaries of important people, eating the right dishes, and drinking the right alcoholic beverages. He is an adaptable entity, ready to pour himself into whatever mold the corporate world desires.

Eating and drinking are paramount to Billy. He prefers softshell crabs to more "niggerish" food, such as the yams that appear in *Invisible Man*. Although his grandmother used to prepare the crabs for him, and his preference could thereby be considered a return to cultural heritage, his grandmother's attitude toward blacks negates that possibility. She is willing to feed him, just as Mary Rambo is willing to feed and nourish the Invisible Man, but she is not willing to have him act "niggerish"; by contrast, Mary Rambo envisions the Invisible Man as a powerful race man, one who will have a sense of mission toward the masses of black people. Billy identifies food with women in his life, for it is another form of gratification, another satisfaction that they can perform for him. Paula cooks pork chops for him on their first date, and when his grandmother dies, women keep him supplied with food during his stupefied existence following the funeral. "Women," he says, "were always preparing food for me" (84), and he looks for some inadequacy in them to account for their actions rather than something in himself that evokes their behavior. Their desire to satisfy him, whether in food or sex, ties in to his expectations for success in climbing up the corporate ladder.

The image of the American Dream, however, is ever elusive. For each successful set of steps maneuvered, another set presents itself. For every favor John Haviland, the CEO of Varitech, expects Billy to perform in return for John recognizing, "appreciating," and promoting him, there is another lurking in wait, for Billy has indeed "sold his soul to the company store." He has become so successful that he has painted himself into the position of being personal mascot to Haviland, "the one person at Varitech most responsible for [Billy's] career" (121). Therefore, when the black machinists in the company, led by a renegade black executive, plan a strike, Billy can call upon neither racial loyalty nor corporate responsibility to sustain him. He finds himself in cultural and professional limbo.

If memory is indeed culture and race a set of social affinities, then Billy has lost the portions that would enable him to reestablish bonds with the black men at the company. For example, the men notify each other of their clandestine meetings by using two African American folk forms: nicknames and folk sayings. A flyer simply reads: "CPT SEE QUARTER TILL." Billy does not have an iota of a clue about what this means. When he is finally forced to retrieve a lost track from the cultural disk of his memory, he vaguely recalls that yes, indeed, once upon a lifetime ago, he had been exposed to the fact that CPT meant Colored People's Time. "I remember thinking, Umph, there's something familiar here" (37)—as the Invisible Man vaguely remembers the blues and the dozens, other cultural signals designed to reclaim the lost. Upon hearing the blues, the Invisible Man thinks, "It seemed that here some memories slipped around my life at the campus and went far back to things I had long ago shut out of my mind" (Ellison, 131). Upon failing to engage in word play with Peetie Wheatstraw, the Invisible Man reflects, "I'd known the stuff from childhood, but had forgotten it; had learned it back of school" (134). If Billy had had any real interactions with the black men in the company, he would have known that one of the machinists, so dark in skin coloring that he was teasingly described as being "blacker than quarter to midnight" (Wade, 107), was logically called "Quarter Till." With this sensitivity to the vibrancy of African American culture that expresses itself even in the midst of white corporate America, Billy would have been able to decipher the code, understand the message, and perhaps begin to see some of the dissatisfaction those black men not so comfortable as him had with Varitech.

Billy's loss of cultural codes is indicated in another striking way in the novel. He is severed from the cultural symbol of the "Buffalo Soldier." Upon hearing the Bob Marley song with the titled reference to those African Americans used to fight Native Americans, Billy has "no idea what it was about" but he likes "its mantic energy and rhythm" (131). This cultural lapse fits the personality he has presented to us, for by failing to recognize the historical significance of Buffalo Soldiers, he simultaneously blinds himself to the contemporary buffalo soldier role he is asked to play in selling out the other people of color, the other blacks in his company.

Billy's inability to respond to these cultural codes sends him careening down a self-destructive path. He lives out the first of his ultimate nightmares—the belief that he will become "thingafied" (132), for that is certainly what happens in his relation to Haviland and the other whites at the company. He is only as valuable to them as he is able to effect their interests; when that no longer obtains, they prepare to dismiss him by claiming sexual impropriety with his secretary. That absurd situation, set against the backdrop of his sexual and professional impotency, clinches his dismissal from the American Dream and the onset of his suicide attempt.

Billy's "thingafication" is in turn set against the backdrop of his cultural passing. When all his volatile props collapse, he ends up in a confounding complex of racial, cultural, sexual, professional, and personal dissolution. In the face of this monumental impotence, he grasps at the only potential power available to him: he begins to write. Like Eldridge Cleaver and many others writing to save themselves, Billy Covington pens his journal entries to Paul Walker, his teenage friend. As it does for the Invisible Man, the power of the narrative restores some of Billy's sense of self and gives back to him an original dream. He says early on in the book that he had always wanted to be a novelist, and at various points he speaks of being a "scenarist," of setting scenes, of his life being a "fiction." He also paints Paula's interactions with his coworkers as a drama of sorts; he is aware of the effect that she, alone, and they, together, have upon their "audience."

The problem with his narration is that it reveals as well as conceals. Even beyond the end of his beginning, even beyond the point of attempted suicide, he tries to hold on to an image of himself as a "good cocksman." He discusses his relationship with Donna, his nurse, and appraises her in ways comparable to his early assessment of Paula's commodities. "She has an ass," he says "that could raise the dead!" (2). Then we learn that his speech is markedly slurred. It is only much, much later in the text that we become aware of the extensive paralysis that he has suffered in one side and of the fact that he drools. This impaired, near vegetable of a man must nonetheless retain a façade of sexual virility in the face of glaring evidence to the contrary.

This self-delusion leads us to suspect that he is probably deluding himself in other ways as well. Is he really physically creating the text that he presents to us, or is he merely thinking the text? Writing presupposes that he actually has a textual audience, Paul, in mind. Thinking means that he has only readers in mind, and their opinion, like the blacks in Harlem, can have no impact upon his image of himself, for it is that image that he is desperately trying to hold in place. Although the novel is ostensibly a series of journal entries, there are no markers to indicate that format—no dates, no letterlike breaks, no salutations. Instead, Billy relies on patterns of informality, references to letters he says he has received, and responses to questions he asserts Paul has posed to him to achieve the effect of an immediate audience-directed narrative. Like the Invisible Man, however, what he reveals contains as much dramatic irony as information, and his capacity for self-parody is extensive.

The façade he wishes to hold in place can be retained only if he perpetuates the myth of manhood, success, and access to the American Dream. Yet the very rationale of the narrative undermines that. He claims to be writing to explain to his friend what has happened. Then we learn that his friend Paul has shattered tradition by writing to their neighbors in the small town of Roberts, Maryland, and publicly professing his homosexuality. Then we later learn that Billy and Paul have had an encounter in which Paul asked:

"Billy . . . you ever wonder what it would be like to hug a man? . . . Well I've thought sometimes . . . what it would be like to hold . . . to hold you." (168)

The text, then, is an elaborate sexual passing, just as the Invisible Man covers his sexual passing, his asexuality, with an elaborate narrative. Billy uses the story to play with the idea of his suppressed homosexuality and finally to try to escape that designation by declaring all the wonderfully successful things he has done. Note, too, that Billy, the closeted homosexual, who has escaped a relationship with Paul, has married a woman named Paula; the names cannot be coincidental. In a rewriting of literary twinning, Billy achieves symbolic forbidden bonding with his childhood friend and is thereby able to embrace homosexuality as well as reject it. The kinds of exotic sexual stimulation in which he and Paula engage have exhibitionism, a stereotypical tenet of homosexual behavior, at their core.

In ultimate nightmare, part two, therefore, Billy is subsumed into the final breakdown in African American literary taboos: blatant, self-confessed homosexuality. Or homosexuality so near the surface of consciousness that it persists as a nagging question that Billy does not dare to shape—"Am I a homosexual?" ("Do I have homosexual tendencies?" "Have I been trying to escape what I really am?") Identity—not racial, but *sexual* identity—is the invisibility that informs Billy's sojourn in America. The question almost reaches his mind on at least six different occasions in the text.

When Billy finally asks the question, it comes out as "Who are you?" (205), which has inherent in it the racial and sexual components of his identity. He asks the question after his dark night of the soul—a drunken excursion through the territory in Atlanta where homeless people hang out—during which he loses his wallet and his Rolex watch, the tangible signs that he belongs in another world (not unlike Milkman Dead's trip south in Toni Morrison's *Song of Solomon*). Only by being "authenticated" by whites (reminiscent of the "front matter" in slave narratives) at his hotel is he able to regain entry to the safety of his room. Ironically, that external verification precedes the giant step that Billy takes to identifying with black people. His experience on the street, where he is humiliated by three black garbage collectors, leads him to sign the petition and join in with the strikers.

The street scene for him parallels the Harlem riot for the Invisible Man. Even the language he uses echoes Ellison:

> But hadn't my entire life been a pilgrimage to this place? It's where you end up when you divide yourself, and it's haunted by the ghost of that other, the invisible man I kept interred in the ivory shell. (205)

He even has an "I was my experiences and my experiences were me" speech that also parallels that of the Invisible Man. Compare the following passages, the first from *Invisible Man* and the second from *Company Man:*

> And now all past humiliations became precious parts of my experience, and for the first time, leaning against that stone wall in the sweltering night, I began to accept my past and, as I accepted it, I felt memories welling up within me. It was as though I'd learned suddenly to look around corners; images of past humiliations flickered through my head and I saw that they were more than separate experiences. They were me; they defined me. I was my experiences and my experiences were me, and no blind men, no matter how powerful they became, even if they conquered the world, could take that, or change one single itch, taunt, laugh, cry, scar, ache, rage or pain of it. (Ellison, 383)

> And a thought came to me so quickly, Paul—so quickly that I knew instantly, without saying or thinking, what the voice had told me. It said: They [William, "Bill," and "Billy"] are who I had always been, no matter who I had assumed they were, no matter who I had thought they were not, no matter who they each dreamt I might have been. It didn't matter. Because we three are all one part of a larger body, this brooding fecund unconsumable blackness. A blackness that I now see will never be fully assimilated. It will always stand abject and separate even to the most well intended, if only on some discrete level of intuition or observance distilled in a nanosecond to a heedless reaction. It's the idea of this blackness

that they see first, regardless. Blackness as the depreciated recipro-
cal of whatever whiteness has come to mean. This is who I am. I
am inseparable from this blackness, its history, its weight, its obligations. Yes, obligations. Perhaps this is the real ghost that haunts
that place I fear within myself. (Wade, 205)

The advantage Billy *seems* to gain in revelation at this point, however,
is nullified when he shoots himself, just as the Invisible Man seems
to take a step backward when he descends into the hole from which
he refuses to ascend.

Although Billy regains temporary potency earlier in the evening before he pulls the trigger, he is still impotent in his job situation, and
chances are Haviland will indeed abandon him. His grandmother's
haunting voice (remember the grandfather's haunting advice to Invisible Man) also keeps resurfacing to let him know that doing the
right thing by signing the petition really just reduces him to the level
of "*just another nigga*" (217). Although that designation might be a call
to cultural heritage and renewed commitment to racial struggle, Billy
finds no comfort in it. Whereas Rufus Scott simply asserted, "This
shit has got to stop" (Baldwin, 217) and took a leap off the George
Washington Bridge, Billy is too self-evaluative, too articulate in his
own therapeutic analyses, too self-consciously analytical to do anything but botch an attempt to kill himself.

He therefore joins Horace in Randall Kenan's *A Visitation of Spirits* (1989) in trying to confront homosexuality, finding the reflection
in the mirror too harsh, and attempting to destroy himself and the
mirror. The public opinion that his friend Paul Walker has defied by
verbalizing his homosexuality, or the public opinion that Miss Maple
in Gloria Naylor's *Bailey's Cafe* (1992) simply ignores, would destroy
the house that Billy built. So he one-ups that possibility by trying to
destroy himself; a gun aimed at his head is the natural consequence
of the "gravity-defying fiction" (Wade, 132) that his life has been.

The Invisible Man's nightmare was more often than not perpet-
uated by others. Billy Covington, however, finds himself in a world

where external forces merely serve as the vessels into which he pours his acquiescent personality—until he reaches a point where the clash between self and society revolves around an issue that he has no way of resolving. How can the superstud black male be impotent? How can the previously "crazy nigger" really be insane? How can a black man show the impact of society upon him by ending up in a psychiatric ward? That is perhaps just a bit less than manly, perhaps the most "sissified" state of all. But most of all, how can the superstud black male really be homosexual? Faced with these contradictions, Billy opts for a permanent vacation from life. What he gets is a permanent vacation from manhood, sexuality, and the American Dream. In this rewriting of Ellison's nightmare, Brent Wade shows that the distance between 1952 and 1992 is no more than the length of a penis propped up by self-delusions, still "niggerish" and funky after all those years.

(1992)

Works Cited

Baldwin, James. *Another Country.* New York: Dell, 1962.

Chesnutt, Charles Waddell. *The Journals of Charles W. Chesnutt.* Ed. Richard Brodhead. Durham: Duke University Press, 1993.

Ellison, Ralph. *Invisible Man.* 1952. Reprint, New York: Vintage, 1972.

Morrison, Toni. *The Bluest Eye.* 1970. Reprint, New York: Washington Square Press, 1972.

Wade, Brent. *Company Man.* Chapel Hill, N.C.: Algonquin Books, 1992.

Four

Zapping the Editor, Or, How to Tell Censors to Kiss Off without Really Trying

Zora Neale Hurston's Fights with Authority Figures in *Dust Tracks on a Road*

 Zora Neale Hurston published *Dust Tracks on a Road* in 1942. The publication was more a directive than a desire. Bertram Lippincott had used his publishing prerogative in requesting that Hurston fall in line with the prevailing "colored person tells all" syndrome that was flooding the American markets at this time. The people at Lippincott obviously knew about the Langston Hughes autobiography that had been published in 1940, and the autobiographical nature of *Native Son* certainly suggested that there was widespread public interest in the 1940s versions of "up from the slavery of racism and poverty," or the inability to make that trip. While the Negro, as Hughes might have said, was "no longer in vogue" in Harlem, he or she was decidedly coming in vogue again in the publishing world of the 1940s. As Robert Hemenway has pointed out, Hurston was not only uncomfortable with the autobiographical form, but she found it hard to retain a consistent voice in the manuscript, and she took an uncharacteristically long time, a year, to complete the revisions on the work. "I did not want to write it at all," she said, "because it is too hard to reveal one's inner self" (Hemenway, 278). Even Alice Walker, mostly sympathetic to Hurston in everything else, has called the autobiography "the most unfortunate thing Zora ever wrote," primarily because "after the first several chapters, it rings false."[1] So Hurston conformed without conforming; she completed a work that defies chronology, drops into essayistic digressions, and offers generalized opinions as frequently as it traces a particular life. Scholars have pointed to its contradictions, its refusal to adhere to its own professed structure, and its general blot upon the reputation of an otherwise respectable author.

Pushed into completing a manuscript that she might not otherwise have completed—or might have completed at a much later date—Zora Neale Hurston could not straightforwardly show her resentment to that coercion, for she was too dependent upon the financial kindnesses of others (she had been particularly strapped financially in the couple of years before she started work on the manuscript). Nor could she wholly retain her own voice, for as Claudine Raynaud has meticulously pointed out, several editorial emendations occurred between Hurston's original manuscript and the final published version of *Dust Tracks*. This was especially true of Hurston's opinions of European and U.S. imperialism, her representations of black sexuality—especially black *male* sexuality—and her depictions of her own subjection to sexism and racism. Raynaud makes clear that "a comparison of manuscript and published versions of *Dust Tracks* retraces the process of Hurston's gradual submission to the control of the white publishing world" (34–64).

On stage and dancing, but without the proper shoes or dress, Hurston decided to change the dance and to show the people who had ordered the performance that she was still her own individual self in spite of their shaping her current reality. In the narrative, therefore, in incidents that were ostensibly drawn from her own life, Hurston could voice her displeasure by refusing to adhere to the expected difference as an *individual* colored person, by violating form and, most important, by creating a series of events and characters who may very well serve as substitutes for the abstract authority that made her sit down at her typewriter and collect the bits and pieces of her life into something of a coherent whole. Hurston exhibits her displeasure in the narrative in a series of events in which she executes physical or psychological violence upon substitutes for authorial coercion.

But first, she thwarted expectations. Lippincott undoubtedly expected a colored version of the up-by-the-bootstraps myth. Hurston, a black woman, had carved out an individual, distinctive face in bas relief against the masses of blacks who were still trapped in poverty and ignorance. Hurston resists that expectation by writing herself into mythic origins and a mythical birth. She's distinctive, all right, but not distinctively, *stereotypically* black. She's distinctive in the best of white male heroic traditions, and her origins reflect those that one might find in Joseph Campbell's *The Hero with a Thousand Faces*, or perhaps the legend of Moses or King Arthur might suffice. At any rate, Hurston carves Eatonville out of the adventurous imaginations of three white wanderers who were drawn back to the territory even as they glimpsed the shores of Brazil. Of course Eatonville itself would eventually be founded by black men, but the important thing, the *impetus* to its creation, came from *white* "educated men of family and wealth" (*Dust Tracks*, 3). The founding of Eatonville thus parallels the founding of the Americas and particularly the United States, thereby landing Zora Neale Hurston and Bertram Lippincott in the same pot instead of placing Hurston in a smaller one.

Hurston further resists the expected stereotypical black difference by casting herself and a white man as the primary agents of her birth (notice how even her mother takes a back seat in this episode). Her mother is weak and alone when her water breaks, so Baby Zora "rushes out" by herself and is squalling when the white man arrives to bring some fresh hog meat to the family:

He followed the noise and then he saw how things were, and, being the kind of a man he was, he took out his Barlow Knife and cut the navel cord, then he did the best he could about other things.

When the mid-wife, locally known as a granny, arrived about an hour later, there was a fire in the stove and plenty of hot water on. I had been sponged off in some sort of a way, and Mama was holding me in her arms. (21)

Again, mythic implications unfold; this is not simply another colored baby born in the backwoods of Florida or Alabama, but one for whom the very gods ensure a fortuitous arrival. Embedded in this occurrence is Hurston's diminishing of racial tension, a denial that undergirds the text. If a white man can cut a navel cord for a black baby, then consort with the child as she grows up, and even use the word "nigger" without such usage being an insult, then all of Lippincott's and white readers' expectations about this being a distinctive black life within a segregated environment are short-circuited. The very questionable nature of this white man's character—and Hurston's forgiving response toward it—again highlights Hurston's *universal* difference and mitigates the individualized, Negro expectations.

The fact that Hurston was anointed and chosen by white women also fits into this schema of the backfiring of expectations. Certainly there have been other instances in which a gifted young black student has been singled out for special attention by a white person visiting a segregated black school. Recall that James Baldwin is similarly singled out as he recounts the incident in the autobiographical *Go Tell It on the Mountain* (1953, pp. 20–21). With Hurston, the difference is in degree. Her teacher asks her to read overly long to impress the visitors. They then in turn invite her to their hotel room, where they treat her like a pet; they give her a cylinder with one hundred bright, shiny pennies; and apparently for quite some time they send her clothes and books. What might initially be viewed as the poor child getting attention from rich white folks becomes larger than life. To the rough and tumble, backwoods Hurston, the women are almost godly in their beauty: "They had shiny hair, mostly brownish. One had a looping gold chain around her neck. The other one was dressed all over in black and white with a pretty finger ring on her left hand. But the thing that held my eyes were their fingers. They were long and thin, and very white, except up near the tips. There they were baby pink. I had never seen such hands. It was a fascinating discovery for me" (*Dust Tracks,* 35). The women's recognition of Hurston's intelligence gives her in turn the ability to elevate them within her text. Thus these women, who would remain relatively unknown to the larger world, are given statue by the very child/woman they presumed to help. Largesse finally turns on its head, and it is Hurston who has the power to immortalize, to write them into her text. Once again, the expectation of the distinctive colored life goes in an unintended direction.

By refusing to retain strict chronology, by setting up a structure of twelve recurring visions and refusing to adhere to it, and by lapsing from narrative into essay, Hurston retains voice and control that she was not otherwise allowed. Her most significant structural and thematic refusal to adhere to the autobiographical mode is chapter eleven, which she titled "Books and Things" (151–56). In a mere *six pages* of the near *three hundred pages* of the originally published manuscript, Hurston treats all of the "things" that have warranted the publishing of her autobiography. Lippincott requested it because her five published books represented a pinnacle of colored success—or any success for that era of American literary history. Yet Hurston reduces the composition and publication of those works to six pages. She gives as much attention to interviewing Cudjo Lewis (144–48) as she does to the whole of her literary career. We have a famous author, therefore, who refuses to deal with the works that have made her famous. Where was she when all the books were composed? Under what circumstances? How did she make contact with the publishers? What did the correspondence look like? We get little of this in *Dust Tracks*. For this autobiographical venture, Hurston essentially said, "I will give you a semblance of form, but I won't give you substance. I will give you a substantially incomplete life, and perhaps you will simply conclude that I was tired, at points, especially here at the end, or that I didn't really know what I was doing." I maintain that she was "putting something outside her mind" for Lippincott and her white readers to play with and going on about her business.

Contrary to the sweet, storytelling image with which we like to surround Hurston, *Dust Tracks* is at times a surprisingly violent book. And the violence is in many cases gratuitous, or at least acutely intense for the offense committed. I read the moments of violence in the narrative, therefore, as Hurston's displacement of aggression onto those over whom she felt a certain amount of linguistic and intellectual superiority, which amounts to an acting out of sorts, a registering of complaint against the very narrative she is in the process of writing. As Baldwin implies of the gang-raped Deborah in *Go Tell It on the Mountain,* the people in the community hate Deborah because hating the white males who violated her would be all consuming in its *powerlessness* as a gesture of reproach. Hurston could not decide *not* to write her narrative, because that would be comparable to fighting against that powerful white male power structure, but she could show her anger throughout.

Of course, in the schema I have developed here, it could be argued that she is stereotypically, then, playing to white expectations in this category of representation because violence would have been one thing associated with black communities. I would say in turn that we have to look at the kind of violence represented, the intensity of it, the circumstances under which it occurs, and finally how Hurston uses it. While we might ultimately conclude that Hurston does bow to white stereotype here, I think there is at least one other explanation as well.

Violence surrounds Hurston in the text; it is as much a part of her growing up as orange trees and jasmine blossoms. Her father is constantly threatening violence to her mother, and her Uncle Jim and Aunt Caroline provide entertainment for the whole community when she goes with her axe to drive him from his lover's house. Aunt Caroline is equally entertaining when she knocks down one of Uncle Jim's lovers just to see if the woman does not wear underwear and, upon discovering the truth, proceeds to spit on the exposed area and grind it in with her foot. These latter instances evoke humor in the text, for, while there is discomfort, there is no actual bloodshed, no broken bones. But Hurston adopts these violent approaches to life. She hits the child who will not go to the end of the world with her (28) and gets into several fights at school (29, 30). When Hurston shows up for a fishing trip scratched and bruised from one such encounter, her mythic white father gives her license to fight—in great detail—but the standing advice is: "don't you never let nobody spit on you or kick you. Anybody who takes a thing like that ain't worth de powder and shot it takes to kill 'em, hear? . . . Can't nothing wash that off, but blood. If anybody ever do one of those things to you, kill ['em] dead and go to jail. Hear me?" (31). Hurston stresses that this is the epitome of the frontier philosophy that guided the actions of many people in the town. When two men end up in court for fighting, the judge fines the plaintiff more than the defendant because "nobody with any guts would have come into court to settle a fist fight" (33). Florida versions of the aggression of the southwestern humor tradition, these ringtail roarers serve Hurston, like her origins and birth, again in an effort to make her history larger than the collective or individual lives of black people.

This penchant for aggression even saturates her reading, for she prefers the violent gods of Norse mythology and the avenging David of the Old Testament to tamer characters. "All David wanted to know from God was who to kill and when. He took care of the other details himself. Never a quiet moment. I liked him a lot" (40). Remember that Hurston starts reading the Bible because her mother has given her a "licking" for repeating something a neighbor has said and has locked her in a room; the only thing available to read is the Bible. Even Hurston's imaginary play has violent overtones. Her doll, Miss Corn-Cob, is the victim of a whipping, to which all the other players respond, "Goody! Goody!" (56). Hurston receives several whippings at the school in Jacksonville (68–69), once for having placed a wet, cold brick in the bed of one of the teachers (78). When she leaves the school to return home, she describes herself as a "wild thing" having been put "back in the jungle" (80). Rather than being stereotypically black, this background sets the stage for the two most violent episodes of the autobiography, both of which obviously have black characters but are intended to reflect white actions.

Many scholars approaching the narrative have focused on Hurston's violent encounter with her stepmother. Indeed, as that woman is represented in the text, readers generally share Hurston's objections to her. The violence, we conclude, is almost justified, for how could such an uncouth, selfish woman not be sensitive to the needs of several small children recently deprived of their mother? So we passively accept Hurston's creation of a legend of herself as an avenging warrior, one who had the audacity historically and the literary skills later to best a problematic stepmother. And not merely to best her, but to humiliate her, to sever the bonds of friendship that the woman professed to have, and to perpetuate the triumph of youth over age. The incident is almost as cathartic for the reader as it is for Hurston. The reader has been drifting with Hurston in her homelessness, wondering as she does if she is going to get the money to stay in school. Hurston, in turn, has been emotionally cramped by her mother's death and her father's dwindling affection, so much so that the attack upon her stepmother almost amounts to sexual release. Hurston certainly enjoys it as much. And the fact that she is the aggressor makes it all the more pleasurable.

Of the fight with her stepmother, Hurston writes:

She called me a sassy, impudent heifer, announced that she was going to take me down a buttonhole lower, and threw a bottle at my head. The bottle came sailing slowly through the air and missed me easily. She never should have missed.

The primeval in me leaped to life. Ha! This was the very corn I wanted to grind. Fight! Not having to put up with what she did to us through Papa! Direct action and everything up to me. I looked at her hard. And like everybody else's enemy, her looks, her smells, her sounds were all mixed up with her doings, and she deserved punishment for them as well as her acts. . . . If I died, let me die with my hands soaked in her blood. I wanted her blood, and plenty of it. That is the way I went into the fight, and that is the way I fought it. . . . She gave way before my first rush and found herself pinned against the wall, with my fists pounding at her face without pity. She scratched and clawed at me, but I felt nothing at all. In a few seconds, she gave up. I could see her face when she realized that I meant to kill her. She spat on my dress, then, and did what she could to cover up from my renewed fury. She had given up fighting except for trying to spit in my face, and I did not intend for her to get away. (74–75)

The stepmother yells for Hurston's father to intervene, but he stands by, crying helplessly. A neighbor woman who responds to the call for help almost meets a hatchet Hurston throws in her direction, thus provoking her hasty retreat. Her father finally pulls Hurston off his wife. But Hurston remains unsatisfied. "Years later," she writes, "after I had graduated from Barnard and I was doing research, I found out where she was. I drove twenty miles to finish the job, only to find out that she was a chronic invalid. She had an incurable sore on her neck. I couldn't tackle her under such circumstances, so I turned back, all frustrated inside. All I could do was to wish that she had a lot more neck to rot" (75–76).

Note in this last passage that Hurston refers to "years later." Less than twenty pages later, however, and still in the same year as the beating, she tries to be reflective about her action, stating that her stepmother "probably did the best she could" (91), but the paragraph of superficial sympathy in which this line appears rings hollow in comparison to the vividness of the anger still lingering "years later." That intensity is also reflected in the fact that Hurston interrupted the chronology of her school years in Jacksonville to relate the incident because it serves ultimately as retaliation for her stepmother having forced their father to whip Sarah, his favorite daughter.

A distanced look reveals that Hurston's stepmother, in spite of her lack of desire for or ability in nurturing skills, is a relatively powerless woman in the grand scheme of things. The anger Hurston felt at the moment of her fight should certainly have been mitigated by the intervening years. Yet Hurston relates the incident with little sobering reflection, with all the vehemence of emotional violence that might have characterized the initial occurrence. To retain such emotion and heap it so gleefully upon the head and body of her stepmother invites the allegorical substitution of other figures of authority for the stepmother. Hurston can eventually walk away from her stepmother; she cannot walk away from the hands that feed her through publishing. But she can retain the intensity of anger that she feels toward being trapped in a situation that has overtones of that earlier one.

The incident, then, begins to gain the same status as several of the folktales that Hurston includes in the volume. It is more than the sum of its parts. Consider language, for example. Remember in *Jonah's Gourd Vine* (1934) how, when Hurston wanted to portray the anger leading to a possible fight between Ned and Amy Crittenden, the anger is all metaphoric language? Instead of voicing specifically what has upset them, they resort to rhymes such as "Don't you lak it, don't you take it, heah mah collar come and you shake it!" (5–6). In fact, the language almost obscures the anger. By contrast, in *Dust Tracks,* Hurston cuts through metaphor—except for describing the fight as corn she wants to grind—and moves immediately to unadorned anger, the kind that we would find in a toast or in some of the folktale encounters between animals. By reducing the number of specific metaphors, Hurston in fact makes her tale more metaphorical. For a comparison in the text, consider how she uses tales of monkeys—unfortunately—to suggest behaviors of black people ("My People! My People," 161–64).

Hurston's stepmother makes the mistake of trying to control her life in the way that editors had in making requests for certain kinds of books and that editorial staffs did in cutting out material she wanted to include in *Dust Tracks.* They all coalesce in the figure of an authoritative, unsympathetic woman for whom Hurston only has value in terms of her labor. All of Hurston's anger can thus be unleashed onto an acceptable target, the figure comparable to Deborah in Baldwin's *Go Tell It on the Mountain,* without in any way undermining the authority of those who have commanded her services, and indeed, they probably concluded that this was a typical incident in the lives of colored people who tried to solve their problems through violence. In the stepmother/editor/editorial staff figure, then, Hurston is able to register her displeasure with those persons who attempt to control other people's lives when those controlled are in a younger, weaker, or more impoverished position. In that larger, macrocosmic arena, they can fight back only indirectly. With the stepmother, Hurston projects violence that she would like to have executed. With Lucy, she reflects that perpetrated against her.

In preparation for her encounter with Lucy, Hurston provides a sometimes rhapsodizing portrait of Polk County. "Primitive minds are quick to sunshine and quick to anger," she writes. "Some little word, look or gesture can move them either to love or to sticking a knife between your ribs. You just have to sense the delicate balance and maintain it. In some instances, there is nothing personal in the killing. The killer wishes to establish a reputation as a killer, and you'll do as a sample" (130). The impersonality of aggression, like the force of destruction that Lucy eventually becomes, is also the impersonal world of destruction of creativity as reflected in publishers. "Nothing personal, just give us what we want. If not, we can metaphorically kill you by refusing to publish your own words." Die for them by giving up your creative mind, and they love you. Declare your right to life, to creativity, and they will bend, break, or utterly silence you by denying you the right to an audience, which amounts to a kind of creative death.

Lucy becomes, then, a metaphor for control, an unleashed destructive control that has only its own interests at heart. When Lucy finally corners Hurston, she starts for her without knowing that Big Sweet, Hurston's protector, is in the room, then

She stopped abruptly as Big Sweet charged. The next moment, it was too late for Lucy to start again. The man who came in with Lucy tried to help her out, but two other men joined Big Sweet in the battle. It took on amazingly. It seemed that anybody who had any fighting to do, decided to settle-up then and there. Switch-blades, ice-picks and old-fashioned razors were out. One or two razors had already been bent back and thrown across the room, but our fight was the main attraction. Big Sweet yelled to me to run. I really ran, too. I ran out of the place, ran to my room, threw my things in the car and left the place. When the sun came up I was a hundred miles up the road, headed for New Orleans. (139)

Being *cornered* into an uncomfortable position is exactly where Hurston found herself in being asked to write the autobiography, a corner in which she spent a year trying to figure out how to write her way out. The aggravation, the frustration at being exposed, the violation of having to tell one's "inner life" are their own kinds of violence, similarly life threatening in their invasion of privacy—threatening in the sense that one is presumably going to reveal things that one does not wish to reveal.

Lucy's is the authority of the switchblade, the authority of the saw-mill camps in which one had no official redress if one's life were threatened—just as Hurston had little redress in producing the auto-biography if she wanted to stay in good graces with the publisher and perhaps get later books, ones that she *did* want to write, published. Lucy's blade of cutting is the blade of cutting up one's manuscripts, one's ideas, one's creative life.

And what of Hurston's escape route? Hurston abandons her song collecting in Polk County and turns to voodoo in New Orleans, an-other genre of folklore, but folklore nonetheless. When Big Sweet tells her to run, she runs into another creative medium, just as the admonition to write autobiography led her into something that crit-ics have consistently complained resists the form of autobiography. In collecting voodoo, Hurston is doing what has set out to do, but doing it in a different way, just as she wrote the autobiography in a different way.

And what role does Big Sweet play in this scenario? Who in real life would have been Hurston's protector, godfather, Big Mama who might have kept the publishing wolves off her, who would have given her the strength to say, "No, I don't want to write an autobiography at this point in my life, and I don't want to suffer any publishing consequences for that decision"? There was no such figure. Her folklore-collecting sponsor and white patron, Charlotte Osgood Mason, had in fact herself held up Hurston's publishing of *Mules and Men* (1935). And Alain Locke, who was Hurston's sometimes intermediary with Mason, could never be altruistically in Hurston's corner for any sustained period of time. Big Sweet is the wish-fulfillment fairy godmother, if the application of such a name to her is not a contradiction in terms. Big Sweet is the mythic arena of resistance to unpleasant life situations. Hurston conjures her up in *Dust Tracks, Mules and Men,* and other of her creative works. Big Sweet is the outlaw side of Zora Neale Hurston (the Cross Damon of Richard Wright's *The Outsider* to Hurston's counterpart in District Attorney Houston), the one who can cuss anybody out publicly, who can wield a knife like a man, and who can indeed stand up and save herself—as well as the wimpish Hurston. Big Sweet is unequivocal violence, not the dressed-up kind that Hurston unleashed upon her stepmother. While Hurston has been reading about killing, Big Sweet has been killing. She says to Hurston:

> You don't know how to handle no knife. You ain't got dat kind of a sense. You wouldn't even know how to hold it to de best advantage. You would draw your arm way back to stop her, and whilst you was doing all dat, Lucy would run in under your arm and be done; cut you to death before you could touch her. And then again, when you sure 'nough fighting, it ain't enough to just stick 'em wid your knife. You got to ram it in to de hilt, then you pull *down.* They ain't no more trouble after dat. They's *dead.* But don't you bother 'bout

no fighting. You ain't like me. You don't even sleep with no mens.
I wanted to be a virgin one time, but I couldn't keep it up. I needed
the money too bad. But I think it's nice for you to be like that. You
just keep on writing down them lies. I'll take care of all de fighting.
Dat'll make it more better, since we done made friends. (138)

Big Sweet not only protects Hurston, but she validates her creative
and sexual reputation. Coming from the mouth of this fast-talking,
quick-striking woman, the evaluations of Hurston the character gain
credibility as Hurston the author manipulates another mythic—folkloristic—means of making a point in the text.

The detail of Big Sweet's advice evokes immediate comparison to
the mythic white father who advised Hurston to kill anyone who
kicked or spat on her and go to jail for it. Parallel placement and positioning in the text gives the white man and Big Sweet parallel roles; it
thus executes another reduction, leveling—or elevation—that white
editors had not anticipated. In portraying Big Sweet as larger than life,
Hurston does not allow the context of seemingly stereotypically black
violence to contain her. She breaks out and stands beside the three
white "educated men of family and wealth" who inspired the founding of Eatonville as well as beside the one who delivered Hurston.

Big Sweet's knife is equivalent to Hurston's defense against creative
encroachment; that is, she epitomizes black folk culture. Hurston's
autobiography is in many ways a tribute to African American folk
culture; it is the cushy couch into which she falls when things do not
go as she would wish them to. That embedding is what she ultimately
uses to criticize those who would control her imaginative energies.
But, in spite of her allegiance to the folk culture, it is also something
that, as she does with Big Sweet, Hurston can abandon at a moment's
notice.

In a counterpart to her absorbing philanthropic whites into her
own mythic scheme, here when it serves Hurston's purpose she similarly subsumes her critics and editorial controllers into a violent folktale. Consider the numerous African American folktales in which

Brer Rabbit commits violence against or cheats other animals. As Bernard Wolfe and Lawrence Levine have convincingly argued, violent actions of the animals are intended to reflect the actions of whites who controlled the lives of blacks.[2] During slavery and the several decades thereafter, blacks obviously could not criticize whites directly. They could, however, signify upon their behavior by presenting anthropomorphized versions of whites. As white collectors embraced the animal tales, they seldom stopped to consider that they might have been laughing at portraits of themselves, their antics as conceived by the black folk imagination.

Similarly, in the bid to get Hurston to write about her own black life and that of others, her publisher and editors did not remotely conceive of the possibility that their actions might be represented in the pages of her narrative. Just as whites generally could not imagine their actions represented by animals, so those contemporary with Hurston and who influenced her fate could not imagine their actions represented in the lives of black characters, actors, indeed the life of Hurston herself. Hurston held the mirrors up, with her cultural history of violence—as well as that of whites—and her cultural history of storytelling to inform her contemporary situation. In the mirror of black folk traditions, she could be simultaneously critical and entertaining. The folk culture saves her from exposure, from literary death, in the same way that Big Sweet does. Ultimately, the folk culture and Big Sweet are one—mythic, violent but enduring, imaginatively engaging, the prototype of what living beings cannot be. Hurston might have tried to live the life of Stagolee, but her pistol was too cute and her fighting skills too paltry in the final analysis for her to do anything but intrude herself into the drama of the story. She could never be the major player.

Hurston's failure as mythic Stagolena the character, however, does not preclude her success as the storyteller, for ultimately the last word is indeed hers. She conceives the characters, she sketches the incidents, she recounts the violence that she uses to criticize as well as to escape from the strictures upon her writing. It is not sufficient simply to say that Hurston is a trickster. It would be more accurate to suggest that, in mythologizing her origins, birth, and anointment, she signaled to the curious that the larger-than-racial text was the one in which she preferred to present herself. Yet in admitting her inability to operate within the black folk world that she admires, she simultaneously cast herself as one who could use the culture to her own advantage or abandon it at will.

Clearly, Hurston's contemporary readers did not scratch below the surface of what they were reading. As Hemenway points out, "*Dust Tracks* was commercially successful. It did not offend whites, it sold well, most critics liked it, and it won the *Saturday Review's* $1,000 Anisfield-Wolf Award for its contribution to 'the field of race relations.' More than at any other point in her life, Zora became a recognized black spokesperson, whose opinions were sought by the white reading public" (288).

The greatest test of any duping is whether or not those so put upon ever realize that they are duped. Hurston's readers concluded that they were getting what her editors intended. Another colored person had revealed a lot about herself, entertained them in the process, not made them feel guilty for being who they were, and equalized blacks and whites by suggesting that they could all end up in hell together ("Maybe all of us who do not have the good fortune to meet, or meet again, in this world, will meet at a barbecue," 209). But nobody really expected to go to hell, so they could dismiss that final note in what they hoped was the spirit of good-natured transracial humor. And for a while, Hurston's compromise in writing the autobiography enabled her to publish quite a bit, particularly between 1942 and 1945. Success and hindsight made the initial uncertainty about writing the autobiography a booger bear.

They did not, however, erase the choices that Hurston had made, the choices that have enabled this reading of the text. The good times following the publication of *Dust Tracks* did not mitigate the reality of publishing control or the anger that had inspired the most vivid scenes in the narrative. Nor did they eliminate the fact that the problems in *Dust Tracks* are as much the fault of others as they are Hurston's. While my reading of the text might not in any way reduce its problematic nature, it might at least encourage us to begin to think that Hurston was somewhat less at sea in the writing of her autobiography than previous critics have suggested.

(1994)

Notes

1. Introduction to Hemenway, *Zora Neale Hurston,* xvii.

2. See Levine, *Black Culture and Black Consciousness,* 118–22. Levine writes that "trickster tales were a prolonged and telling parody of white society."

Works Cited

Baldwin, James. *Go Tell It on the Mountain.* New York: Dell, 1953.

Hemenway, Robert. *Zora Neale Hurston: A Literary Biography.* Urbana: University of Illinois Press, 1977.

Hurston, Zora Neale. *Dust Tracks on a Road.* 1942. Reprint, New York: HarperCollins, 1991.

———. *Jonah's Gourd Vine.* 1934. Reprint, New York: Harper and Row, 1990.

Levine, Lawrence W. *Black Culture and Black Consciousness: Afro-American Folk Thought from Slavery to Freedom.* New York: Oxford University Press, 1977.

Raynaud, Claudine. " 'Rubbing a Paragraph with a Soft Cloth'? Muted Voices and Editorial Constraints in *Dust Tracks on a Road.*" In *Decolonizing the Subject,* ed. Sidonie Smith and Julia Watson, 34–64. Minneapolis: University of Minnesota Press, 1992.

Wolfe, Bernard. "Uncle Remus and the Malevolent Rabbit." In *Mother Wit from the Laughing Barrel: Readings in the Interpretation of Afro-American Folklore,* ed. Alan Dundes. 1973. Reprint, Jackson: University of Mississippi Press, 1990, 524–40.

Five Architecture as Destiny?

Women and Survival Strategies
in Ann Petry's *The Street*

 In *The Street* (1946), Ann Petry anticipates Toni Morrison in that her fictional world is one in which houses and apartments play as significant a role in the construction of female character and the shaping of destiny as 7 Carpenter's Road in *Sula* (1974) or 124 Bluestone Road in *Beloved* (1987). Indeed, Petry's architecture may be even more determining than Morrison's, for the options available to characters center around the larger enclosure of the city of New York, of which the smaller, domestic enclosures are but a microcosmic representation. At least Morrison's characters have sky and open spaces surrounding the houses in which they reside. The very street on which Petry places her characters serves its own destructive, defining constrictions, for that street is controlled by the men who in turn attempt to control the lives of the women as well as their domestic spaces. Against the backdrop of the construction of the street is the American Dream that tempts black people with its promise of fulfillment, then withholds that fulfillment from them. Male domination and failed cultural ideology go hand in hand, therefore, to shape attitudes toward space and to undermine the best intentions of the women in the novel to acquire safe and secure spaces.

For Lutie Johnson, Mrs. Hedges, and Min, the three major black female characters in *The Street,* the psychological impact of their encounters with men and the society, and the confinement of the domestic spaces in which they are forced to live, combine to ensure rather bleak futures for them. Or so it would seem at a glance. A more careful examination of the novel and its uses of space, however, reveals that while Lutie ultimately ends up a victim of such spaces, Mrs. Hedges and Min are able to forge different futures for themselves. Lutie Johnson believes that she can claim the American Dream (home, good job, security) as her own, that she can fight the men who would control her, and that she can find a safe space for herself and her son, Bub. Mrs. Hedges, by contrast, almost literally becomes a part of the apartment she inhabits, which means that she tries to merge with the patriarchal world into which she has bought. Min learns to survive abusive men and failed dreams by "melting into chairs," an important feature of flexibility and adaptability that the ambitious Lutie Johnson never masters.

The tales of these three women are tales of wood, stone, and concrete on the one hand, and flesh on the other, finding or not finding that they are compatible. Of the black female characters in *The Street,* Min, the nearly invisible woman, and Mrs. Hedges after her, are the malleable bodies and personalities that adjust successfully to the world in which they must live. Lutie Johnson, who sees physical structures as objects to step over on her way to somewhere else instead of forces to blend with, ultimately turns out to be less the central focus of the novel than the other two women. With their trait of adaptability, Mrs. Hedges and Min illustrate that physical surroundings are only part of destiny. The major part lies within an individual who recognizes and assesses clearly the circumstances of her life and determines to flow *with* instead of *counter to* those circumstances. Such attitudes would suggest, then, that an understanding of environment and architecture should precede the imposition of an alien, absolute morality upon a world where survival depends upon mutability.

As Hazel Arnett Ervin and Gloria Wade-Gayles point out, all of these women desire the security of family and home that was commensurate with prevailing cultural expectations in the 1940s.[1] Following her divorce from a philandering husband, Lutie goes to the street in an effort to escape from the morally compromising home environment of her father's apartment. Mrs. Hedges arrives in New York from the South with the expectation of finding love, marriage, and the home that accompanies those states. Min, who is also no longer with her husband, nonetheless desires the security and safety represented by the American ideal. All of the women, Ervin argues, desire the usual American status of wife at home and husband working, but none, because of her blackness and gender, can find that ideal on the street. The stated and unstated cultural expectations informing their quests for space, therefore, undergird their individual attempts to wrest security from a society with which their very existence is incompatible.

Grandmother Said All I Needed Was a Husband and a House

By aligning herself with Ben Franklin (63, 72) and all his legacy represents in the up-by-the-bootstraps American tradition of success, Lutie Johnson buys into the American Dream and begins the imposition of an alien morality and worldview onto the world in which she lives. By adhering to her grandmother's straitlaced and simplistic absolute morality, Lutie similarly fails to recognize that the evil forces around her do not abide by the same standards of behavior. Consequently, she is set adrift in a world where she believes that the mastery of where one lives is key to climbing out of poverty, out of unpleasant living conditions, and into white-collar jobs where employers will eventually recognize one's talents and reward one accordingly.

Space for Lutie initially means finding the resources to retain the home she shares with her husband, Jim, and her son, Bub. This rather understandable dream or need quickly accelerates into something else when she meets the white family for whom she goes to work. Lutie's sense of space as escape is then shaped by her work for the Chandlers in their home in Lyme, Connecticut. A domestic dreamland to the woman who has been forced to hire herself out to pay the mortgage interest on a rather paltry home in Jamaica, New York, the house in Connecticut becomes emblematic of the idea that the kind of domestic space one owns has a direct correlation to one's success in society. The Chandler home represents what one can achieve if one strives desperately enough, that is, a secure physical place in society, while the house in which Lutie and Bub live with her father and his many girlfriends exists at the other end of the scale: confinement and imprisonment in a "crowded, musty flat on Seventh Avenue" (55). For Lutie, Pop's house is one where alcohol and sex flow freely, where almost anyone can enter at any hour, and where Bub will very early discover the vices that will prevent him from ever aspiring to a space comparable to that of the Chandlers, even if that space were toned down to allow for the working-class young black man into whom Bub will probably grow.

Her efforts to transcend spatial and psychological confinements and to find a home for herself and Bub begin with Lutie's move onto 116th Street, the street of the novel's title. In the very graphically depicted opening chapter of the novel, the text makes clear during Lutie's quest for better housing that escapes and confinements are merely matters of degree. While Lutie herself similarly recognizes that the apartment house before which she stands and the apartment she eventually sees are comparable to many others at which she has looked, she still holds to the idea that escape is possible. She knows that the tenants portend patterns of behavior and cycles of interaction that will keep poverty and illiteracy ever before her. Yet optimistic and determined, Lutie seeks to transform space to suit the images she has in mind, for she is still very much in the tradition of a young woman seeking safety for herself and her son.

Textual representation of space in the apartment, however, makes clear that Lutie's sense of things is a case of her awareness of reality operating against her knowledge of what the Chandler house represents. She notes the darkness of the hallway, the fact that she can touch both sides of the hall without really trying, and the seemingly interminable steps to get to her fourth floor walk-up apartment. The higher she walks, "the walls were reaching out for her—bending and swaying toward her in an effort to envelop her" (12). The climb is up a stairway that will never be crystal, no matter how much light will enter, no matter how much painting will be done. The smallness of the apartment and the same smell in all the rooms similarly convey an environment where human energy exerted against its stifling effects is more likely to cripple the exerter than transform the landscape. A bedroom without a window, a bathroom with "old-fashioned and deeply chipped" fixtures, and a living room from which the only view is an alleyway littered with trash and dogs further illustrate the improbability of transformation here.

To extend this impossibility, Petry introduces Jones, the super, as the satanic figure responsible for upkeep in this hell of a place to live. His great height and gauntness highlight his sexual hunger as well as his separation from other human beings. Through Lutie's evaluation of him as a brooding, dangerous man—even as he initially shows her the apartment—and our sensing of his desire to contain her in the same way that the apartment will, the text makes clear that the American Dream is absent from this environment. Just as Lutie must compromise and settle for much less than what she wants in an apartment, so are other forces at work to try to extract moral and sexual compromises from her. With the presentation of the apartment, the text suggests that Lutie is being locked into a new set of negative expectations, not freed from her previous existence.

Locks and keys serve a crucial function in the depiction of Lutie's life, as well as in the lives of Mrs. Hedges and Min. They are used so frequently in a space that protects so little that the question immediately arises: what is being locked in or out? The super is careful to unlock the door to the apartment Lutie examines, and, within that apartment, there are doors that Lutie has to open as she tries to examine the size and quality of the apartment. The fact that the super holds the keys, that he is able—against her will—to silently persuade Lutie to climb the stairs in front of him, and that he physically dominates the space that will later become home for her and Bub is further testament to the male control of locks and keys as well as to the lives of *most* of the women in the novel—and Lutie Johnson is not the exception.

Petry uses locks and keys to suggest a mazelike construction of domination as well as sexual desire. Where domestic space is traditionally associated with women and deemed "safe," Petry allows violation of the space Lutie selects—even as she is selecting it as well as after she moves in. We later learn that her suspicions about the super's thirsty lust for her are accurate, for he has indeed imagined violating her sexually as he has shown her the apartment; her awareness of "the hot, choking awfulness of his desire for her pinioned her there so that she couldn't move. It was an aching yearning that filled the apartment, pushed against the walls, plucked at her arms" (15). It has only been with superhuman effort that he has contained himself. Lutie's awareness of his lust for her on this first visit ties into the vividness with which she is able to analyze some situations and contrasts with the shortsightedness she shows about others. From her first sight of the apartment, therefore, a force that would reduce her to the essentialist body of a youthful black female dominates her assessment of where she is to live.

Jones the super is symbolic of the impersonal, almost animalistic forces on the street that would similarly reduce Lutie to a voice, a body, a potential for exploitation rather than a struggling young woman who is just looking for a relatively safe place for herself and her son to live. By reducing Lutie to her youthful body, Jones anticipates the reactions to Lutie of Boots Smith, a local bandleader, and Junto, a nightclub owner, when they will later seek to control her because of how she looks and sings; they will similarly ignore her aspirations for herself and her son. In the junglelike environment of the street, where those in power, or those with money, or those who are physically stronger prey on those who are weaker, Lutie's initial and accurate reaction to Jones shows that he belongs in this environment. And not only does he belong there, but he has also made his peace with it. He has lived in basement apartments for so long as the super of various buildings that he has lost a certain amount of human sensitivity; his basest emotions are blatantly obvious, whereas jungle residents like Boots and Junto try more subtle means to get Lutie to give in to them.

Jones's desire for Lutie is striking in the scene in which he enters the apartment after she has moved in. The combination of violation of safe space and base animalistic desire illustrates the relationship between architecture and sexuality. The men in the novel seem to believe that if they can control or at least have access to women's domestic space, then they can control the women's bodies. Jones has no qualms about entering Lutie's apartment when she is absent, fraternizing with Bub, and sending him out on an errand so that he can examine Lutie's personal space more thoroughly. Violation of physical space is equivalent to sexual violation, for Jones claims Lutie's most personal things as his own. He looks through her kitchen and bathroom, examines the talcum powder on her dresser, and invades her closet. Like the warped sexual pervert that he is, he crushes one of Lutie's blouses in his hands as he lives out the sexual fantasy of owning her body in the same way that he owns her physical space and clothing. The blouse "had a low round neck and the fullness of the cloth in the front made a nest for her breasts to sit in. He took it out and looked at it. It smelt like the talcum and he crushed it violently between his hands squeezing the soft thin material tighter and tighter until it was a small ball in his hands except the part where the metal hanger was near the top" (108).

For a woman who seeks safety but who must suffer this kind of abnormal violation from a source from which she least expects it, Lutie can have no peace on 116th Street or anywhere else in New York. Her womblike domestic space serves only to lock violators in, not to lock them out. If she can have no protection within her own small apartment, then she can surely expect none from the more public space into which she ventures, such as the Junto Bar and Grill. Not only does Jones violate her space, but also she constantly feels its power to oppress. "Yes, she thought. The trouble is that these rooms are so small. After she had been in them just a few minutes, the walls seemed to come in toward her, to push against her. Now that she had this apartment, perhaps the next thing she ought to do was to find another one with bigger rooms" (78–79). For the time being, however, architecture is oppression, especially during one disturbing evening when Lutie's bedroom "grew smaller and the pieces of furniture larger until she felt as though she were suffocating" (194).

The bigger room for the moment, therefore, is the Junto Bar and Grill, with its "gracious spaciousness" (144) that makes her feel "free here where there was so much space" (146). It is in that particular space that she meets Boots Smith and where she observes Junto watching her after her loneliness drives her to sing a bluesy song. In contrast to Jones thinking he can control the space in which Lutie lives, Junto knows that he can control her destiny by withholding her pay and controlling her access to a singing career at the casino he owns. In the Bar and Grill, space is allocated so that sexuality is as dominant as the beer and the music. A woman like Lutie, sitting at the bar area in the light, can be observed with impunity by Junto, who is sitting farther away and in a more darkly lit area. The space arrangement puts Lutie on display, almost on an auction block, as two powerful males, one black and one white, gauge her sexual value to each of them. Boots sees her as a potential singer and sexual partner; Junto sees her simply as a body he wants to possess. Coming to the bar to elude the confinement of her apartment puts Lutie in another prison, one where her grandmother's advice and her own common sense do not serve her in good enough stead for her to save herself.

Space in *The Street* is always sexual space, whether it is a female-rented private apartment, such as Lutie's or Mrs. Hedges's; a public space such as the Junto; or a male-rented private apartment, such as Jones's or Boots's. All of these spaces are sites of contestation between males and females, between the forces that would control women and turn them into whores or kept females, and the forces—much more feeble—that seek escape from these influences. For Lutie, the final confrontation with the space that determines destiny occurs when she goes to Boots Smith's apartment seeking the loan of two hundred dollars for the lawyer to defend Bub from the accusation of mail stealing. Boots uses this as the opportunity to present Lutie to Junto; if she becomes Junto's concubine, Boots explains to her, the two hundred dollars will be hers immediately. When Lutie screams and Junto leaves, the confrontation with Boots escalates into him trying to seduce her and slapping her when she refuses. Angered beyond reason, Lutie beats Boots to death with an iron candlestick. It is not surprising that architecture surfaces as one of the main causes for her blows: "First she was venting her rage against the dirty, crowded street. She saw the rows of dilapidated old houses; the small dark rooms; the long steep flights of stairs; the narrow dingy hallways; the little lost girls in Mrs. Hedges' apartment; the smashed homes where the women did drudgery because their men had deserted them. She saw all of these things and struck at them" (430). Boots and Junto, in their desire to keep women like Lutie confined to such spaces, to make whores out of them, are symbolic master builders for the architecture that destroys wills, futures, lives.

When Lutie attempts to leave Boots's apartment, she further discovers the extent to which he was determined to make a whore out of her: "The foyer door was closed because she backed right into it. Just a few more steps and she would be out. She fumbled for the knob. The door was locked. She didn't believe it and rattled it. She felt for a key. There was none. It would, she was certain, be in Boots Smith's pocket and she felt a faint stirring of anger against him. He had deliberately locked the door because he hadn't intended to let her out of here" (431–32). Determined to exert his will over Lutie's, Boots was sure that his domestic space would provide the sexual interlude he desired, so he confidently put the key "in his pocket." Lutie forces herself to fumble through the clothing of the dead Boots to effect her escape from the apartment and from New York, but Boots Smith, though dead, along with Junto, has indeed had a hand in architecture determining Lutie's destiny. Although she kills Boots in this skirmish, she has lost the war to escape from the street, which means that she has lost the war to secure a safe domestic space.

Certainly she will *leave* the street, but she will leave as a fugitive who has abandoned her son to the very forces from which she has tried to keep him safe. She recognizes the walls that have been built to contain and ultimately to destroy her: "From the time she was born, she had been hemmed into an ever-narrowing space, until now she was very nearly walled in and the wall had been built up brick by brick by eager white hands" (323–24); she has been "neatly caged" (324) on 116th Street. When she encounters Junto in Boots's apartment, therefore, she realizes that he "has a brick in his hand. Just one brick. The final one needed to complete the wall that had been building up around her for years, and when that one last brick was shoved in place, she would be completely walled in" (423). And if we were to write beyond the ending of this novel, it would not be difficult to envision a substantially morally weakened Lutie Johnson whose trek to Chicago under the double burden of having killed a man and left her son will soon combine to force her into a deterioration from which no grandmother's advice will be able to raise her.

Using physical space as the measure of upward mobility led Lutie down a dangerous path, yet that path is easy to understand. It is indeed within the tradition of Ben Franklin with whom she identifies, and it upholds the tenets of the American Dream—at least as Lutie interprets them and tries to apply them to herself. Yet Lutie fails to average in accurately how all the components of her being—youthfulness, beauty, and blackness—would work to the detriment of her larger objective. Because she could not respond sexually to Jones the super, or bend the morality that singing for a Boots Smith would mean, or become Junto's whore, she discovers that all the houses of potential safety have been locked away from her. Set outdoors, in the general lack of safety of "the Street," she falls prey to the forces that control all the "safe" spaces because she cannot give of herself sufficiently to warrant their protection.

Acquiring Property with the Big Guys

Unlike Lutie Johnson, Mrs. Hedges learned early that it was better to blend with the landscape than try to reshape it. Arriving in New York as a large woman who believed that she was too unattractive to reap genuine love and affection or even the possibility of prostitution, Mrs. Hedges had ravaged through garbage cans to survive. It was on one such food-finding mission, gnawing on a chicken bone, that she met Junto, who was collecting junk. Instead of becoming involved in a potentially lengthy contestation of territory, Mrs. Hedges showed her first sign of adaptability: she agreed to work with Junto. That alignment proved profitable for both of them. In Mrs. Hedges, Junto got a hardworking, honest partner who gave him good advice about possible investments (in apartments, whorehouses, and nightclubs) and became janitor and collector of rents in the first apartment building he bought. In Junto, Mrs. Hedges got the power and whiteness from which her blackness excluded her. As a white male, Junto could easily make the business deals that might have been more or too difficult for Mrs. Hedges, and he could make the investments that would ensure a bright future for both of them.

In the absence of some of the attributes that Lutie Johnson has— good looks and youth—Mrs. Hedges has a clarity about her existence that serves her well. Yet at a glance her force of will compares favorably to Lutie's, especially when she is caught in a fire in one of Junto's apartment buildings. Her effort to escape is almost superhuman:

> It was a narrow aperture not really big enough for the bulk of her body. She felt her flesh tear and actually give way as she struggled to get out, forcing and squeezing her body through the small space. Fire was blazing in the room in back of her. Hot embers from the roof were falling in front of her. She tried to keep her face covered with her hands, so that she wouldn't see what she was heading into, so that she could keep some of the smoke and flame away from her face. . . .
>
> There was nothing but smoke and red flame all around her, and

she wondered why she kept on fighting to escape. She could smell her hair burning, smell her flesh burning, and still she struggled, determined that she would force her body through the narrow window, that she *would make the very stones of the foundation give* until the window opening would in turn give way.

She was a bundle of flame when she finally rolled free on the ground. The firemen who found her stared at her in awe. She was unconscious when they picked her up, and she was the only survivor left from that house full of people. (244; emphasis mine)

The desire to survive, and the will to make the adjustments to do so, no matter how repulsive those adjustments might be—this is the area in which Mrs. Hedges's will surpasses Lutie Johnson's. Mrs. Hedges's actions in the fire are emblematic of her actions in life. Make the adjustments, bend to the changes that are necessary to keep on being a part of the world. By contrast, Lutie would probably have died in the fire.

The house fire represents the possibility in which architecture could have shaped Mrs. Hedges's destiny, but she transcended it. That becomes the measure by which she lives. After the fire, Junto offers Mrs. Hedges the apartment in the building on 116th Street in which Jones and Lutie reside. She, like Jones and Boots, turns domestic space into sexual space by transforming her apartment into a brothel and hiring "girls" to work for her. Becoming a pimp is another of Mrs. Hedges's concessions to the street on which she lives, to the New York world of which that street is a part. She realizes that, as an already unattractive and rather large black woman now severely scarred by burns, she will never garner sex, love, or affection. But she, like Boots Smith, can at least control access to sex. That control makes her one of the exploiters instead of the exploited. As she examines Lutie and determines that she is a high-priced commodity to be set aside for Junto, she shows further that the morality that constrains Lutie is not a part of the world in which she operates.

Yet Petry makes clear that Mrs. Hedges is not simply a villain. She does provide a home for her girls, and on at least one occasion she allows a young man who cannot pay immediately to have sex with one of the girls. She also looks out for children in the apartment building when their parents are not at home, and she is rather kind to Min when she recommends the Prophet David to her. Equally important, she saves Lutie when the sex-crazed super attempts to drag her into the cellar and rape her—either because she is genuinely appalled by his actions or because she is protecting what she perceives to be Junto's "property": " 'I just wanted to tell you [Jones] for your own good, dearie, that it's Mr. Junto who's interested in Mis' Johnson. And I ain't goin' to tell you again to keep your hands off' " (238). By contrast, however, without any consideration for Lutie as a separate, living, breathing, self-determining human being, Mrs. Hedges can plan her future as callously as the men. She muses: "Mr. Junto would be willing to pay very high for [Lutie]. Very, very high, because when he got tired of her himself he could put her in one of those places he ran on Sugar Hill" (256). In other words, Mrs. Hedges exhibits the kind of flexibility necessary for survival on the street that Lutie, in her absoluteness, cannot envision. Instead of "going with the flow," as Mrs. Hedges does, Lutie wants to stop it, or reroute it; she can only find herself crushed in the process, just as Jones crushed her blouse in his hands.

Perched in her open window on the coldest of days, Mrs. Hedges is the blend of adjustment and adaptability that presages success on the street. She blends not only with the setting, but also with the weather. When Lutie is pulling her coat tightly around her neck to stop the raging wind, Mrs. Hedges is calmly enjoying the weather, without coat or jacket and with just her trademark scarf on her head. From her lookout position as near oracle, she is able to gauge, access, and act upon what she observes. She has no need to leave her apartment, as Lutie seeks escape in Junto's Bar and Grill, for she has made peace with herself and peace with her surroundings. The absence of restlessness and a seeming lack of ambition give her an advantage over many women on the street. Yet she has acquired what she judged to be available to her in life—property and as much money as she needs, in addition to control over the lives of the girls who live with her; she has joined the patriarchy, at least at its lower rungs.

Again, Mrs. Hedges is by no means a suggested model for altruistic behavior, but she has not allowed the spatial confinements of her surroundings to determine her destiny. She is much freer sitting at her window on the coldest of days, looking out on the street and meddling in people's business, than Lutie Johnson is with her typing certificates, her quest for a white-collar job, her good singing voice, and her wonderful looks.

Melting into Chairs

Of the three women on whom this study focuses, Min would appear to be the least likely to survive, but that first impression ultimately needs altering. Min is initially presented as a broken, beaten-down woman who has acquiesced in her own abuse over several decades:

> During the years she had spent doing part-time domestic work she had never raised any objections to the actions of cruelly in-different employers. She had permitted herself to be saddled with whole family washes when the agency that had sent her on the job had specified just "personal pieces." When the madam added sheets, towels, pillowcases, shirts, bedspreads, curtains—she sim-ply allowed herself to be buried under the great mounds of dirty clothes and it took days to work her way out from under them, getting no extra pay for the extra time involved.
>
> On other jobs the care of innumerable children had been added when the original agreement was for her to do the cooking and a little cleaning. The little cleaning would increase and increase until it included washing windows and walls and waxing floors. Some of her madams had been openly contemptuous women who laughed at her to her face even as they piled on more work; acting as though she were a deaf, dumb, blind thing completely devoid of under-

standing, but able to work, work, work. Years and years like that.
(126–27)[2]

A human doormat—that is what Min has been and remains during
the course of the novel; never once had she protested or left any of
the jobs on which she was exploited. And the doormat image is appropriate for the spaces she has inhabited. Not only has she allowed
her madams to treat her without respect, but she has also allowed
her many "husbands" to do so. She has given up dignity in exchange
for space, and her clinging to whatever little space she has found has
usually meant that she would be financially exploited and physically
beaten. Min has judged the "safety" of space to be more important
than the abuses.

By literally presenting her body to be beaten, however, Min has
executed the ultimate transformation in adjusting to the spaces in
which and the men with whom she must live. Her body becomes
almost an inanimate physical structure on which her "husbands" im-
print their right to abuse her however they want and to take whatever
she has. This grammar of violence trains her to accept abuse from
one husband to the next, for her body knows the script and is pli-
able enough to contain the violence without Min being ultimately
destroyed. When Jones overcomes his fear of her spell casting and
moves toward beating her, she remembers the script:

> she waited for the feel of his heavy hands around her neck, for
> the violence of his foot, for he would kick her after he knocked
> her down. She knew how it would go, for her other husbands had
> taught her: first, the grip around the neck that pressed the windpipe
> out of position, so that screams were choked off and no sound
> could emerge from her throat; and then a whole series of blows,
> and after that, after falling to the ground under the weight of the
> blows, the most painful part would come—the heavy work shoes
> landing with force, sinking deep into the soft, fleshy parts of her
> body, her stomach, her behind. (357)

Becoming one with her environment means that Min has learned the "art" of molding flesh and blood to wood and stone, especially when that wood and stone comes in the shape of men who hold the keys to the lodging she needs.

Min has "melted into the furniture," as Lutie observes her doing on the night she puts down a deposit on the apartment on 116th Street. Whereas Lutie holds her body sacred, and Mrs. Hedges presents hers to be burned, Min shapes hers to whatever the situation demands. She thereby becomes the ultimate adapter, the ultimate survivor, for, before meeting Jones, she has found nothing too ugly, no situation too compromising for her to exist in it without a measure of peace. She has blended with wood and stone, made her very body the site on which contest and compromise can be effected.

Architecture becomes for Min the bottle into which she pours the wine of her body. That is where we find her with Jones the super. When he casually suggested that she move in with him, she had done so two years before Lutie arrived, because, being a flexible person, "she didn't have any place in particular to go to" (116). And those two years had been the most pleasant of her life. Jones had not beaten her, had not stolen her money as other men had. With Lutie's arrival, indeed the very night on which Lutie appears in Jones's apartment to pay the deposit, Min knows that her safe haven is no longer safe. Jones's desire for what he perceives as the sexually more vibrant Lutie will lead to Min taking the only constructive action of her paltry little life: going to the Prophet David for spells that will allow her to stay in Jones's apartment.

Our first glimpse of Min tells the story of her life. She has spent it being as unobtrusive as possible; she "whispers" when she speaks and gives over physical space to more dominant personalities. Lutie observes Jones's apartment and Min: "Next to the sofa there was an overstuffed chair and she drew her breath in sharply as she looked at it, for there was a woman sitting in it, and she had thought that she and the dog and the Super were the only occupants of the room. How could anyone sit in a chair and melt into it like that? As she looked, the shapeless small dark woman in the chair got up and bowed to her without speaking" (23). "Shapeless" is a good word to describe Min, for it shows her potential adaptability, her willingness to be molded into any shape her domestic living condition requires. Lutie's evaluation of Min is equally indicative of Min's ability to survive. Lutie thinks of her as "a drab drudge so spineless and so limp she was like a soggy dishrag" (57), and Lutie decides that she will never allow herself to succumb to the same fate. But all those images of Min—spineless, limp, dishrag—reiterate malleability, the trait of free-flowing adaptability instead of the frigidity that will cause Lutie to break. In living with Jones, Min has learned how to disappear through meaningless chatter or through quiet, near invisible sitting postures.

Her posture and the dog's are not dissimilar in response to Jones, a situation that further sheds light on Min's willingness to be abused. Jones yells at the dog and kicks it, but it still wags its tail and itches to be near its master. When Lutie first enters Jones's apartment, "the dog had been lying near the radio that stood under a window at the far side of the room. He got up when he saw her, walking toward her with his head down, his tail between his legs; walking as though he were drawn toward her irresistibly, even though he knew that at any moment he would be forced to stop" (21). At the "Lie down" command of the super, "the dog moved back to the window, shrinking and walking in such a way that she thought if he were human he'd walk backward in order to see and be able to dodge any unexpected blow. He lay down calmly enough and looked at her, but he couldn't control the twitching of his nose; he looked, too, at the Super as though he were wondering if he could possibly cross the room and get over to her without being seen" (21–22). The dog and Min share the same relationship to Jones, existing in his space at his whim and subject to whatever brutality he would commit against them. Indeed, Min feels the dog's pain when Jones abuses it: "When he beat the dog, it made her sick at her stomach, because as each blow fell the dog cried out sharply and her stomach would suck in against itself" (363).

The dog's irresistible attraction to Lutie and inability to control his twitching nose parallel Jones's inability to control his lust for Lutie. At one point, Jones is described as being drawn to Lutie's apartment "like a magnet" (232). On another occasion Lutie has a disturbing dream in which the super and the dog become one in chasing her (191), and she links Min and the dog: "She couldn't decide which was worse: the half-starved, cringing dog, the gaunt man or the shapeless whispering woman who lived with him" (75). Buddy the dog thereby represents features of both his keepers—the desire for unleashed animalism on Jones's side and the desire for a safe haven on Min's side. More often than not, however, Petry ties dogs and dog imagery to heightened sexuality of domestic spaces, to leashed and unleashed sexual desire, not unlike a similar use of dogs on leashes in relation to Jadine's sexual desire for Son Green in Toni Morrison's *Tar Baby* (1981). When Lutie expresses approval at Jones's cleaning of the apartment windows after his painting job, "he had looked like a hungry dog that had suddenly been given a bone" (69), a kind of pleasurable orgasmic response. On the night before Min visits the Prophet David, "when she leaned over to take some beans out of the oven, [Jones] kicked her just like she was the dog" (117), because he realizes how sexually undesirable her rear end is in comparison to Lutie Johnson's.

Like Buddy, Min is willing to exist in whatever small space Jones allots to her. The key she holds to Jones's apartment is one she "timidly" uses for entry and exit because it is too precious to risk Jones's displeasure by being loud in her actions. It is only after her visit to the Prophet David that there is a change in her use of the key, which Jones notes:

> It was the sound he had been waiting to hear, but it came to his ears with an offensive, decisive loudness. Normally Min's key was inserted in the lock timidly, with a vague groping movement, and when the lock finally clicked back, she stood there for a second as though overwhelmed by the sound it made. This key was being thrust in with assurance, and the door was pushed open immedi-

ately afterward. He frowned as he listened because on top of that
she slammed the door. Let it go out of her hand with a bang that
echoed through the apartment and in the hall outside, could even
be heard going faintly up the stairs. (138–39)

With the prophet's assistance, Min is finally able to claim the space
she has shared with Jones as her own. She proceeds to do so further
by hanging the cross the prophet has given her above the bed, thereby
preventing Jones from beating her or even sleeping in the room, by
burning her sacred candles, and by putting in Jones's coffee the potion
the prophet has advised. For the first time in her life, Min has taken
action to influence her relationship to space. By creating a situation
in which Jones cannot put her out—either because of the spells or
because of his own past history—she tries to triumph over rather
than blend with space. It is this Lutie Johnson–type action that finally
creates the most turmoil in Min.

She watches as her space is transformed from a safe haven to a
place unfit to live. Initially, after the visit to Prophet David, the series
of cleanings Min performs enable her to "dominate" (293) Jones's
space; she claims it through the cleaning process and makes Jones
uneasy with her handiwork. However, even cleaning cannot change
the size and oppressiveness of the apartment, and Min occasionally
feels the need for "a breath of air" because "sometimes it seems awful
close and shut up inside here" (296). In addition, Jones's increasing
sexual desire for Lutie rather quickly makes his apartment increas-
ingly unbearable for Min: "The change in him had transformed the
apartment into a grim, unpleasant place. His constant anger, his sullen
silence, filled the small rooms until they were like the inside of an
oven—a small completely enclosed place where no light ever pen-
etrated" (352), and "living with him was like being shut up with an
animal—a sick, crazy animal" (354).

Although the prophet has ensured Min's stay in Jones's space, she
finally decides that *she does not wish to stay.* Another strong decision, this

one returns her to her more normal course of action, that is, flowing with the circumstances around her instead of trying to change them. Min decides that "having room to breathe in meant much more [than not paying rent]. Lately she couldn't get any air here" (362). Jones's "evilness," fueled by his sexual desire for Lutie, "made the whole apartment grow smaller and darker; living room, bedroom, kitchen— all of them shrinking, their walls tightening about her" (362), and Jones becomes "more than flesh and blood could bear" (364). Having a key to Jones's apartment had reflected Min's desire to cling to safety; her separation from it makes clear the significance of her decision to leave:

> She stared at the key. She had held it in her hand when she left for work in the morning, because the last thing she did before she went out was to make sure she had it with her; and at night, too, she'd clutched it tight in her hand when she approached the door on her return. Leaving it here like this meant that she was saying good-bye to the security she had known; meant, too, that she couldn't come back, never intended coming back, no matter what the future held for her. (368)

Leaving the key is the last step in Min recognizing that the illusion as well as the reality of her safety is gone: "she knew she would never be safe here again" (365); "It wasn't safe here any more" (368). Her life, she decides, depends upon her leaving, "not necessarily that Jones would kill her, not because it was no longer safe here, but because being shut up with the fury of him in this small space would eventually kill her" (368). By leaving Jones's space, Min returns to the level of adaptability that has ensured her survival for so many years. She will probably return to being abused, but she also returns to familiar grounds of flexibility—within limits that fall just short of life threatening.

As the ultimate survivor, Min makes the practical decision to save herself. She has a bit of pride left, and she is hurt when Jones stops even sleeping beside her. She has been able to tolerate his silence and earlier rages, his kickings, and his general unpleasantness, but when it comes to a question of her life, her ability to breathe—even in a constricted space—then she chooses life, the larger desire for safety, over the temporary desire for lodging.

In observing the pushcart man whose services she has sought to help her move from Jones's apartment, Min gives us further indication of her adaptability. She is still flirtatious enough to realize that the man is desirable; as a woman alone, she knows that she is too much a victim, and she hints to the man that there is a possibility for a liaison if he so desires it: "This was a very strong man. His back muscles bulged as he pushed the cart. She moved closer to him. 'Say,' she said, and there was a soft insinuation in her voice, 'you know anywhere a single lady could get a room?' Then she added hastily, 'But not on this street'" (371). Like Mrs. Hedges, Min is too realistic to expect romance, but, unlike Mrs. Hedges, she is not so conscious of her own unattractiveness that she will not try to find sexual as well as physical shelter.

Strikingly, of the three prominent women characters in the novel, Min is the one who most effectively blends architecture and destiny. By not expecting too much of the world, she is seldom disappointed. By presenting her body to be abused, she manages to retain the small spaces of "security" in which she finds lodging. I am not suggesting that Petry presents Min as a model for behavior, one superior to Lutie Johnson or Mrs. Hedges. What we see in Min is basic survival, survival without the qualifications and niceties of a Lutie Johnson or the financial security of a Mrs. Hedges. We see survival in its raw, unembellished condition in an environment that obviously has the potential to destroy anyone. Min becomes the roach after the nuclear holocaust. While more ambitious species target themselves for extinction, she simply finds the nooks and crannies where she is allowed to thrive. Her unstated awareness and comprehension of her surroundings give her the edge over Lutie Johnson and make her perhaps even more adaptable than Mrs. Hedges.

Living Buildings

Petry conveys the possible blending of bodies and buildings by anthropomorphizing the spaces in which her major characters reside. Walls and rooms are active agents; they "reach," "bend," "sway," "rush," "push," "grow," "suffocate," and exert profound psychological influences upon the people who inhabit them.[3] They "shrink" symbolically as the events in the lives of the characters in turn cause them to shrink. Animate and inanimate forces come together to create several environments in which the domination of human bodies and the control of human destiny are as much physical as psychological states. Spaces loom so large in the text that they warrant as much consideration as "characters" as the human characters.

Projection of life into walls provides the physical manifestation of the psychological traumas these women experience by trying to live up to the standards of American familial and feminine ideals in the 1940s. They are caught in a set of imperatives that did not take into consideration the facts of their lives. Indeed, *black* women must bend their bodies to fit the American ideal as surely as Min tries to blend into furniture. The script was never written for them, therefore any attempt to fit their lives into it was doomed to frustration if not certain failure. Petry seems to suggest, therefore, that the class and race factors impinging upon the lives of a great portion of the American population cut them effectively and unapologetically out of the American Dream. Modeling their lives on Ben Franklin or any of his descendants would not ensure them that they would matter to anyone, and certainly not to the men who controlled the spaces and places they tried to make safe for themselves.

(1994, 1999)

Notes

1. See Ervin, "Subversion of Cultural Ideology"; and Wade-Gayles, *No Crystal Stair.* I am particularly grateful to Hazel Ervin for reading a copy of this chapter and making suggestions for improvement as well as for generously sharing a copy of her dissertation.

2. Gloria Wade-Gayles was one of the first critics to offer more than passing commentary on Min. She focuses on Min's work as a domestic, her submissiveness, and her sexual exploitation. See *No Crystal Stair,* 118–22. Hazel Arnett Ervin offers even more extensive commentary on Min in "The Subversion of Cultural Ideology."

3. Wade-Gayles also comments on walls "reaching," "walking," and "swaying and bending" toward Lutie in keeping her confined. *No Crystal Stair,* 151.

Works Cited

Ervin, Hazel Arnett. "The Subversion of Cultural Ideology in Ann Petry's *The Street* and *Country Place.*" Ph.D. diss., Howard University, 1993.
Petry, Ann. *The Street.* 1946. Reprint, Boston: Beacon, 1985.
Wade-Gayles, Gloria. *No Crystal Stair: Visions of Race and Sex in Black Women's Fiction.* New York: The Pilgrim Press, 1984.

Six

Chocklit Geography

Raymond Andrews's
Mythical South

 Scholars who had come to know Raymond Andrews in the eight or ten years before his death and who were instrumental in inspiring new critical interest in his work were understandably puzzled and saddened when he committed suicide near Athens, Georgia, in the fall of 1991. His three previously published novels—*Appalachee Red* (1978), *Rosiebelle Lee Wildcat Tennessee* (1980), and *Baby Sweet's* (1983)—had been reissued by the University of Georgia Press, and three new works, the autobiographical *The Last Radio Baby: A Memoir* (1990) and the novellas *Jessie and Jesus and Cousin Claire* (1991), had been published within a year of his death. He had recently completed "Once upon a Time in Atlanta," the sequel to *The Last Radio Baby,* which was to focus on his life from the age of fifteen.[1] Andrews's literary reputation and requests for lecturing and reading appearances were comfortably on the rise when he chose suicide.[2] With that action, Andrews joined, whether intentionally or coincidentally, the ranks of several American fiction writers who have taken their lives. Andrews always desired to be a "great writer," but his imitation of Hemingway unfortunately has not earned him the same critical or objectionable accolades. His southern birth and seasoning place, however, have aligned him with William Faulkner, Eudora Welty, Flannery O'Connor, Alice Walker, and others who have made the Deep South their point of creative departure.

I have entitled this essay "Chocklit Geography" because of the peculiar twist that Andrews puts on his imagined southern soil in *Appalachee Red,* the novel on which I will focus for this discussion and which won the first James Baldwin Prize for Fiction. While created southern literary territories have engaged the imaginations of readers since Faulkner made Yoknapatawpha a routine word in American literature classes, few of them have been conceived with the overall lighthearted tone and self-conscious narrative presentation that Andrews adopts, which provide a striking contrast to the final reality of his own life. There are certainly some funny stories in Faulkner's canon, and there are certainly some funny scenes in many of the larger works, but the dominant tone is heavy, if not downright pessimistic, and the ultimate endings are more tragic than not. Gloria Naylor's Willow Springs, that mythical world off the coast of Georgia and South Carolina, but belonging to neither, invests the setting of *Mama Day* (1988) with a mystical, fantastic aura of powers beyond this world drawn upon to effect events in this world. Andrews shares with Naylor and Faulkner a love of good storytelling, but he stops short of the otherworldly phenomenon. Perhaps he has closest ties to Randall Kenan, who has made Tims Creek, North Carolina, the territory on which he explores everything from tobacco pulling to the impact of homosexual behavior upon small-town morality. In his novel, *A Visitation of Spirits* (1989), as well as in his collection of short stories, *Let the Dead Bury Their Dead* (1992), Kenan, like Andrews, has been uncompromisingly iconoclastic in his disturbance of southern rituals and patterns of behavior. Like Kenan, Andrews takes pleasure in expanding expectations for what is possible in the South. He achieves his purpose with an inspired knowledge of history, an intimate awareness of black-white relationships, a bluesy serio-comic self-positioning, and an unflinching and unapologetic desire to tweak his nose at what others hold sacred, whether that is a southern attitude toward football, expected sexual mores, or the use of language deemed inappropriate for polite southern storytelling.

Andrews keeps readers constantly aware in *Appalachee Red* that he is narrating, that he is having fun with his narration, and that he is relating his tale from a black vantage point that pokes fun at blacks as frequently as it pokes fun at whites. His "chocklit geography" is tangible as well as intangible, for patterns of relationships are just as important as the territories on which they are carried out. The land is situated in Muskhogean County, Georgia, whose county seat is Appalachee, the city in which all Andrews's fictional inhabitants reside. Located in the Piedmont Belt of North Georgia, Appalachee is slightly more than eighty miles east and south of Atlanta, which becomes the big city mecca in which many of the residents aspire to sojourn. Made up of poor blacks who are trapped in pre–Civil War jobs and relationships with whites, and of a white elite willing to perpetuate the old patterns of masters and enslaved persons, Appalachee is slow to change. For most of the period between 1918 and 1963, the span of time Andrews covers in the novel, blacks in Appalachee are no better off than they were when they were legally enslaved. The geography is thus "black" in the sense that African Americans are stymied into historic patterns that determine their destiny and make it almost impossible for them to become educated, own desirable property, or climb to any heights of which the local whites do not approve.

In these neoslavery conditions, Andrews manages nonetheless to transcend the limitations upon human spirit that the corresponding limitations upon human activity would warrant. Black people may work in the peach fields all day, every day, all week, but they have their ritual excursions into town on Saturday and their own environments in which to escape, momentarily, from the pressures of being black in a white universe. The dark worlds that Andrews creates consist of Dark Town and Light Town, unfortunate divisions based on a pigmentocracy within the black community, but nonetheless more W. C. Handy than Mozart. He also creates Sam's Café, which starts out as the center of the eating, drinking, dancing diversions in black Appalachee and quickly becomes the site on which the title character carves out a new space for black people to be in Appalachee.

Andrews tells his story in a meandering, panoramic way. He relies more on narration than dialogue not only for its functional value in narrative, but also because it enhances the mysterious, legendary qualities of characters by smoothing over some details, thereby leaving those to reader conjecture. Andrews exhibits a love of language with constant plays upon it as well as upon familiar names and places. A central site in the text is called the White House. A two-block street in the heart of the black community's business district—and sometimes blood bank—is called Wall Street (there is also a wall there literally separating the black and white communities). Big Apple is the name of a character who, on his way to New York, got sidetracked in Appalachee for several decades. A dance that peach pickers develop is called the "Fuzz Shake" (as in shaking the peach fuzz off their bodies). The constant and humorous surprise in such usage prevents these plays on language from becoming boring. Surprises also come out of the mouths of southern ladies. The wife of the most prominent white man in town decries football by declaring that it is "a silly-ass game played by sillier-assed people and watched by the silliest asses of them all" (57). The lady's seven-year-old daughter is the conveyor of her mother's sentiment, thus making it even weightier in undercutting the myth of the proper, polite southern lady.

I call the southern world Andrews creates "mythical" not only for its basis in fiction, but for its presentation of a particular set of circumstances and interactions between characters that history tells us would probably have had other patterns of interactions—or perhaps the ones that do exist would have manifested themselves in slightly altered forms. For example, there might have been occasions when black men and white men decided to go into business for their mutual benefit, but seldom with the black man completely in charge. White southern law officers have often been mean and vicious, as the legacy of Alabama's Bull Conner makes clear, but probably not with the style of Clyde White. There might have been an instance or two historically when a black woman razored a white man's face—and lived—but I would doubt that that man would have been the white chief of police.

History, therefore, is merely a polite jumping-off point for Andrews to create larger than life characters, ones with almost superhuman abilities to influence the actions of other people. It is in this realm of imagination, the space where the real gives way to the possible, that Andrews offers mythical, fantastic possibilities for his fiction. And yet he offers them with enough basis in the perceived reality of his fictional characters that there is a blending effect that makes even the fantastic subject to credibility.

To achieve this larger than life effect, Andrews makes legendary characters of his primary protagonists, Clyde "Boots" White and Appalachee Red. Since *how* we perceive them is as much a part of land as it is a part of genealogy, Andrews creates a genealogy of land and property as well as a genealogy of people; in addition, he traces transgenerational exploitation and suffering. To get to the battle of wits and wills between Boots and Red, Andrews must make it clear how they came to be, how social circumstances and history have prepared for them. His narrative posture, therefore, is understandably meandering, and his vision is always panoramic, for he clearly prefers the wide shots to the narrow ones. He creates characters and life stories as he needs them to flesh out the major story. Andrews adopts a technique similar to that of Toni Morrison, who creates seemingly peripheral characters who turn out to be central. Boots and Red are surrounded by many actions and people that do not touch them directly but obviously prepare the way for them.

Andrews also prepares the way for the battle between Boots and Red by using excerpts from the poetry of Langston Hughes and by drawing upon the biblical passages in Revelation that refer to the four horsemen of the apocalypse. Hughes's poetry explores problematic relations between blacks and whites in the South, including lynching, miscegenation, and pride in blackness (the poems Andrews includes are "Song for a Dark Girl," "Cross," and "Me and the Mule").[3] Balanced against the passages from Revelation, the epigraphs structure the novel as a clash between injustice and justice, with an aggressive blackness thrown in for good measure. Red, in various guises as the "horsemen," will presumably right the wrongs done to his family and his people.[4] The biblical overtones of vengeance reflect the imagery Andrews uses to describe Boots and Red, both of whom are called "de devil" or Satan at various points in the text. Their questionable actions are grounded in a history they share.

The characters and land that serve to place Appalachee Red begin with the patriarch of the town's elite white family, John Morgan, in conflict—perhaps unknowingly—with one of the town's black couples, Big Man and Little (Lil) Bit Thompson. One week after his marriage to Lil Bit in 1918, the twenty-one-year-old and strikingly honest Big Man (whose name reflects his size) mistakenly goes to the site of a still to repay a debt he owes. He is arrested and sent to Yankee Town, the local prison. In his absence, eighteen-year-old Little Bit seeks work at the home of young John Morgan, who makes sex a condition of her job, "thus launching another white-man-and-black-woman love affair, a then-prevalent Southern pastime" (7). The business-minded Little Bit, still very much in love with Big Man, concludes that she might as well take practical advantage of her situation and profit from the relationship with Morgan. She persuades him to give her a small lot and build a two-story house on it, which becomes known as the White House. When a baby arrives " 'as red as a green blackberry' " (9), Little Bit sends the "red baby" to Chicago to live with her sister. Upon returning home after a year in prison, Big Man "gave unto his wife the whipping of her young life" (11) but was not otherwise perturbed by her involvement in the "Southern pastime"—at least not until she insisted that they live in the White House. Thus begins their legendary status, for their fights become known throughout the community, the previously nondrinking Big Man takes to drink, and Little Bit takes to "specializing" in cursing him out and to carving up his face with a razor.

Such commotion along the back street did these battles create that the town's blacks soon began telling the bit about the family Blackshear, owners of the undertaking parlor sitting directly across the dirt street from the White House, each evening stuffing cotton into the ears of their dead so that they wouldn't be kept awake nights by the brawling couple and have to appear "tetchy" at their funerals. (12)

Readers are very much aware, therefore, of the potential for violence that the red baby, who will grow up to be Appalachee Red, has inherited, although none of the townspeople—other than his mother and his younger and blacker brother—will ever know who the mysterious Red is. The mystery surrounding him, as I will illustrate later, is central to his positioning as a mythic character.

The legendary fights eventually end only when Sam Wallace, a stranger to Appalachee, buys the White House and Big Man and Little Bit return to a smaller place in Dark Town. It is not until the Depression, in 1935, when Little Bit returns to work for John Morgan, who immediately reestablishes the job's sexual basis, that the Thompson fights begin again. Out of work Big Man simply broods in Sam's Café until a fateful encounter in 1936 with Boots White. Big Man's positioning in the tale to this point, however, makes clear the options for black men in rural southern communities. The concept of manhood can be manifested only in the domestic arena, either in bed or beating one's wife. In despair, the black man must finally acquiesce in his wife's degradation and accept the fact that he cannot get her to voluntarily give up the job he knows she needs in order to support both of them. Yet, what is fascinating about Andrews's treatment of Big Man is that he makes him larger than life nonetheless. In the primarily male world of Sam's Café, as well as in the streets in which he and Little Bit have their fights, Big Man Thompson is considered a king. Crowned the "King of Dark Town," Big Man is also king of the "poolboard" (checkers); he spends his days during the Depression enticing people to challenge him. He is also king because the Hard Labor Holers, the hard-core, mean guys who make their weekly trek from peach picking into town looking for drink, gambling, and "female in-between-legs" (22) entertainment and who would cut a person as soon as look at him or her, have learned not to "mess with" Big Man Thompson because his reputation as a fighter extends far beyond his escapades with his wife; "he was the biggest and respected as the toughest black in the area and all without having to carry a knife. Over the years his big stone-like fists had broken enough of other people's bones to convince those who had seen him in action that he, Big Man Thompson, did not need a blade" (37).

Locating Big Man and Little Bit in Appalachee is central to Andrews's creation of legendary characters, for their interactions make it clear that the townspeople applaud such "entertainment" even as they might eventually call the law to try to stop it. It also makes clear the atmosphere of violence and potential violence that captures the imaginations of Dark Town's inhabitants. The antics of the couple further serve to show that black people's reactions to exploitation might be self-destructive, but they earn admiration from others who are equally oppressed (a part of Big Man's reaction to his wife's relationship with John Morgan is that there are few secrets—black, white, or otherwise—in Appalachee; everybody knows everybody's business, which means that pride is the only response available). Big Man and Little Bit Thompson also set the stage for someone else who is as larger than life as they are to capture the townspeople's imaginations.

The White House, as part of the geography, is thus key to the anticipated battle that will occur in 1945, after an adult Red returns and takes over the running of the café. It is also important for Andrews to position two other characters who will be central to that geography as well as to Red. Their histories and relationships to land and race are equally as significant as Big Man and Little Bit's. These characters are Baby Sweet Jackson, who will become Red's lover, and Clyde "Boots" White, who will become his antagonist. Baby Sweet is the youngest of thirteen children of the black overseer for Mist' Ed (I wonder if that television show was on then . . .), a descendant of Jake "Ol' Crip" Turner, who used black convict labor from Yankee Town to clear a "wilderness," fill it in, and plant the peach trees that stretch for miles across "the entire southwest end of Muskhogean" (26).[5] The fierceness with which Ol' Crip used his laborers earned the place the nickname "Hard Labor Hole." And the fierceness of Ol' Crip himself, who is clubfooted, earned him the nickname "Satan," a whip-carrying, gun-toting demon astride a white stallion who rains down punishment on his workers. With Ol' Crip (and some believe that the devil himself has one clubbed foot), Andrews intertwines the mythical and biblical effects that he will pursue throughout the text. At various points, the narrator and characters will identify both Boots and Red with Satan, thus making such identification one of the features tied to the larger than life figures. It is also noteworthy that Ol' Crip evokes Frederick Douglass's Mr. Covey in the pace at which he expects his workers to produce, his snake/Satanlike demeanor, and the unexpectedness with which he pops up on the work site.[6]

Andrews also uses Ol' Crip to show the absurdity of man trying to exert his will over nature and God. During picking season in 1925, Ol' Crip urges his workers beyond capacity because he wants all the peaches picked before a storm comes. Whipping laborers from their huddled spots under trees during the blinding downpour, Ol' Crip insists that the picking continue in spite of blasting lightning. The scene ends with a prayer and a benediction when Ol' Crip and his horse suffer a blasting fate. The stallion falls, and Ol' Crip is pinned between him and a tree with the handle of his infamous whip protruding from his dying throat. This legendary villain suffers an implied divine punishment for his actions; though that divinity will not play as dominant a role with either Boots or Red, the underlying theme of justice meted out to deserving culprits nonetheless surfaces in relation to Boots. On the other hand, if we view Red in the light of the avenging passages from Revelation that structure the novel, then perhaps we should not so readily dismiss an element of the supernatural.

The genealogy of land and property that meanders toward Red's fate continues when Ol' Crip's only son, Mist' Ed, inherits the land as well as its tradition of having young black girls work in the "Elberta Orchard," which means they are near his house and sexually available

to him anytime of the day. Poor Boy Jackson, Mist' Ed's black overseer, inherits from Ol' Crip an uncompromising love of labor and of
pushing his laborers to the limit:

> Except for the one hour it took him each day to get home, dis-
> pose of the noon meal, and return, Poor Boy spent his daylight
> hours from Monday through Friday among the peach trees. And
> as a result of this total dedication of his the black overseer over the
> years was to prove harder for many Hard Laborites, especially the
> younger males, to stomach than had been Ol' Crip. (33)

Ol' Crip thus writes a violent pattern of existence upon Poor Boy's
life, a pattern that will influence not only his treatment of the laborers
but his interactions with his daughter. Poor Boy uses his "Poor Boy
Whip," "a thick, rounded, long oak stick, which when standing upright came midway between the overseer's high waist and wide shoulders" (33), to "bust heads" and keep the workers in line. He makes his
contribution to the events destined to occur in Appalachee when he
acquiesces to Mist' Ed's request that he send his youngest daughter,
Baby Sweet, to join in the brigade in the "Elberta Orchard." Baby
Sweet's attempt to rescue herself by running away from home puts
her squarely in the hands of the immoral Boots White, who, upon
seeing Baby Sweet walking down the highway, "arrests" her, installs
the fifteen-year-old black beauty in a room above Sam's Café, and
nightly uses her as a sperm depository.

The genealogy of people necessary for this scenario ends with
Red's antagonist. Clyde White, a white man named White and called
"the Man," wears shiny black boots in manifestation of another kind
of geography with which Andrews teases readers in the novel—that
of color—just as he teases them with the color geography relevant to
Dark Town and Light Town. Clyde White, from slightly out of town,
grew up in Yankee Town, where his father, Ezra White, "the Original
Bastard of Yankee Town" for having organized the Ku Klux Klan
and run all the black folks out of town, worked his way from guard
to prison warden (prison is the only place where blacks are allowed

to live in Yankee Town). Determined not to follow in the line of his father and six older brothers and run the cotton mill or the prison, young Clyde, identified in biblical terms as "the son of Ezra," chose to become a civilian lawman instead. Quickly developing a fetish for dress, Clyde dons a uniform and high-top black boots that become known throughout Dark Town, where he walks down the Alley every Saturday to instill fear in the black population. He ends his sojourn by walking into Sam's Café, glaring around the room, posturing for effect, spitting on the floor, and stomping out (43). Clyde earns a reputation among blacks not only for violating their space, but also for the violence that becomes his trademark. On the occasion when a drunken black man actually staggers against Clyde and rips buttons from his picture-perfect uniform, he stomps him into oblivion, thus earning the nickname "Boots" for his "nigger-stomping" boots. The sound of those boots alone becomes enough to send black folks scrambling out of Boots's way. The boots allow the black population to separate Clyde from the rest of white humanity; there are white folks and "the Man," personified in Boots White.

Inevitably, "the son of Ezra" meets "the King of Dark Town." Annoyed that Big Man never seems perturbed by his floor-spitting activity and equally annoyed by the fact that the current chief of police complains about young Boots locking up so many blacks every Saturday night, Boots strides into Sam's Café on Easter Sunday 1936 and initiates a confrontation with Big Man by declaring that "ain' no checkah play'n 'lowed in heah on Sunday!" (48). Big Man's playing partner quickly disappears, but Big Man still ignores Boots. Then Boots commits the unforgivable sin by knocking over the checkerboard: "nobody went around mistreating Big Man's poolboard . . . not even the white Man. The next thing everyone in the place knew was that Boots was lying flat out on his ass on the floor up near the front door, where Big Man had sent him flying with one blow from the back of his big fist" (49; Andrews's ellipses). Boots pumps "six bullets into Big Man's wide body. But even carrying all of this lead, the King, like a big bear, continued advancing towards Boots, who

AMERICAN RIVER COLLEGE

after firing his last shot somehow managed to scramble up and reach the front door just ahead of Big Man" (49). Boots is knocked back by Little Bit, who responds upon realizing that her husband is dying: "with one swipe of her razor the southpaw-swinging Little Bit carved a streak down the right side of the policeman's face, beginning just above the eyebrow and extending downward to the middle of his smooth pink cheek" (50). For her effort, she is pistol-whipped, kicked, unattended at the hospital (the doctor is trying to save Boots's eye), and comatized for a week shortly after giving birth to a true black baby fathered by Big Man.

The King of Dark Town's exit from the narrative creates more presence than absence, for he becomes the measure for how larger than life characters can act toward the law when the confrontation is a matter of saving one's dignity and one's reputation in the community. His becomes the life and the tale to overcome, the touchstone against which other would-be bad men, especially a couple of youngsters from Hard Labor Hole, are measured. And he provides the standard for chocklit heroic geography against which Appalachee Red will also be measured and whose pattern Red will expand and exceed.

On that evening of the fateful encounter with Big Man Thompson and Little Bit in 1936, Boots may have killed Big Man and pistol-whipped Little Bit, but they leave tangible evidence of black resistance written on his face. Big Man breaks Boots's nose and Little Bit razors out one of his eyes, thus causing Boots to become meaner than ever (the eye patch he must wear will later earn him a new nickname—"ol' One-Eyed"—but it does not replace "Boots"). It is not enough that Big Man dies or that Little Bit suffers a mental breakdown; Boots must still heap punishment upon the family. His father, Ezra, sends members of the Ku Klux Klan to burn down the home of Little Bit's parents, with them and two of her younger siblings in it. This is the nadir of black-white relations in Appalachee, for Boots's "one-man law" is institutionalized, blacks are terrorized, and there is no one strong or crazy enough to stand up to him in an effort to change things. That is the state of affairs from 1936 to 1945, by which time Boots has become chief of police.

Andrews has been fairly straightforward in his presentation of Boots White, the power he derives from his father's position, and the fear he instills in all those around him. By 1945, one of his favorite pastimes is catching unsuspecting motorists who do not stop for a traffic light deliberately placed above their line of vision. His partic-ular targets are blacks and Yankees. Andrews pokes fun at Boots in an encounter with a Yankee even as he illustrates his power. "Asking the Yankee where he was from, Boots got the smart answer 'Chi-cago' before quickly pointing out to the wiseguy that his license plate said 'Illinois.' Realizing he had been caught lying to an officer of the law, the red-faced Yankee couldn't do a thing but laugh at his own self and pay up" (61). This straightforwardness changes, however, in Andrews's presentation of Appalachee Red.

From the moment Red arrives in Appalachee on Thanksgiving Day in 1945, mystery surrounds him. That feature highlights his unusual status as more and more citizens wonder about him. By making him the object of so many different gazes, Andrews intensifies the sense of power that accrues to him and the larger than life status that he holds. He is identified as "the man," and we first see him through the eyes of his seven-year-old white half-sister, Roxanne Morgan, and the Morgan maid, who is none other than the senile Little Bit Thompson working yet again for the family that has caused her family so much pain. Roxanne watches "the man" staring up at her family house and wonders why he is not coming to Thanksgiving dinner (just as she will watch him for years after this point when he pauses briefly at the same gate every Sunday morning to contemplate the heritage from which he has been cut and of which Roxanne remains unaware). To match Roxanne's gazing at "the man," Little Bit Thompson stands "transfixed as if in a daze" (59).

Readers barely catch their breaths from pausing over Little Bit's reaction before they see the as-yet-unnamed Red through the eyes of Boots White. What Boots sees has a profoundly disturbing effect upon him: "A cold chill which was not brought on by the weather began creeping slowly up the back of Appalachee's Chief of Police" (63). Unfamiliar with the man, but still believing him to be white, Boots is particularly annoyed that "the stranger" does not recognize his existence by speaking to him:

> Boots had a strong urge to run up to the corner and down Freedom Road behind the stranger and scream out to him: *Just who in the goddamn hell do you think you are that you can walk right past me, Clyde White, the Chief of Police of Appalachee, county seat of Muskhogean County, Georgia, without so much as a look of respect in my direction? Don't you know that this is my town? And if you don't stop that crazy walk and walk like a white man ought to walk and turn around and tell me who you are and just what it is here in my town that you came looking for then I am going to kill you right here on the spot!* Then, if the man still refused to stop, turn around, and recognize an officer of the law, Boots would pull out his well-oiled pistol and shoot the big stranger through the back of the head. (64–65)

Since Boots has this much antagonism directed toward a total stranger that he thinks is white, one can only imagine how his assessment will be altered when he knows that Red is legally black (although Boots will have difficulty with that definition). Boots's observation of Red thus sets the stage for the impending confrontation even at the level of intuition. In essence, Red has disturbed the very air that Boots breathes; that disturbance is enough to earn his enmity.

Distance and *imagination* become the means through which Andrews allows us knowledge about Appalachee Red. Andrews's strategy of making Red larger than life is to force us to see him through the eyes of others, especially through that of characters such as Boots. We peek over their shoulders, become secondary camera eyes, and become part heir to the anxiety they feel in trying to categorize a man, indeed a *force,* they do not understand. We watch with the watchers, although we may have more information than they do about the person they are watching. By encouraging us to fill in the "spaces" and "holes" of characterization, as Toni Morrison would say, Andrews invites us to join imaginatively in the creative process, for we form opinions about Red as well as about the people who are watching him. We shape the object of our gaze in ways slightly different than do the textual characters, but we shape him nonetheless.

Sam the café owner is the first person with whom Appalachee Red actually makes contact; Big Apple, a café hanger-on and local gossip par excellence, is glued to his usual spot upon Red's arrival and witnesses the scene. The uneasiness Red creates in Sam and Big Apple expands Roxanne's, Little Bit's, and Boots's fascination with "the man": "Both remained paralyzed in their places, their gazes fixed on the man's every move lest he vanish before their very eyes or, worse, lest they be swallowed alive by such a big, mean-looking creature" (70). Their reactions certainly are not shaped by the fact that they believe "the man" is white, for they have seen other white men, particularly Boots White, in this space. Carriage, demeanor, and attitude inspire their reactions to Red. Big Apple, who will become the primary source through which we witness the townspeople's reactions to Red after Sam disappears to his second-floor room, is a pulse for the community. What he feels, they feel; what he thinks, they think. These initial reactions, therefore, are but the shore for the deep waters of fear and intimidation—primarily self-imposed through their overly active minds—that Red inspires in the townspeople. With lesser knowledge but more willing to let their imaginations run away with them, the townspeople mirror readers in their responses to Red. Who is he? Why is he there? What plans does he have in mind?

Sam finally indicates that he "ain' 'lowed to serve white folks" and barely regains his voice when Red utters his first words in the text: "I ain't white folks" (70). That revelation brings no diminishing of fear and paranoia, for Sam is so unsettled that he allows Red to rent one of the rooms upstairs from the café, thereby putting another man in proximity to Baby Sweet, over whom he has been assigned guardian duties. Sam's greatest uneasiness is caused by his knowledge that Boots will be making his nightly visit to Baby Sweet (sounding out the "nigger-stompers" to announce his arrival) in a few hours after Red has appeared. There is great irony in the fact that Sam is playing the role of "Mammy," watching over the "virtue" of a young girl who has already been violated by the person who has set Sam to do the watching. Even more ironic is the fact that the girl is black. With these few strokes of connection, Andrews is able to evoke an entire history of sexual interactions among some members of the South's black and white population. On the scene of the White House, therefore, all the forces move steadily toward the inevitable confrontation between Boots and Red.

With very few words uttered thus far in the novel, Red has done several things. He has generated curiosity in Roxanne and paralyzed Little Bit. He has upset the chief of police, creating such fear in him that, when he does arrive on that fateful Thanksgiving night, he is not able to perform to his usual standards sexually (and those standards are already low).[7] He has set Sam to drinking more heavily than usual. And he has given Big Apple a new reason for being, a topic for gossip unmatched by any of his previous subjects.

Absolutely central to the portrait of Red is the figurative language Andrews and his characters use to describe him and how their feelings about Red, in turn, are described. Boots, with his comparison of Red to a cat, begins the focus on images that will recur. Big Apple observes the "catlike grace" (73) with which Red follows Sam up the stairs to his bed for the night. The cleanup man, who witnesses Boots's unsettling reaction to Red, asks him, "Whassa matter, Chief White? You look lak you jes seed de devil" (65). The chief's face is described as being "as white as a haint" and he tries to shake an "ominous feeling" (65) that comes over him after Red passes on the street. Indeed, many other characters will consider Red a demon and will specifically refer to him as the devil (108, 130, 131, 159, 184). Big Apple expects "some wild beast" (97) to appear at Sam's on the morning after Red's arrival, which picks up again on the animal imagery that seems to be the metaphorical base for describing Red.

Categorizing language is also relevant to elevating Red from man to something more than man. From the indefinite "a man" to the definite "the man," Red becomes "the stranger," with emendations such as "that goddamn stranger!" (93, 94) and "the big stranger" (97). He progresses to being "De big red niggah" (Big Apple, 98) and "that big red nigger," "*the Big Red Nigger!*" (Andrews, 99, 108, and many times thereafter) and finally, once his identity is known, "The Big Red Nigger" (used about thirty times in the text). Big Apple soon begins to "gasp" for breath and "tremble" "from the Big Red Nigger fear" (108). The unknown certainly guides these epithets being attached to Red, but the extensive use of the word "nigger" also brings to mind connotations of the BAD NIGGER syndrome documented in history and literature. Red is "bad" physically because of the potential he has to wreak havoc on the little community's conception of itself and "bad" in psychological terms because of his potential to mess with people's minds, to disturb the status quo, to upset comfortable patterns. Even later, Roxanne will categorize Red as "the Hawk" when she watches him watching her house on his Sunday drives. She purchases binoculars to indulge in this quickly developing sexual fantasy suggested by the bestiality implied in her nickname for Red.

One reason the mystery surrounding Red works so well is that Andrews refuses to portray relationships or conversations that would clarify who he is. For example, we never see Little Bit and Red interacting at all; the mother-son relationship may well have never existed beyond Red's promise to Blue (who does not know at that point that Red is his brother) that he will take care of Little Bit when Blue goes off to college. Also, in those instances in which Red is in proximity to other characters, in the initial scenes we always follow the other characters' points of view—Roxanne, Little Bit, Boots, Sam, and Big Apple. Their register of various degrees of unsettledness dovetails with the overall intentions of the text.

The long-anticipated encounter between Boots and Red works itself out on three battle sites—the sexual, the mental/physical (both involving what it means to be a man), and the financial (what it means to be a *white* man). All of these sites entail Red recognizing patterns that have been set, then consciously, deliberately deciding to rearrange them. The sexual arena shapes itself on Red's first night in the rented room upstairs at Sam's. We are left to imagine how he must have felt or what he thought as the "nigger-stompers" crunched their way up the outside stairs for Boots's nightly violation of Baby Sweet. We are left to imagine what he did, what he felt during that period of violation. When he acts, it is in direct reaction to and revision of what Boots has done. Baby Sweet nightly cleans her body after Boots leaves, then turns on her radio (her only pleasure) and dances in front of her mirror (in various of the clothes she has bought with no place to wear them). It is while she is dancing that Red emerges (à la Son Green in Jadine Childs's bedroom in Toni Morrison's *Tar Baby*) and seduces her. A comparison of the difference in sexual techniques between Boots and Red during their first encounter with Baby Sweet is noteworthy. Boots leaves Baby Sweet crying and bleeding—and with the parting directive that she should report for work at a local restaurant the next day. Red comes as a mirror image "Great Massager" who soothes away the horror of the damage that Boots has done and "massages" Baby Sweet into the ecstasy of true sexual pleasure. Without words and without exchanging names, Red and Baby Sweet enter a fantasy world of sexual fulfillment, one that will sustain them throughout their relationship. The scene epitomizes the larger than life, potentially folk heroic nature of the character destined to have a totally disturbing impact upon the entire community.[8]

By seducing and thereby trespassing upon Boots White's "personal honey pot," then keeping the girl from work the next day, Red signals to all—especially Boots—that he is a powerful force. He transforms Boots's nightly rituals and gains the upper hand in the sexual arena of competition, something that black fictional characters historically have not been able to do in conflicts in interracial liaisons (I think especially of Bob Stone, Tom Burwell, and Louisa in Jean Toomer's "Blood Burning Moon").[9] What goes on with Red and Baby Sweet, beyond the nearly surrealistic mirror lovemaking, the townspeople—

and readers—can only speculate about, for Baby Sweet essentially disappears into her bedroom. Although we later learn, from Baby Sweet's point of view, some of the details, for the time being, the mystery continues.

The mystery intensifies as well because Sam also disappears, which sets the stage for a clarification of Red's manhood before he must have that tested with Boots. When the regulars arrive at the café two days after Red's arrival, they find "the big red nigger" behind the counter. His apparent takeover (and the death of Sam three weeks later) sends local imaginations into territory they have not previously explored. With all those in town too old—or too frightened—to challenge Red, they await the arrival of the Hard Labor Holers on Saturday, including the Bird ("the blade king" who is former dance partner and secret admirer of Baby Sweet) and the Snake (Baby Sweet's brother), reputed to be the "baddest" of the Holers. When these two "baddest" of the local Hard Labor Holers come threatening Red, he runs them out of Sam's Café by brandishing a forty-five.

Having dispatched the best the black folks have to offer in terms of mean mothers, Red mysteriously starts doing business with "the Man," who is seen making several trips after hours to and from the café. It remains unclear how Red has effected a truce with Boots after having taken his "honey pot," but the truce is obvious from the actions of the two men working together to control the town's bootleg whiskey industry as well as its illegal gambling activities. Forced to be watchers again, the townspeople and the readers can only speculate on what is built up to be the most important confrontation in the book. This strategy thus forces textual characters and readers to use their imaginations to fill in the blanks for the time being. Though some of the details will be revealed later, the mystery serves to push forward constantly the process of elevating Red to legendary status.

In the arena of the financial, Red easily bests Boots by proposing the whiskey and gambling schemes to him and by advising him on how to expand his profitable and fast-growing empire. Since Red is a genius at business, which to Boots's mind no black man can be,

Boots *exempts* Red from colored, "nigger" status. To Boots, Red is a "foreigner." Boots is pushed to that conclusion because Red buys a Cadillac, the only one in Muskhogean County. When whites come to the chief of police to complain that his business partner has entered into "white man's business!" (215) by owning a Cadillac, Boots simply replies, "Red's no niggah" (216) and thereby ends the controversy. Boots reasons thus:

> nowhere under God's sun did there strut a nigger with balls enough to walk into Appalachee, or any *real* American town, and take away a white man's black gal or anything else belonging to a white man. He started to get the feeling while he listened all that evening to the man's plans for the future of the building, and this planning had sent Boots away believing him to be much too shrewd and bold a person to be anybody's nigger, yet too mystic to be a "real" white man, and he appeared too four-square, from what he'd heard about Jews, to be one of them—all of which meant to the lawman that he had to be something else . . . a foreigner being the only other answer. (220; Andrews's ellipses)

As with the matter of the traffic light, readers can sense Andrews poking fun at his character even as he explodes the implied stereotypical and racist attitudes inherent in Boots's reasoning. Designating Red a foreigner enables Boots to stomach, so to speak, a nonwhite man being smarter than he is and to save some sense of dignity in the process. After all, Red comes up with the plan to get Boots elected sheriff, and the two of them enter into a strange and strained relationship that exists almost twenty years, until 1963.

For Red's positioning in the text to work in the heroic tradition, it is necessary for the fear the townspeople feel toward him to change to admiration. Red therefore achieves legendary status by what he comes to represent to local blacks. His power, his sexual trespassing, and his car give the townspeople a different way of seeing a black person interact with whites. Red refurbishes Sam's Café and makes it *the* center of social activity not only for the town, but for the county. In the tradition of Wyatt Earp, he prevents the Hard Labor Holers from creating chaos in town. He hires Big Apple and the Snake and thereby gives them new status (the Snake starts to view Red as a god by developing "unmitigated belief in Red the Risen, the Way, the Truth, the Light . . . Appalachee Red the Absolute" [207]). Red turns Baby Sweet into the closest thing to a movie star the town has ever seen. And he takes care of Little Bit Thompson. Yet, almost like a ghost, he does all of this with a silence and invisibility (he seldom talks or appears) that keeps everyone in awe. When he buys the car and makes the Snake his chauffeur, that is the crown for this new king of Appalachee. For black people, the car is the tangible symbol of Red's power.

> The area's blacks immediately took Appalachee Red's Cadillac to their hearts and souls, as to them the car not only represented an object too rich even for the blood and apparently the pocketbook of the county's richest, but by owning such a vehicle Red had changed from being the villain to suddenly becoming the good guy, as far as most of these blacks were concerned, by having the nuts to show up the white folks right to their faces by outdoing them at their—supposedly—own thing! (215)

For these black folks, Red's car is the final touch in shifting his identity from Satan to businessman to hero. He becomes a local Joe Louis, a weaver of spells over white folks with his audacity and his money.

Most of the black citizens of Appalachee willingly give up something to Red in exchange for their identification with his new status in the town, which makes for a fairer trade than some readers are willing to accept. Critics of the novel have claimed that Andrews locks most of his female characters into traditional stereotypical roles. Baby Sweet, for example, is identified primarily for her sexual value—not only to Boots White but to Red as well. From this perspective, it could be argued that Baby Sweet gives up a kind of autonomy or self-determination in order to become the lover of the new authoritarian figure instead of the old one. Counterpoints to this argument must average in, first of all, the rather conspicuous fact that Baby Sweet has never had any autonomy. Poor Boy Jackson, her father, was about to turn her over to his white boss before Boots White captured her and locked her away in Sam's Café. Counterpoints to this argument must also weigh in Baby Sweet's reaction to what this particular exchange with Red means for her. To Baby Sweet, the exchange value of becoming Red's lover as opposed to remaining Boots's sperm depository is obvious. Instead of Baby Sweet working in a restaurant in which she has absolutely no authority, Red gives her responsibility for running the café and, eventually, the entire downstairs operation as he retires to the gambling business in the upstairs part of Red's Café. From having no place to wear her many colorful clothes, Baby Sweet progresses to being able to wear them around Appalachee as well as on her one memorable trip to Atlanta, the trip on which Red purchases the infamous Cadillac. From being repeatedly raped, Baby Sweet moves to having a lover who is sensitive to her feelings and body, who understands and helps her to terminate the pregnancy that has resulted from Boots's violation of her, and who trusts her perhaps more than anyone else in the town. Under Red's tutelage, support, and care, Baby Sweet grows into womanhood. The enlightenment that accrues to her, her increased awareness of the world and of herself in it, provides the education that no other institution or force in the novel could provide. The gains from her association with Red, therefore, far outweigh any feminist categorization of her as being relegated to a particular role or place. She has more freedom within Red's Café than she could possibly have had in the "Elberta Orchard" or with Boots White.

It is especially important to note that, though Baby Sweet might fit a traditional role in relation to Red to some critics, never is there any violation or coercion in that relationship. That significant contrast to all of her previous experiences again makes it clear that her present circumstances are far preferable to her previous situation. Readers judging otherwise are superimposing their own expectations upon Andrews's world and failing to perceive the world that he has created.

If one assesses that world from the inside out, Baby Sweet's situation is a strong one. Her acquiescence in the transformation of Red from man to more than man epitomizes the pattern essential to any shaping of folk heroic possibilities. Persons over whose imaginations the legendary figure holds sway willingly accede to that implied domination. While that power dynamic might, on the surface, look like more exploitative comparable situations, the nuances of difference in Andrews's novel make it acceptable to characters as well as to those readers willing to suspend disbelief as they enter into that fictional world.

The situations of Big Apple and the Snake, like that of Baby Sweet, mirror the implied requirements for creating legendary characters. Initially two of the most skeptical characters responding to Appalachee Red, they shortly become his employees and gain a status that dwarfs their previous condition. Big Apple, who lives on charity, gains respect and financial security when Red hires him to put his natural snooping talents to work in the service of Red's Café. Purists might be offended by the trade-off, but in the flexible moral world that Andrews creates, Big Apple's exchange is a definite improvement over his previous circumstances. By earning his keep and gaining a modicum of financial security, he no longer has to rely solely on the generosity of the people who run the local poor house. Having been on his way to New York to visit his daughter when he was sidetracked in Appalachee, he becomes a member of a family by working for Red; we might view him as Baby Sweet's father or grandfather, perhaps, or even Red's uncle. Big Apple quickly develops loyalty to Red comparable to that we would expect in biological families. And to round out this analogy, Red's Café quickly becomes Big Apple's home in a much more secure way than it ever served when Sam owned the building. Andrews uses figures like Sam, then, to highlight the conversion process that takes place in the general populace toward Red—from skepticism to acceptance to idealization. He uses the Snake in a similar way.

As the Bird's second in command, the Snake could rarely voice opinions, had no authority, and could use the symbol of his violent nature—his knife—only if the Bird allowed that. When Red saves him from a police raid on the blood bank (one he and Boots have planned), he begins to see other possibilities in the man who initially looked to be no more than a dangerous enemy. When Red takes the Snake to Atlanta on that Cadillac-buying trip and then, with no preliminaries, makes him the chauffeur of the *only* Cadillac in Muskhogean County, the Snake achieves status superior even to that of Big Apple. Not only does the Snake acquire the uniform of authority (the chauffeur's outfit and cap), but he also acquires responsibility for taking care of the car, a responsibility that he elevates to the form of art. He washes the car, checks it constantly for engine and other needs, and takes as much pride in it as does its owner—if not more. By assigning the Snake the additional responsibility of running the pool tables and by showing him the socially political reasons for allowing the customers to win on occasion, Red further assists in his growth and development as an adult. From a young man who could envision nothing to look forward to beyond a rowdy Saturday night excursion into Appalachee, the Snake becomes a man of responsibility and justifiable pride.

His association with Red leads the Snake to give up his friendship with the Bird. As readers learn more about that character, however, we discover that the loss of his friendship is not a very great one. The Snake must also give up his knife-wielding, hard-drinking days, along with his identification with Hard Labor Hole. These things are also not appreciable losses. As with Baby Sweet and Big Apple, what the Snake gains is far more valuable than what he has lost. His prominence beside Red is matched only by that of his sister, Baby Sweet. Red has allowed him, as he has allowed Baby Sweet, to travel away from Appalachee and experience the potentially broadening effects upon the mind that such travel can have. Such actions on Red's part succeed in creating loyalty, if not downright worship, in the Snake. The family metaphor serves here as well. Whereas the Snake could not even see Baby Sweet when Boots White had her locked away in

Sam's Café, he can see her every day, almost anytime, now that he and she work for Red. The Snake's estimation of Red is naturally bolstered by the fact that Red has rescued not only the Snake's favorite sister, but also the Snake himself. His elevation of the rescuer to a lordly status is understandable and acceptable within the schema Andrews has created.

Critics of *Appalachee Red,* therefore, cannot successfully argue that, with Red's assumption of power, the traditional pattern of male substitution in the power scheme has taken place. Red is sufficiently different from Boots White to make such an argument absurd. In addition, the fact that Red is a black man in a southern town usually run by powerful whites also makes the substitution argument fallacious. In a world where a black man was never intended to have power, and certainly not the kind of power that Red acquires, the fact that he acquires it makes him something more than a mere equation to white man. As Boots wanted to elevate Red to "foreigner," so the circumstances of his existence in Appalachee elevate him to more than man. This process is essential to the folk heroic creation that undergirds the structuring and presentation of the novel. Andrews transforms all expectations of what stereotypically *would, could,* or *ought to* occur in this environment and introduces something else altogether. That something else is the site on which legends are made, the site on which human imagination creates the larger than human in a symbolic sustaining of itself.

Appalachee Red's relationship with Boots White ends with the death of Little Bit Thompson. Although she and Red do not interact openly, she has established a ritual of walking to the café late at night and standing outside staring at the space she knows her son occupies. And Baby Sweet has assumed responsibility for taking care of Little Bit once Blue went off to school. Little Bit's death, therefore, brings an era to an end in Appalachee. It also brings to an end Red's sojourn in the town. The site of Little Bit's funeral, which John Morgan attends with his daughter, Roxanne, becomes the occasion for Roxanne's reflections about Red and her revelations about watching him through the years. Too saturated with sexual thoughts of Red to sit through the funeral, she dashes out, opens the back door to the curtained, chauffeured Cadillac where she knows Red is sitting, and jumps in. It is the first ever encounter between these two characters. However, we are not allowed to enter the door with Roxanne, only to witness it with the other watchers, as they stare "in disbelief at the big cloud of Georgia red dust hiding the Kitty from their view and smelling the still-burning rubber of those speeding tires rolling down the road toward town hauling the Big Red Nigger and Mist' John Morgan's gal in the back seat" (282). The sheriff sent presumably to reclaim the girl is found dead "lying over the threshold of Red's office": "He had been shot through the center of his good eye with a .45 caliber bullet, and Appalachee Red was long gone in his brand-new black Cadillac" (282).[10]

Yet absence again simply highlights presence, for Appalachee Red leaves the text in a swathe of mystery and myth just as he entered it. But since the text also ends after one more paragraph, the "What happened?" questions abound. Did Roxanne indeed throw her hot, still virginal at twenty-five body into his lap? Has Red been long waiting for and wanting a relationship with his stepsister? Did he kidnap her just to get back at John Morgan and his lost heritage? What are his plans for Roxanne—since he always plans? Has he been watching her and planning something as long as she has been watching him? To what end? Did he think that with the onset of civil rights activity in Appalachee his days of control were limited? Did he feel he had truly paid his respects to his mother and the memory of his stepfather and it was now time to go? Did he kill Boots? Did he kill Boots in vengeance for all his violations? If so, why now? Has he been playing trickster with "the Man" all along? Why would he go off and leave Baby Sweet without a word, especially since the two of them have been so devoted to each other (he has even taught her to read and write)?

By leaving so many questions unanswered, Andrews not only makes cocreators of his readers, but he also turns them into voyeurs.

Andrews forces readers to become participants in events that border on a peepshow. He teases us, titillates us, and leaves us without fulfillment as far as the story line is concerned. Andrews positions us not unlike Boots White on his weekly visit to Red's Café to get his share of the whiskey and gambling money. Boots sits in agony, drinking and talking, trying to imagine what one more sexual encounter with Baby Sweet would be like. The click of her high heels on the bare floorboards over their heads (Red has refused to let her buy a rug for that reason) epitomizes his agony. We witness Boots's frustration, share his lack of sexual release, see in it our own lack of narrative closure.

We become voyeurs in our superiority, for we know that Boots's desire will never be fulfilled. We know as we watch Big Apple and the townspeople respond to the stranger that Red is the famed "red baby" born to Little Bit Thompson. While we may not know what his intentions are, we can surmise more accurately than the townspeople the reasons for his intentions. As victims of recurring dramatic ironies, the locals can at times appear like the title character in the Little Moron jokes. "How can they be so stupid?" we ask. And we feel superior to small-town southerners whose prejudices, violence, and general backward behavior are so extensive that they consume their very lives. Few people in Appalachee actually *live;* their histories more often than not have merely allowed them to exist in superimposed patterns determined long before they were thought of.

Ultimately, Raymond Andrews's mythical South exists in the prompted formulations of our imaginations. The patterns and interactions that have been upset can never be reinstated, yet the questions remaining are numerous. The final paragraph of the text, however, gives us yet another path on which to take a stroll with yet another concept of the New South. Little Bit is buried, Boots dies, and Red disappears—all on 22 November 1963, the day President John F. Kennedy was shot. The mythical road on which Red disappears in his brand-new black Cadillac is just as filled with mystery as Kennedy's death, and just as filled with promise as Kennedy's election. The referential date brings Appalachee into the national arena that Blue had insisted was necessary by sitting in and demanding to be served at the Pine Room restaurant in the Morgan House. An era of racial repression and exploitation is ending in the country. Since Red has served his purpose in awakening the blacks of Appalachee to other possibilities and ways of being in the world in relation to whites, perhaps it is only fitting that his exit mirror his entrance, wrapped in whatever legendary connotations we and the townspeople shape to suit our fancy.

With his willful act of suicide, Raymond Andrews has become as much of an enigma as Red. By taking his life, he wrote his way into his own script of southern history and southern eccentricity. His death writes him into the competition for grotesqueness that seems to plague the South. A mystery not quite resolved, a talent not quite fulfilled, a life lived too much in some ways and not enough in others, Raymond Andrews is now locked into the car in which Appalachee Red made his getaway with Roxanne. He is claimed by the very southern territory and penchant for imagination and storytelling that guided all of his works. Just as he created art, his life has become art, and he has perhaps won out over many of his competitors by becoming one of the most mysterious—and thus one of the most southern—of the South's plethora of weird, if not downright crazy, writers.

(1995, 1997, 2001)

Notes

1. *The Last Radio Baby* is a memoir from Andrews's childhood until the time he was fifteen, when he moved to Atlanta. While several sources indicate that "Once upon a Time in Atlanta" was scheduled for publication by Peachtree Publishers in Atlanta in the fall of 1992, the volume has not yet appeared. A conversation with an editor at that house revealed that the volume is "on hold" until some matters with Andrews's estate can be resolved.

2. Sometime between 24 November 1991, when he typed a letter to his brother Benny, and 12:20 P.M. the following day, when his body was found, Raymond Andrews went into his brother's yard, put a revolver to his head, and pulled the trigger. In the letter, Andrews discussed pain in his joints and

digestive system and an inability to get proper medical care without health insurance. He selected the spot he did because he did not want to mess up the gazebo or disturb the animals' habitat; he asked his brother to use the least expensive way of disposing of his ashes (even handling them by paper cup, if necessary). Without mentioning his plan to shoot himself, Andrews indicated that if what he had in mind failed, then Benny should not allow him to be kept alive on life-support systems [I have paraphrased these comments from Andrews's suicide letter, which is on file in the Special Collections Library of Emory University, Atlanta, Georgia]. Andrews was fifty-seven when he killed himself; he had returned to the Athens area in 1984 after sojourns in Atlanta, Michigan, and New York.

3. See *Selected Poems of Langston Hughes,* 172, 158, 125.

4. In chapter 6 of Revelation, the four horsemen are presented as follows: the white horse is to conquer, the red horse has the power to take peace from the earth, the black horse represents balance/justice, and the pale horse represents death (hell follows him).

5. It is noteworthy that Andrews selects "Jake Turner" as the name for this character, for it immediately evokes the legendary "Joe Turner," a white man of blues song fame who abducted black men and turned them into convict laborers. August Wilson develops this tale in his play, *Joe Turner's Come and Gone* (New York: Plume, 1988). I discuss the implications of the Joe Turner connection in "August Wilson's Folk Traditions," 49–67.

6. See the scene as described in Frederick Douglass, *Narrative of the Life of Frederick Douglass, an American Slave,* chap. 10.

7. We later learn through Baby Sweet just how unnerved Boots had been: "But on this particular night she kept thinking of the nervousness, or the fear, she had sensed in the Man that night, feelings that the Man couldn't conceal and that she couldn't easily wash away [in her nightly cleansing ritual]" (91).

8. It could also be argued, however, that in some ways Red takes Boots's leavings by claiming Baby Sweet. Another perspective allows for Baby Sweet to become merely the pawn in the power game between Red and Boots. When they both deposit their sperm in her, there is a commingling of the two men on the site of her body, which locks them into mortal competition. For a comparable portrait of black and white men, whose racial hatred for each other is keen, depositing sperm in the same women, see Yusef Komunyakaa's "Tu Do Street," in which black and white soldiers in Vietnam use the same prostitutes. The men are so intent upon their own racial hatred and sexual competition that they fail to consider the female bodies upon which their battles are carried out. See *Dien Cai Dau,* 29.

9. Toomer, *Cane.*

10. Cadillacs have a long-standing history—at times upgraded to stereo-type as the car of choice—in black communities. They also play a part in black men asserting themselves against the restrictions imposed by whites who frown upon black men owning "white" things. See my discussion of this conveyance in "Adventures in a 'Foreign Country': African American Humor and the South." Daryl Cumber Dance discusses the tradition of black men who commit crimes being "long gone" in *Long Gone*. "Long Gone" is also the title of a poem by Sterling Brown; see *The Collected Poems of Sterling A. Brown*, 22–23. Red's disappearance, therefore, places him in a long line of black folk and historical figures who earn the approbation of their communities with their unprecedented actions against white authority.

Works Cited

Andrews, Raymond. *Appalachee Red*. 1978. Reprint, Athens: University of Georgia Press, 1987.

Brown, Sterling. *The Collected Poems of Sterling A. Brown*. New York: Harper Colophon, 1980.

Dance, Daryl Cumber. *Long Gone: The Mecklenburg Six and the Theme of Escape in Black Folklore*. Knoxville: University of Tennessee Press, 1987.

Douglass, Frederick. *Narrative of the Life of Frederick Douglass, an American Slave*. 1845. Reprint, Cambridge: Harvard Belknap, 1960.

Harris, Trudier. "Adventures in a 'Foreign Country': African American Humor and the South." *Southern Cultures* 1, no. 4 (summer 1995): 457–65.

———. "August Wilson's Folk Traditions." In *August Wilson: A Casebook*. Ed. Marilyn Elkins. New York: Garland, 1994, 49–67.

Hughes, Langston. *Selected Poems of Langston Hughes*. New York: Vintage, 1974.

Komunyakaa, Yusef. *Dien Cai Dau*. Middletown, Conn.: Wesleyan University Press, 1988.

Morrison, Toni. *Tar Baby*. New York: Knopf, 1981.

Toomer, Jean. *Cane*. 1923. Reprint, New York: Norton, 1988.

Seven

The Necessary Binding

Prison Experiences in Three August Wilson Plays

 Given the fact that their encounters with the legal system have been so extensive and unpleasant, it is probably a historical truism that the majority of African American men would not find such encounters to be happy occurrences. Families shy away from talking about incarcerated sons and male relatives, and popular lore depicts girlfriends and wives selecting other partners after jail and chain gangs cause long absences. The men can survive the experiences, but some of them also can be broken by them. While folklorists and other cultural analysts who have studied prison populations have observed the communities and patterns of interactions jailed men create, the rich lore that saves them, few have asserted that incarceration is a prerequisite for growth into manhood and/or into learning about the self. Yet that is precisely what August Wilson seems to assert in several of his plays. Prison can break black men or stunt them emotionally, but it also can be the preparation ground for them to move into a different state of being.[1]

Wilson's inclusion of the various experiences of black men in prison (all of which take place in the South) does not mean that he actually goes behind prison walls in his stage representations. Instead, prison experiences are memory, a part of the distant and at times not so distant pasts of the male characters who inhabit Wilson's dramas. The men have served the time that the legal system has required of them, or they have escaped from that system (Jeremy is running from the law in *The Piano Lesson*—1987). The point at which audiences see them on Wilson's stage is one from which they look back upon the experience of incarceration. In looking back, they may wax nostalgic about that particular time in their lives, or they may recount the brutalities that accompanied their incarceration. In other instances, recounting the prison interlude might be only a brief, seemingly insignificant narrative that a character relates. Read against the character's current actions in the drama, however, the narrative takes on much more importance. Whether the men are innocent or guilty of the charges for which they have been incarcerated—and Wilson depicts both—they often embrace their prison experiences as much as they see them as a form of punishment.

What has led to the imprisonment of the characters is frequently couched in terms of the overall racial climate that existed in the repressive South in the early decades of the twentieth century. Historically, the possibility of prison as well as the actual fact served equally to keep the majority of black men in line. Prisons notorious for their brutality or their inescapability scarred the landscape of the American South, including Parchman Farm in Mississippi, Angola Prison in Louisiana, and Huntsville Prison in Texas. Guards were violent and brutal, workdays long and hard (in some instances, black prisoners were required to build roads with just the use of hoes), and the prospect for a change of status rare and improbable. Finding the space within the self to contemplate removal from such an environment took more imagination than men dulled by extreme physical labor could muster. Although their work songs, as Sterling Brown documents in *Southern Road* (1932) and Bruce Jackson documents in *Wake Up Dead Men: Afro-American Worksongs from Texas Prisons* (1972), might have incorporated visions of life beyond the prison walls, the majority of the black men who entered such brutalizing environments as adolescents or teenagers did not leave until they were very old—if at all (those who died—or were killed—on the premises were buried there).

Atrocities that Wilson's characters experience or to which they

allude continue to have their historical counterparts. Disproportion-
ate numbers of African American men are incarcerated even in these
early stages of the twenty-first century. A general statistic is that one
in every four young black men will have some unpleasant encounter
with law enforcement and may end up being incarcerated. The contemporary prison-industrial complex is big business; indeed, many
staid white communities have opted to have prisons located in their
communities purely for the economic value of keeping men incarcerated, the majority of whom are African American. While it is true that
many of these young men historically have learned trades and liter-
acy skills while in prison, or been converted to a permanent change
in their lifestyles through such organizations as the Black Muslims,
the fact remains that prison is too often an assumed part of African
American male existence—as Wilson makes clear in his plays.

Wilson's characters who have experienced prison not only survive
those experiences, but they talk about them with other men who have
been incarcerated or with those who show a willingness to listen.
The rare exception is Loomis in *Joe Turner's Come and Gone* (1988).
He has been so blighted by his time in prison that it is difficult for
him to articulate what it means, let alone to speak with others about
it. However, of all the male characters in Wilson's dramas who have
been imprisoned, Loomis is the one who is most transformed by
that environment; he is forged into a being receptive to the tran-
scendent spiritual forces that descend upon him at the end of the
play.[2] It might reasonably be suggested that his prison time is the
preparation period that leads to his calling to carry the word of a
higher power to nonbelievers. Prison shapes Loomis, in other words,
to be a preacher/priest/prophet who offers a vision to the characters
around him.

For the majority of Wilson's previously jailed male characters,
prison provides a shaping force for their lifeworlds as well as the shaping material for their post-prison imaginations. Prison is the stuff of
which their tales are made—or inspired, and many of Wilson's male
characters love to talk. In addition to providing fuel for their stories,

shared prison experiences create the bonds and the male communities through which stories are transmitted. Indeed, it could be argued that prison creates fraternity for Wilson's black male characters, fraternity that permits camaraderie as well as trespass within the groups that claim that brotherhood. With one notable exception in Wilson's plays (Berniece's attitude in *The Piano Lesson*), a stint in prison is never a stigma that the community or other previously imprisoned men use against the characters. Even the incommunicative Loomis is not dismissed *because* he has been in prison; he is considered strange because of his post-prison behavior. Boy Willie *(The Piano Lesson)* and other previously jailed black male characters loudly vocalize their pasts, consider them a casual and perhaps necessary part of their personal history, and are not in any way embarrassed because of them.

How prison shapes Wilson's male characters is obvious with Troy Maxson *(Fences*—1986), Boy Willie *(The Piano Lesson)*, Loomis *(Joe Turner's Come and Gone)*, and minor characters in these plays. Long before the current action of *Fences*, Troy was jailed for robbery, a crime of which he was unquestionably guilty. His encounter with the law, however, has grown out of the particularly virulent racial oppression that did not allow for the incorporation of peoples of African descent into the great American democratic experiment. Wilson focuses in his preface to the play on immigrants from all over the world who found their way to America and into American society. Not so African Americans. As bottom-rungers who "settled along the riverbanks and under bridges in shallow, ramshackle houses made of sticks and tar-paper," who "collected rags and wood" and "sold the use of their muscles and bodies" (xvii), black people in cities in the early decades of the twentieth century and their descendants at mid–twentieth century inherited conditions of racism and poverty that shaped their attitudes toward the world and their possibilities in it. What is unarticulated by the characters is covered by the blanket indictment of prejudice against black people that Wilson uses to preface the play. A victim of these circumstances, Troy Maxson found himself in the southern city of Mobile, Alabama, trying to make a living during the 1920s (he has escaped a brutal father and a sharecropping environment when he arrives at this point). By his own account, he robbed people to survive. When his need to prove his manhood in spite of his poverty led him to marry and have a child, he then had to rob sufficiently to support three people. He lands in prison when an attempted robbery goes awry and he kills a man.[3]

Viewers or readers might reasonably be surprised to learn that good-loving, hard-drinking Troy Maxson has spent fifteen years in prison and even more surprised that it was for robbery and especially murder. Indeed, Wilson never allows us to engage fully with the fact that Troy has murdered a man (perhaps it is in keeping with the overall attitude throughout his works that prison offenses for which his characters have been imprisoned are not for the viewer/reader to judge). By revealing that information slightly more than halfway through the play, when viewers have formed a substantial impression of Troy, Wilson forces readers to return to what they have learned about Troy and to reevaluate his character in light of this new information. What happens is a process of inference. We infer that Troy's relationship to his son Lyons is probably influenced by the fact that he was forced to leave Lyons and his mother for those fifteen years, thereby forcing Lyons's mother to scrounge for a living for herself and the child; these circumstances must have weighed heavily on Troy's mind and his notion of manhood during those fifteen years. Indeed, he takes "responsibility" very seriously, and not having been able to fulfill his responsibility to his first wife and child must have hurt terribly. It explains the fact that he constantly allows the thirty-four-year-old Lyons to borrow money from him, though he denigrates him verbally each time he does so. We infer that Troy's relationship to Cory, the son of his current marriage to Rose, is similarly informed by his experiences in prison. Troy learned to play baseball in prison, and it is the sports arena on which he and Cory clash. Rather than allowing Cory to go to college on a football scholarship, Troy prefers instead to remember that he was not allowed to play professional baseball when he was released from prison, and he blames that on racism. He stifles Cory's future by refusing to accept the fact that his forty years of age and less than stellar batting performances might have influenced his inability to play in the majors.

Prison, then, has shaped the way Troy views life and the world. Indeed, his image of fighting death is a baseball image—"a fastball on the outside corner" of the plate—the game he learned in prison. Prison has also shaped his friendships. He has only one companion/friend in the play, and that is Bono, whom he met while he was in prison. They share work (collecting garbage and building the fence around Troy's house), liquor, and talk of women, activities that represent the range of their social existence. The reason for Bono's imprisonment is never clear, but he, like Troy, suffers no social stigma for it. As former prisoners who have paid their debt to society, they have married, have had children, and now have "respectable" jobs, though they may be less than ideal.

During the course of the second half of the play, and with retrospective analysis of the first half, it becomes clear that prison has had a profound impact upon Troy's outlook on life. Having learned his lesson about robbery and murder, he is content to remain in a fairly safe relationship to the world. He does challenge his union to get a job as a driver on a garbage truck, but he is not similarly willing to challenge his own perception of racism sufficiently to enable Cory to pursue his life's dream to play football. His worldview is about containment, as the title of the play so vividly suggests. Certainly racism is prominent, but Troy has willingly fenced himself in. No white person stands over his shoulder to assert that his son Cory cannot play football (indeed Cory's white coach encourages Cory); Troy sets that mental limitation with its consequent physical outcome.

Prison, combined with the traumatic experiences with his father, seems to have made Troy unaffectionate, except in expressions of sexuality, and generally unwilling to be a father beyond providing the necessities of food, clothing, and shelter. In a strikingly dramatic moment in the play, when Cory asks Troy if he likes him (when he learns that Troy does not want him to play football), Troy's response is comparable to that of Toni Morrison's Eva Peace when her daughter Hannah asks her if she ever loved her children:

> Like you? I go out of here every morning . . . bust my butt . . . putting up with them crackers every day . . . cause I like you? You about the biggest fool I ever saw.
>
> *(Pause.)*
>
> It's my job. It's my responsibility! You understand that? A man got to take care of his family. You live in my house . . . sleep you behind on my bedclothes . . . fill you belly up with my food . . . cause you my son. You my flesh and blood. Not 'cause I like you! Cause it's my duty to take care of you. I owe a responsibility to you! (38; Wilson's ellipses)

With Troy, as with Eva, responsibility is what one owes one's off-spring.[4] Responsibility, however, is not love or affection. To fulfill responsibility with the attitude that Troy has is to stunt the development of the person on the receiving end of such largesse, which is precisely what happens with Cory. Troy's sense of responsibility in the current action has certainly been shaped by his inability to carry out similar responsibilities with Lyons and his mother during his fifteen-year stint in prison. His notion of manhood, therefore, is still driven by the lack he suffered for his youthful crimes.

Troy also has other problematic interactions with Cory. He insists that Cory use "yessir" in addressing him and that Cory remember always that Troy is "boss" (note, as well, Troy's use of "my" in the quoted passage). While it is certainly understandable to say "yessir" to a male parent, the use of "boss" harks back to Troy's imprisonment, when he himself probably had to refer to his imprisoners with such an appellation. The containment in the father-son relationship, therefore, duplicates to some extent the prison-guard relationship that Troy has endured. Troy wants to make it clear to Cory that he is in charge, that Cory's actions can ensue only with Troy's permission, and that Cory has absolutely no rights that Troy need respect. Again, Troy fences in his son in the same way that the prison guards have fenced him in. As a parent, he is an unemotional, unaffectionate tyrant who does not go beyond the biological fact of fatherhood. His time in prison has assuredly informed these dynamics. The ultimate indication of this warping of parental affection is the scene in which Cory and Troy square off with the baseball bat. Troy wrestles it from his son, and a couple of beats pass before it is clear that he will not swing it at Cory. The murder that sent him to prison looms large in the morality informing his decision to swing the bat or not.

Having been forced to leave one wife through imprisonment perhaps also influences indirectly Troy's decision to leave Rose—figuratively—in the current action of the play. It is a reflection of the mental defeat Troy suffered as a prisoner. No white person stands over Troy and insists that he cheat on his wife; he makes that decision. But prison has perhaps conveyed to him that leaving a woman can be explained as due to circumstances beyond his control. Troy argues that Alberta, the woman with whom he has an affair and who never appears as a character in the play, makes him feel like a man, which means that manhood, in the convoluted way in which he thinks, is partially identified with absence of responsibility even as it is simultaneously loaded with responsibility; manhood is also, due to Alberta's absence, suggestively a fantasy. In prison, Troy could not care for Lyons and his mother. Out of prison, he cares for Cory and Rose, but it makes him feel as if he is in prison, that is, weighed down by responsibility; he asserts that he has "*locked* [himself] into a pattern trying to take care" (69; emphasis mine) of Rose and Cory. So he goes to Alberta to feel more manly, less weighed down, and thereby less imprisoned by the very things that he asserts are a contrast to prison. Even to his death, he remains unrepentant and unapologetic about his infidelity, which might reasonably be read to assert that his very sense of morality, the one he went to prison to have straightened out, has been irrevocably altered by that experience.[5]

In the schema that Wilson outlines for black men who have served time in prison, therefore, Troy Maxson takes problematic lessons from that experience. He certainly survives the experience; *how* he survives is the problem. The big, husky, hard-drinking, storytelling man is damaged in places that are not immediately visible to the eye. Only through the series of his interactions during the course of the play are the depths of his flaws revealed, flaws that have their genesis in a system that confined him, flaws that are compounded by the fact that he is unable to separate out from that system a place he could name Troy Maxson. The Troy Maxson who appears before viewers and readers is one who carries with him the mental scars of a stifling life that he can measure only by the rules of baseball. That simplification of life and living, without an attendant reflective mode with which to assess his mistakes, reduces Troy to an almost tragic figure who could have transformed his destiny if prison had not transformed his mind.

To a greater extent than Troy Maxson, Boy Willie in *The Piano Lesson* uses words to buffer his relationships with the characters around him (though he makes small talk more frequently than sharing fully formed stories as Troy does). It is impossible for him to shut up, no matter whom he disturbs or what the circumstances are. His voice becomes the weapon with which he bullies his way into his Uncle Doaker's house in Pittsburgh at 5 A.M.; it is what he uses to put distance between himself and any pain he may feel for the loss of family members; and it is what he uses to keep before himself and others his vision of becoming a landowner. He is loud and ill mannered (though certainly not mean spirited or violent), and unapologetic about both. While his character in the current action of the play may be less directly traceable to his prison experiences than is Troy Maxson, it is clear that encounters with "the law" have played a prominent part in his life. They have apparently contributed to the laissez faire attitude he has toward living. Talking is a part of that personality, and talking about prison is as casual a part of his conversation as is talking about selling watermelons.

Like Troy, Boy Willie is guilty of the crime for which he was convicted. He and his friend Lymon have been skimming lumber from their deliveries in Mississippi. It is on the evening that they go to retrieve their confiscated goods that the sheriff and several of his men catch them. For their offense, they spend three years in prison. Boy Willie is free after that, but Lymon still has the law looking for him (on a trumped-up vagrancy charge). For Boy Willie and Lymon, having gone to prison is no more significant than having driven a truckload of watermelons from Mississippi to Pittsburgh; indeed, the Pittsburgh venture might be more dramatic. As presented in this drama, prison and encounters with the law are almost expected parts of African American male coming of age experiences in the South. In the middle of a conversation about his Uncle Wining Boy's musical career, in which Boy Willie and Doaker are making it clear to Lymon who Wining Boy is, note the casualness with which Boy Willie mentions having spent time in prison:

> DOAKER: He [Wining Boy] made one or two records a long time ago. That's the only ones I ever known him to make. If you let him tell it he a big recording star.
>
> BOY WILLIE: He stopped down home about two years ago. That's what I hear. I don't know. Me and Lymon was up on Parchman Farm doing them three years.
>
> DOAKER: He don't never stay in one place. Now, he been here about eight months ago. Back in the winter. Now, you subject not to see him for another two years. It's liable to be that long before he stop by. (8)

And there is no more mention of the prison stint at this point. It is several conversations later before the incident surfaces again. For viewers unfamiliar with Parchman Farm, therefore, the reference might pass over them, except for the phrasing "doing them three years," which is a colloquial formula for discussing prison terms. Because everyone on stage at this point knows the history of the other two, there is a silent brotherhood that informs what is not stated. Within the fraternity that Wilson establishes among his male characters, there is again no stigma attached to such a background and no explanation necessary to cover black male trespasses against the law.

In discussing the situation he has encountered in prison, Boy Willie presents it from one perspective as another brotherhood that one thrives in because of one's connections or blood relations to other black men who have spent time there and whose reputations still linger behind those walls. Going to prison has been barely more painful to Boy Willie than perhaps going to the dentist, because inmates know who he is from other members of his family who have spent time there. Doaker, who lives with Boy Willie's sister, Berniece, in Pittsburgh, is now a respectable railroad cook who has a background of incarceration. That information is revealed when Boy Willie asserts: "Hey Doaker, they still talk about you down on Parchman. They ask me, 'You Doaker Boy's nephew?' I say, 'Yeah, me and him is family.' They treated me alright soon as I told them that. Say, 'Yeah, he my uncle'" (40). And while Doaker asserts that he "don't never want to see none of them niggers no more" (40), he is nonetheless a part of that brotherhood, one with which Boy Willie exhibits a certain amount of pride in claiming identification; indeed, with the testing from the other inmates, he has experienced a rite of passage into that brotherhood. It is also noteworthy that some of the prisoners have spanned generations of incarceration, which means that their offenses are far greater than the lumber stealing for which Boy Willie and Lymon have been imprisoned. Although Doaker's offense is never revealed, the *fact* of his imprisonment is another link in the chain of evidence supporting the contention that black male encounters with the law are the expected, southern casualty of being born black and male, another version of Richard Wright's "Ethics of Living Jim Crow."

Doaker's brother, Wining Boy, has also spent time at Parchman. "Doaker say they had you and Lymon down on the Parchman Farm," Wining Boy says to Boy Willie. "Had you on my old stomping grounds" (37; as with Doaker, Wining Boy's offense is never made known). Passing through Parchman has become almost a tradition for the men in this family. That camaraderie is expressed in one of the most powerful creative moments in the play, the scene in which

Boy Willie, Doaker, Lymon, and Wining Boy sing "O Alberta," one of the work songs characteristic of prison experience. They *"stamp and clap to keep time"* and sing with *"great fervor and style"* (39). It would undoubtedly be erroneous to conclude that the men have enjoyed their time in prison (Lymon says "they work you too hard down there. All that weeding and hoeing and chopping down trees," 39), but it has influenced them and has initiated them into the sharing of this creative moment. No matter the repression that they suffered for being jailed, they can still appreciate the power and perhaps beauty of what they shared/learned in that environment. Since the men were imprisoned at three different points in time, this sharing is also testament to a prison culture that thrives beyond the presence of individual inmates.

For all their acceptance of their own individual and collective trespasses against the law, the men are not as acceptable to Berniece. She represents the rare instance in a Wilson play in which a character passes severe moral judgment on black men who have been accused of crimes. Berniece is therefore a striking contrast to Rose, who accepts Troy where he currently is. Although Berniece seems to have accepted Doaker's past (after all, she lives in his house), she remains unforgiving of Boy Willie and Lymon. It is understandable that she would be angry because her husband, Crawley, was killed on the night that Boy Willie and Lymon went to retrieve their stolen wood (they had asked him to help load the wood, and he had stupidly brought along a gun and tried to fight off the sheriff's men when the wrongdoers were discovered); however, Berniece's attitude toward Boy Willie borders almost on hatred. To Boy Willie's assertion that Crawley would be alive if he had not had the gun, Berniece retorts:

> All I know is Crawley would be alive if you hadn't come up there and got him.
> BOY WILLIE: I ain't had nothing to do with Crawley getting killed. That was his own fault.
> BERNIECE: Crawley's dead and in the ground and you still walking

around here eating. That's all I know. He went off to load some wood with you and ain't never come back.

BOY WILLIE: I told you, woman . . . I ain't had nothing to do with . . .

BERNIECE: He ain't here, is he? He ain't here!

(BERNIECE *hits* BOY WILLIE.)

I said he ain't here. Is he?

(BERNIECE *continues to hit* BOY WILLIE, *who doesn't move to defend himself, other than back up and turning his head so that most of the blows fall on his chest and arms.*) (53–54; Wilson's ellipsis)

Ever unforgiving, Berniece allows the past to inform her every action with Boy Willie. She is inhospitable when he arrives in Pittsburgh, insulting to Boy Willie and Lymon, and totally absent of any trace of the presumed southern hospitality that she has left a mere three years before. She implies that Boy Willie is a murderer (she verbalizes her belief that he might have pushed Sutter down his well) and generally thinks ill of him. She lumps all of the men into the same violent, criminally oriented pile. "You," she says to Boy Willie, "Papa Boy Charles, Wining Boy, Doaker, Crawley . . . you're all alike. All this thieving and killing and thieving and killing. And what it ever lead to? More killing and more thieving. I ain't never seen it come to nothing. People getting burned up. People getting shot. People falling down their wells. It don't never stop" (52). Echoing Sarah in Wright's "Long Black Song," Berniece refuses to see the part that institutionalized racism has played in the fates of the men in her life. That shortsightedness is a rarity in Wilson's plays. Bernice's opinions are so formed from the beginning of the play that there is little growth throughout; that refusal to see beyond the surface makes her an aberration in Wilson's dramas. Her consistent blaming of the men for the situations in which they found themselves with the law sets her firmly outside the brotherhood/sisterhood of sympathy that most characters exhibit toward black men who have been incarcerated.

Berniece's reaction to Boy Willie and his seeming insensitivity to and lack of implied responsibility for Crawley's death highlight the dysfunctionality in all of the familial relationships in *The Piano Lesson*. The characters yell at each other, argue constantly, threaten violence against each other, force payment for hospitality, are not generous in sharing food and drink, and generally sound more like bickering children than adults—but for the seriousness of their disagreements (Berniece is prepared to pull a gun on Boy Willie if he tries to remove the piano, and it seems at one point as if Doaker is willing to support her). The "Boy" portion of several of the male names supports the accusation of immaturity in the characters and illustrates again the generally negative impact that violation of the law and the prison backgrounds have had upon all the characters, not just the men who served the terms. The historical disruption of imprisonment is almost as detrimental to the family as the history of slavery iconized in the piano and the carvings on it. While Boy Willie's seeming truce with Berniece after fighting Sutter's ghost and his planned return to the South might presage some future transformation, the mental states of characters during most of the play are ones largely informed by prison and its consequences.

In contrast to Troy Maxson and Boy Willie, Herald Loomis is *not* guilty of any crime when he is imprisoned for seven years in *Joe Turner's Come and Gone*. Caught in circumstances that have acquired the status of legend in African American history and folklore, Loomis is snatched up for vagrancy by the infamous Joe Turner and bartered into the new form of slavery, convict leasing, that followed Reconstruction.[6] Black men so caught were imprisoned for purposes of free labor that white southerners had been denied by the outcome of the Civil War. A precursor to sharecropping, the convict lease system was perhaps psychologically more damaging because those imprisoned under its dangerous reaches could not claim even a miniscule portion of the profits that their labor produced. Arrested outside Memphis and subjected to the whim of a man who "generously" released a few prisoners on his birthday each year, Loomis waited seven years before that generosity reached him. In the meantime, he has lost his wife and daughter, and he is changed forever.

The gaunt, brooding man we meet at the beginning of the play, whose silence and wearing of a heavy coat even in warm weather set him apart as unusual, strange, someone to be wary of, is obviously a ghost of the man he was (a deacon in a church) before those seven years. He maintains at one point, "Loomis done seen some things he ain't got words to tell you" (53). The incongruity of his physical appearance and oppressive silence, combined with his apparent caring for his young daughter, presents an enigma to the residents of Seth Holly's boardinghouse in Pittsburgh, at which Loomis ends up in his three-year search for his wife, who had left her daughter in Tennessee a few years after she was evicted from the land she and Loomis had worked before his imprisonment. Loomis is now a tightly strung bundle of emotional containment that might explode at any moment. Silence and dysfunctional relationships are his counterparts to the talking, talking, talking that characterize Troy Maxson and Boy Willie. Loomis has been so stunted by his imprisonment that his search throughout the play is for psychological release. That will come in part when he hands his daughter over to her mother, but it also comes in part when he finds his song, as Bynum (the resident conjurer) asserts, which means that he will create a space within himself to believe in his own value and that he can have a purpose in the world.

Nowhere in Wilson's plays is the psychological impact of incarceration upon black men more apparent than in the character of Herald Loomis. His imprisonment has destroyed his family, turned his wife from affection to abandonment with a casualness that is not fully explained beyond her religious fervor, left him with a daughter whom he does not understand and has difficulty parenting, deprived him of the ability to be affectionate with women, and isolated him from general human contact. In fact, the impact is so strong that, when Bynum recognizes that Loomis is "one of Joe Turner's niggers," Loomis's response is, "You lie! How you see that? I got a mark on me? Joe Turner done marked me to where you can see it? You telling me I'm a marked man" (71). Loomis is certainly marked, but the marks, like Troy's, are mostly on his mind and imagination. He manifests consequences of imprisonment that Troy Maxson turns toward baseball and that Boy Willie covers up with words. He therefore becomes the most dysfunctional of the characters treated in this study. That dysfunctionality is even more painful to read about or watch because of Loomis's innocence. Readers enter the play, then, with some expectation that this wrong can somehow be righted in the psychological realm where it apparently means so much to Loomis. That correction can come only in the arena of the spiritual that borders on the otherworldly.

Through Bynum, Wilson introduces the ideas of the legend of "shiny men" as well as those who are given special songs, such as his father's healing song or his own binding song. Men who are fortunate enough to become shiny men inspire others with their visions. By finding his own song, Loomis effectively breaks the mental bonds with which Joe Turner has bound him far beyond the actual fact of his imprisonment; he therefore becomes one of the shiny men Bynum has reported seeing on one rare occasion. He in turn is able to inspire those around him.

Wilson thus uses the fact of Loomis's prison experience to introduce a new mythology or a new spirituality. When Loomis's estranged wife, Martha, finally arrives at Seth's boardinghouse and Loomis hands over their daughter to her, Martha can see only sin in Loomis and begins spouting the Twenty-third Psalm and the need to believe in Jesus. When she touts the importance of the blood that Jesus shed for others to be cleansed, Loomis slashes his own chest and bleeds for himself. He thereby transcends Christianity, finally rejects Martha and Joe Turner, and inaugurates a new definition of himself. In this scenario, Christianity and Joe Turner are placed in the same relation to Loomis (Joe Turner had caught Loomis because he stopped on a street to preach to a group of gamblers); both are sources of stymieing and repression. For Loomis to grow, the text posits, he has to reach for a different spirituality; it comes from his own body and his own imagination. By symbolically bleeding for himself, Loomis assumes responsibility for his place in the world. He will no longer be bound by the definitions of others, including Martha and Joe Turner, because he can now stand on his own legs (as in the dry bones vision he has seen) and move to a different psychological space. After seven years of prison and almost four years of looking for his wife, therefore, Loomis is finally *free*. His freedom has come at the price of giving up a daughter, but that seems to be a lesser issue to Wilson. The man coming into his own *as man* supersedes his coming into his own *as father*. He has not been the most affectionate father, but he has taken care of his daughter; in the schema that Wilson creates, that seems to be enough, and given the sympathy afforded Bynum, whose ideas guide Loomis's development, Loomis's choice at the end of the text is clearly posited as the right one.

While the idea of founding a religion might be an attractive one, as it is with Baby Suggs in Toni Morrison's *Beloved* (1987), that possible celebration must be weighed against the violation of human spirit that characterizes incarceration, especially when one is innocent and particularly when one has been snatched away from one's family as Loomis has been. It is a hard price to pay for Wilson to make his point about black men's susceptibility to imprisonment just for being black in the South. While Loomis might form a community with thousands if not hundreds of thousands of black men in the South, he is, unlike the previously imprisoned black men in other plays, more alone than not. Mattie, the boarder in Seth's house whom Loomis has not been able to touch, dashes out after Loomis at the end of the play; whatever connection they can forge, however, is left to the imaginations of readers and viewers.

The solidity of Troy's baseball bat and Boy Willie's watermelons is not matched in Loomis's post-prison experiences, which could make him, the innocent man, the most pathetic of those previously imprisoned. Wilson avoids that outcome by taking the play to the level of spiritual reward. Still, the indictment of the racist white southern legal system remains constant, so much so in fact that Wilson runs the risk of sacrificing his black male characters to stereotypical conceptualizations of black males to make his points. Since so few black men in his dramas do not have encounters with the law, it might reasonably be assumed that Wilson specializes in the pathologies of violence and criminality that paint black men as perpetrators of violent and objectionable behavior, paths to which they adhere with or without the law looming large around them.[7] Wilson has avoided that potential outcome through his well-publicized intention to create a ten-cycle play about African American life in the twentieth century. He has therefore created an expectant audience that is willing to give him broad leeway in his creative endeavors. That audience has waited and continues to wait patiently as he moves toward his ultimate goal. The cultural, racial, historical backdrop against which he has set that goal seems to make audiences less willing to indict him for little tears in the fabric of his larger objective—at least for now.

(1995, 2001)

Notes

1. One of the most striking representations of prison experience in African American literature is James Baldwin's *If Beale Street Could Talk* (1974), in which a young black man is erroneously jailed for rape. In folkloristic representations, Bruce Jackson's *Get Your Ass in the Water and Swim Like Me* (1974) depicts the culture and the lore of imprisoned black men. Jackson's book *Wake Up Dead Man* (1972) also documents black male prison culture. There is also a film version of this project.

2. His transformation in the fiery prison of racism evokes Claude McKay's expression of his ability to enter the fire of American racial hatred in "Baptism" and emerge "a stronger soul within a finer frame." See *Selected Poems of Claude McKay,* 35.

3. Although Troy's brother, Gabriel, has not suffered a long period of incarceration, he is in constant trouble with the law in the current action of the play. Shell-shocked from World War II and truly believing that he is the archangel Gabriel, he occasionally disturbs the peace, including one instance in which he reportedly chases children. The payoff from Gabriel's war wound has enabled Troy to buy the house in which he and his family live; Gabriel has lived there until the current action of the play.

4. For Eva's speech that is equivalent to Troy's, see Morrison, *Sula,* 69.

5. Troy's life circumstances and the issues surrounding infidelity and love relationships might be read in a blues mode, which is what Sandra G. Shannon does in *The Dramatic Vision of August Wilson,* chap. 4.

6. Joe Turner is the subject of song and legend. For a more extensive discussion of his impact upon the development of the play, see my "August Wilson's Folk Traditions" (essay on *Joe Turner's Come and Gone*) in *August Wilson: A Casebook,* 49–67.

7. Although I have limited my comments in this essay to three of Wilson's plays, there are instances of violence in other of his plays. In *Ma Rainey's Black Bottom* (1984), for example, a murder takes place on stage when Levee, one of the four musicians supporting Ma Rainey, stabs Toledo, another of the musicians, to death. In *Seven Guitars* (1996), Poochie is killed (offstage) by a policemen, and musician Floyd "Schoolboy" Barton's throat is cut onstage.

Works Cited

Baldwin, James. *If Beale Street Could Talk.* New York: Dell, 1974.

Harris, Trudier. "August Wilson's Folk Traditions." In *August Wilson: A Casebook.* Ed. Marilyn Elkins. New York: Garland, 1994, 49–67.

Jackson, Bruce. *Get Your Ass in the Water and Swim Like Me: Narrative Poetry from Black Oral Tradition.* Cambridge: Harvard University Press, 1974.

———, ed. *Wake Up Dead Man: Afro American Worksongs from Texas Prisons.* Cambridge: Harvard University Press, 1972.

McKay, Claude. *Selected Poems of Claude McKay.* New York: Harcourt, 1953.

Morrison, Toni. *Beloved.* New York: Knopf, 1987.

———. *Sula.* New York: Knopf, 1974.

Shannon, Sandra G. *The Dramatic Vision of August Wilson.* Washington, D.C.: Howard University Press, 1995.

Wilson, August. *Fences.* New York: Plume, 1986.

———. *Joe Turner's Come and Gone.* New York: Plume, 1988.

———. *Ma Rainey's Black Bottom.* New York: Plume, 1984.

———. *The Piano Lesson.* New York: Plume, 1990.

———. *Seven Guitars.* New York: Plume, 1996.

Wolfe, Peter. *August Wilson.* New York: Twayne, 1999.

Wright, Richard. "The Ethics of Living Jim Crow." In *Uncle Tom's Children.* 1938. Reprint, New York: Perennial, 1965, 3–15.

———. "Long Black Song." In *Uncle Tom's Children,* 103–28.

Eight | Hands beyond the Grave

Henry Dumas's Influence on
Toni Morrison

 When Beloved made her appearance at
124 Bluestone Road in Cincinnati, Ohio,
in 1987, Henry Dumas had been dead for
nineteen years. Readers, teachers, and scholars praised Morrison's creation of the story surrounding a ghost child's return to her mother.
Morrison's imagination and the lyricism of her prose won accolades
worldwide and culminated in her being awarded the coveted Nobel
Prize for Literature. We applauded the creativity that continued to
move Morrison into a class by herself. We celebrated her taking us
into difficult new worlds and keeping us safe and sane after the journey. Certainly we accepted her discussion of the influence of Margaret Garner's life upon the creation of Sethe and Beloved, and we
recognized that she had provided a point of entry for many persons
to begin to wrestle with the traumatic history of slavery. Even those
of us who read her works especially closely did not immediately find
reason to look for influence beyond the sources to which we had been
pointed. Occasionally someone would comment that Morrison had
been the editor at Random House for Toni Cade Bambara's *The Salt
Eaters* (1980), and we might begin to see some connections between
that novel and *Beloved*. Hardly anyone stopped to consider that there
might be other works that Morrison had edited that could have influenced her creation of various characters. And while I certainly do not
intend this possibility in any negative way, it is worthwhile to consider

the relationship between Morrison and Henry Dumas, another writer whose works she had a hand in bringing to public readership.

A poet, short fiction writer, and budding novelist, Henry Dumas was born in the small town of Sweet Home, Arkansas, in 1934.[1] He grew up in New York City and did a short tour of military duty, during which he explored Eastern religions and got married. He fathered two sons, participated in the civil rights movement in the mid 1960s, and taught in writers' workshops in East Saint Louis, Illinois, in 1967, where he met the poet Eugene B. Redmond, who would prove instrumental to his career. This incipient, talented writer was shot to death by a New York City transit policeman on 23 May 1968 in what was apparently a case of mistaken identity. Dumas's death at thirty-three initiated a Henry Dumas cult; here was another young black man killed under mysterious and questionable circumstances, but this one had the good fortune of having well-known writers and editors, including Redmond and Morrison, who could speak for him once his voice was silenced. Redmond, who devoted much of his life from Dumas's death through 1989 to the publication of Dumas's completed and unfinished work, has edited and coedited six volumes of Dumas's prose and poetry.[2] It was Redmond who contacted Morrison at Random House about publishing the works.

Dumas's works are informed by his interests in religion, spirituality, and mythology; they frequently focus on the intersections of the natural and the supernatural. Dumas is as interested in the magically real as is Toni Morrison; indeed, the ending of "Ark of Bones," the story on which I will focus more attention shortly, anticipates the ending of Morrison's *Tar Baby* (1981), in which Son Green goes "lickety-split" into myth and history. As Arnold Rampersad observes of Dumas's writing, "the most fascinating aspect of his work may well be the tension between his interest in realism and his interest in the surreal. Side by side with his concrete, tactile sense of reality is Dumas's imaginative determination, fed no doubt by his interest in Eastern culture, to render the world and experience in a mythic and symbolic sense"

(331). The critic Clyde Taylor comments that "Dumas aspired to the oldest, most honored version of the poet, that of poet-prophet to his people. He sought to incarnate their cultural identity, values, and mythic visions as well as to codify and even reshape those myths into modalities of a more soulful existence" (354).

Indeed, Dumas may be viewed as developing his own mythological system, a strikingly different way for black people to articulate their ontology and their ties to western civilization. Consider the title story of *"Ark of Bones" and Other Stories,* in which Dumas uses his trademark natural setting to effect something beyond the natural. Set in a small town in Arkansas and featuring two young boys, Headeye and Fish-Hound, "Ark of Bones" centers upon an encounter with an ark and the ancient priests, griotlike men, who have been selected to guide the Ark and watch over the millions upon millions of bones the Ark contains. These are the bones of Africans and African Americans who have died violently as a result of the Middle Passage and other encounters with Western civilization, and this is the "soulboat" upon which the evidence of their existence and their demise resides. Headeye, in the tradition of black preachers and others who are selected for a special tie with the supernatural world, has been called to join the fraternity of the attenders of the bones. He disappears into myth and history in a manner comparable to that of Son Green.

The story focuses upon African American caregiving responsibility for deaths that occurred in the Middle Passage, a responsibility that supersedes racism and centers upon preservation and reverence. Racism may be the backdrop for the Ark's existence, but the bas relief is the more important thing. Headeye and Fish-hound learn that there is a history that cannot be washed away with water. The Ark becomes the "tracks in water" that enslaved persons in Caryl Phillips's fiction assert cannot exist. These tracks lead Headeye to communion with forces much larger than the forces that took the flesh and blood of the bones stored in the Ark. In an Africanized version of the story of Ezekiel, Headeye and his initiators make clear that bones can live and that they *can* tell stories. Slave ships that transported Africans through the Middle Passage recede in comparison to the Ark. With its over-tones of biblical history (particularly Noah's Ark) and slave history, the Ark moves African American history beyond both. The myth that Dumas creates is one in which black people recognize their oppres-sions and move beyond them to the possibility of creating something else. There is a timeless vigil that these keepers maintain, and that vigil is the basis for transcendence of the reductive history that would de-fine black Americans solely as the descendants of enslaved persons. Slavery definitely is a part of the history, but to believe that it is *all* of the history of black people on Western soil is to be subsumed with a mentality that does not recognize the eternity, the immortality, of African American existence. Communal memory that exceeds a hu-man sense of time is what the keepers of the bones pass on to Fish-hound and Headeye, and it is with the knowledge that Headeye is to become one of them that they induct him into his extranatural calling. Certainly there are echoes of Minnie Ransom from Bambara's *The Salt Eaters* in this process, for Minnie has out-of-body experiences and communes with the dead, but there are also anticipations of Sula's demise, of Pilate's sight beyond sight and similar communion with the dead, and of Beloved's uncommon residence. Morrison's *Beloved,* the story not to be passed on, that is, not to be passed *over,* is also Dumas's tale, of which generations upon generations of black people on Western soil must ever be aware. It is the impetus to redefinition of self, to the claiming of cosmic ties for people of African descent.

"Ark of Bones" and *Beloved* draw upon Christian traditions and imbue them with other influences, whether we call those influences Eastern, African, or African American. In African American commu-nities, it is generally recognized that preachers in most folk churches are "called," that is, specially selected by God, to their profession. One of the most vivid documentations of such callings is Bill Ferris's film, *Two Black Churches,* in which a black minister in New Haven, Connecticut, recounts the physical ailments and psychological dis-comforts he suffered before he said yes to God and became a preacher. Dumas adheres to the African American tradition by making it impossible for Headeye to resist the call, but he modifies it by not allowing Headeye to become a preacher. If there is a prophet in the story, it is Fish-hound, for he is left to tell the story, although he leaves out significant details and modifies the narrative in keeping with what he believes Headeye wants. Headeye's role goes beyond even what Baby Suggs attempts in *Beloved*. Remember that Baby Suggs in effect creates a religion, one based in humanistic and practical principles. She is as much god as any other god. Her calling, perhaps more self-induced than not, is to encourage black people to reclaim the best in themselves by erasing the trauma of slavery. The keepers of bones in "Ark of Bones" recognize that the bones of slavery are the very base from which something else has to emerge. Headeye's calling, therefore, is to the shaping of a different kind of myth, one not based in Christianity or any other established religion. As Clyde Taylor notes, "Dumas tries virtually to excavate the spiritual core of Black Christianity, leaving behind the husk of deadening and diversionary forms of what he calls 'the Jesus disease.' He then tries to unite that core with the syncretistic mythology of great subtlety that he was obviously fashioning in his work" (360).

Not only do Morrison and Dumas share kinship in their attempts to transform Christianity, but also in their recognition that planes of existence can be crossed easily. By merging the lines between life and death, this world and the other side, they intertwine folklore and history, fact and fiction, life and death. "I am very much concerned about what is happening to my people," Dumas once wrote, "and what we are doing with our precious tradition." This statement, writes Redmond, "echoes [Dumas's] earlier call for 'full-time, devoted scholarship' designed to establish a proper perspective on the Black heritage and simultaneously to create appropriate vehicles for utilizing traditional folk forms in the service of serious literary expression" (xiv). In an early story, Dumas gave fictional life to supernatural events that shape African American folklore. In the lore, there is the generally held belief that if it rains and the sun shines at the same time, the devil is beating his wife. Dumas brings that belief to life in "Rain God" by having his three young protagonists encounter just such a scene when they are running through the woods one day.[3] They come upon a stump on top of which they see the devil and his wife in miniature, with the devil carrying out his proverbial switching, literally with a whip. Blue, the narrator, races toward home with the others as he envisions the devil growing to gigantic proportions and pursuing him. Morrison brings to life the tar baby story in a more extended narrative in her novel of the same title. She allows myth and folklore to take on flesh and blood before she rerelegates them to the realm of the mythical. Giving narrative flesh to the bare bones of folk tradition, therefore, is an experiment in which both authors engage.

With Dumas, as with Morrison, events beyond the natural exist in the same space as the natural. A soulboat can appear on the Mississippi River. The devil and his wife can be on a stump almost in our backyards. The fantastic world of speaking animals can become the reality of black men and women. Both writers domesticate the supernatural, make it so familiar that its ability to frighten is severely diminished. And they simultaneously domesticate extranatural events. The blurring of usually accepted divides, the merging of traditional lines of demarcation inextricably links these writers and encourages us to think more extensively about intertextuality, influence, and creativity. Perhaps Henry Dumas, the mostly forgotten young writer, had a greater impact upon our most revered contemporary writer than the majority of readers and critics would suspect.

When *"Ark of Bones" and Other Stories* and *Play Ebony: Play Ivory* were both published by Random House in 1974, Toni Morrison penned a letter to potential buyers and supporters. She began that letter, which invited recipients to a book party, this way:

Dear . . .

In 1968, a young Black man, Henry Dumas, went through a turnstile at a New York City subway station. A transit cop shot him in the chest and killed him. Circumstances surrounding his death remain unclear. Before that happened, however, he had written

some of the most beautiful, moving, and profound poetry and fiction that I have ever in my life read. He was thirty-three years old
when he was killed, but in those thirty-three years, he had completed work, the quality and quantity of which are almost never
achieved in several lifetimes. He was brilliant. He was magnetic,
and he was an incredible artist.[4]

Morrison went on to say that she was sending copies of both works
under separate cover, and she encouraged readers of her letter to
choose passages that they were moved by, and come to this rather
unusual book party prepared to read from Dumas's work. She was going to read, she declared, as would Angela Davis, Jane Cortez, Melvin
Van Peebles, John A. Williams, and Eugene Redmond. She wanted to
offer "a meaningful tribute to this extraordinary talent."

This magnanimous praise from a writer to whom these same descriptions would be applied a few years later is included in the summer 1988 special issue of *Black American Literature Forum* devoted to
Henry Dumas's life and work; Morrison joined nearly sixty other writers, scholars, and activists in celebrating Dumas's unique talent. Also
included in that issue is a copy of the letter Morrison sent to book
clubs announcing the discovery and publication of Dumas's novel,
Jonoah and the Green Stone. She referred to the "spectacular reviews"
the earlier books had received and heralded the novel as "fulfilling the
enormous promise of Dumas's briefer works" (311). It is reasonable
to expect that a person so appreciative of Dumas's work would, deliberately or inadvertently, be influenced by him. Keep in mind that
Morrison wrote these words in September 1974 and the spring of
1976, when only the first two of her novels, *The Bluest Eye* and *Sula,*
had appeared. Her picture had not yet graced the cover of *Newsweek;*
she had not yet won the National Book Award, the Pulitzer Prize, or
the much-coveted Nobel Prize for Literature. She was herself an up-
and-coming writer, one still looking for ways to carve her name into
literary history.

In her role as editor, she was also perhaps effusive in her praise of Dumas from the practical point of view of wanting to sell books. Even a cursory reading of Dumas's volumes published under Morrison's supervision reveals that several of the short stories were fragmentary and certainly would have been revised. Yet the most polished ones do reflect an exceptional mind at work, and the unfinished novel is an impressive creation. I would argue, therefore, that not only did Morrison help Henry Dumas by agreeing to publish his first three books, but also he in turn helped her by encouraging her to expand her imagination in ways that have led to her becoming a household name around the world. While there may be no visible tracks in the waters that tie them together, as surely as Morrison's legacy lives on, so too does Henry Dumas's.

(1996)

Notes

1. Is it mere coincidence that Morrison names her most famous plantation in her most famous novel "Sweet Home"? Eleanor W. Traylor has also commented on this echo; see "Henry Dumas and the Discourse of Memory," 366.

2. These volumes include *"Ark of Bones" and Other Stories* (1970, 1974), *Play Ebony: Play Ivory* (1974; originally published as *Poetry for My People* in 1970), *Jonoah and the Green Stone* (1976), *Rope of Wind and Other Stories* (1979), *Goodbye Sweetwater: New & Selected Stories by Henry Dumas* (1988), and *Knees of a Natural Man* (1989).

3. The story first appeared in *Negro Digest* in January 1968; it was one of the few of his publications that Dumas saw in print before his death. The story is collected in the "Goodbye, Sweetwater" section of *Goodbye, Sweetwater: New & Selected Stories by Henry Dumas,* 319–22.

4. "On Behalf of Henry Dumas," 310.

Works Cited

Bambara, Toni Cade. *The Salt Eaters.* New York: Random House, 1980.

Dumas, Henry. *"Ark of Bones" and Other Stories.* New York: Random House, 1974.

———. *Goodbye, Sweetwater: New and Selected Stories by Henry Dumas.* Ed. Eugene B. Redmond. New York: Thunder's Mouth Press, 1988.

————. *Jonoah and the Green Stone.* New York: Random House, 1976.

————. *Knees of a Natural Man: The Selected Poetry of Henry Dumas.* New York: Thunder's Mouth Press, 1989.

————. *Play Ebony: Play Ivory* (originally published as *Poetry for My People* in 1970). New York: Random House, 1974.

————. *Rope of Wind and Other Stories.* New York: Random House, 1979.

Morrison, Toni. *Beloved.* New York: Knopf, 1987.

————. *The Bluest Eye.* New York: Holt, Rinehart, Winston, 1970.

————. "On Behalf of Henry Dumas." In *Black American Literature Forum* 22, no. 2 (summer 1988): 310–12.

————. *Sula.* New York: Knopf, 1974.

————. *Tar Baby.* New York: Knopf, 1981.

Rampersad, Arnold. "Henry Dumas's World of Fiction." In *Black American Literature Forum* 22, no. 2 (summer 1988): 329–32.

Redmond, Eugene B. Introduction to *Goodbye, Sweetwater: New and Selected Stories by Henry Dumas.* New York: Thunder's Mouth Press, 1988.

Taylor, Clyde. "Henry Dumas: Legacy of a Long-Breath Singer." In *Black American Literature Forum* 22, no. 2 (summer 1988): 353–64.

Traylor, Eleanor W. "Henry Dumas and the Discourse of Memory." In *Black American Literature Forum* 22, no. 2 (summer 1988): 365–78.

Nine Salting the Land but
Not the Imagination

William Melvin Kelley's
A Different Drummer

 Various fictional works that depict parts of
the American South depend for their landscape upon completely imagined territo-
ries that the authors have created out of whole cloth. Gloria Naylor
has her Willow Springs, a mythical island off the coasts of South Carolina and Georgia; Raymond Andrews completed three novels about
Muskhogean County, Georgia, somewhere in the northeastern part
of the state, near Athens; Randall Kenan has centered a novel and a
collection of short stories upon Tims Creek, North Carolina; and of
course William Faulkner has his Yoknapatawpha. One of the lesser
known literary lights who has contributed to this southern imaginary
space is William Melvin Kelley, who, in *A Different Drummer,* published in 1962, creates a mythical southern state to enact his narrative
of black and white relationships. That unnamed state, with the capi-
tal site of Willson City named after the most prominent family in the
region's history, is uniquely situated. *"An East South Central state in the
Deep South, it is bounded on the north by Tennessee; east by Alabama; south by
the Gulf of Mexico; west by Mississippi"* (11). Its geographical location is
matched by an equally noteworthy demographic fact: *"In June 1957, for
reasons yet to be determined, all the state's Negro inhabitants departed. Today, it
is unique in being the only state in the Union that cannot count even one member
of the Negro race among its citizens"* (12).

The novel anticipates Douglas Turner Ward's *Day of Absence* (1964), a play set in a southern town in which black people simply disappear for a day. During the course of that day, nothing goes right in the town. White women cannot cook or take care of their babies, no garbage gets picked up, no white businessmen can be chauffeured to their places of business, and there are no loiterers on the streets. The mayor makes a crying, begging plea for the blacks to return, and because of this plea or for other reasons, the next day things are back to normal. Or are they? While Ward focuses on absence and return and an implied permanent though subtle disruption of the status quo, Kelley spends his narrative exploring the *process* of disappearance and the one man who, inadvertently or deliberately, is responsible for that disappearance. The man who, in the Thoreauvian tradition, hears the different drummer is Tucker Caliban, a diminutive black man who is the fourth generational descendant of "the African," a huge black man whom slave traders tried to enslave.

What Tucker Caliban does and why ties the African, the Willsons, and the white "men on the porch" into a cycle of history and psychological and physical violence. A couple of months after Tucker convinces David Willson, the current patriarch of the Willson dynasty, to sell him seven acres of the original Willson plantation on which early descendants of the African had lived and worked, he severs the bonds of paternalism and history that have tied the two families together. The most dramatic part of his declaration of independence is what Tucker does to his land. He orders ten tons of salt and essentially plants it on the land. When his neighbors, both black and white, hear about this extraordinary deed, they come to watch Tucker carry out, patiently and methodically, what they judge to be a peculiar brand of insanity. One observer notes:

> *Just like he's planting seed. Just like it's spring planting time and he started early and don't have to worry none about missing the first good days. Just like all of us every spring, getting up early and eating and then going out into the field and tossing in seed. Only he ain't planting nothing; he's surely killing*

the land and he don't even look like he hates it. It ain't at all like he got up one morning and said to hisself, "I ain't busting my backbone another day. I'm getting that land before it gets me." Not running out like a mad dog and putting down the salt like it WAS salt, but putting it down like it was cotton or corn, like come fall, it'd be a paying crop. He's so tiny to be doing such a terrible thing, no bigger than Harold even, doing that like a boy building a model plane or working with a little hoe beside his daddy, pretending he is his daddy and it's his field and his own little son is working beside him. (45)

I include the neighbor's observation about Tucker's size because it is a consistent comment in the portraits of him. Everyone seems to think that his boyish size, his stunted growth, makes it impossible for Tucker to have complex ideas. Indeed, his size has occasioned a kind of invisibility with Tucker. For such a man—small, quiet, generally obedient, seemingly always acquiescent—to kill his land intrigues and stupefies his neighbors. And not only does he kill the land, but he shoots his horse and cow, chops down General Willson's favorite tree, chops up the grandfather clock he has inherited from the Willsons, and burns his house to the ground before he and his pregnant wife begin their trek away from Sutton and the unnamed state in which they live. Tucker's actions to liberate himself become the primary topic of conversation at the local porch gathering site, the impetus for all the Willsons to reflect upon their relationship with Tucker as well as their relationships among each other, and the starting point for all the blacks leaving this mythical southern state.

What is especially striking about the novel is that we never enter Tucker Caliban's head space. We see him through the eyes of the people upon whom he has an impact—the Willsons, his wife, the gawking neighbors. Through his actions and the neighbors' evaluations of them, Tucker becomes as much a legend in Sutton as the African became when he arrived in the area several generations before, as much of a legend as the mythical state in which they all reside. To understand Tucker and what the land has come to mean, it is necessary to know the story of the African. A giant of a man who stood two heads taller than any other man, the African was chained in the hold of a ship and eventually brought to the city of New Marsails to be auctioned off. He arrived on the day that Dewitt Willson, one of David's ancestors, arrived to pick up a grandfather clock he had imported from Europe, the same clock that has been passed down to Tucker. Fascinated by the African, Dewitt bid for him, only to witness the African kill the auctioneer and escape to the swamps—all of this with a baby under his arm. The African then proceeded to free enslaved blacks on various plantations in the area. After obsessively pursuing him for several months, Dewitt Willson caught up with him when the African was betrayed by a man he trusted, and, recognizing that the African would never be enslaved, Dewitt shot and killed him. He took the baby, named him *First* Caliban, and established the pattern of field work, carriage driving, and chauffeuring that interlinked the Willson and Caliban families for the next several generations.

The African's death, however, is far less important than the legendary status he holds among the men on the porch, chief among them Mister Harper, who relates the tale of this extraordinary man. Everything about the African is larger than life—his size, his ability to kill, his commitment to the baby, and his freeing of enslaved persons. He roars loud enough to bulge out the sides of the slave ship, tears a hole in the wall of the ship on which he is chained, needs twenty or thirty men to bring him to the auction block (even with chains on him), slices the auctioneer's head off with one of the chains, runs with three hundred pounds of chains on him, and grabs a man from a horse racing toward him and snaps the man's back across his knee. Mister Harper maintains that the African's *blood* yet runs through Tucker Caliban's veins, and it is for that reason that Tucker kills his land. If these are the legends that the more skeptical whites believe about the African, it may reasonably be assumed that his descendants, down to Tucker, would believe them even more fervently.

Like those flying Africans who returned to Africa, or those who preferred death by drowning to slavery in the New World, the African lives and dies by a standard that none of his descendants has been able to match. He becomes the icon of freedom from laboring on land that does not belong to him. He becomes the icon of freedom in choosing death to enslavement, for none of his descendants has been able to make that choice. He provides not only an abstract standard for Tucker Caliban, but a physical standard as well. Tucker is described as barely being able to reach the top of the car he drives for the Willsons, he is several inches shorter than his wife (who is over six feet tall), and he generally spends his life looking *up*. He is an unhappy, brooding man whose angry appearance is a contrast to his boyish exterior. He is insulted when his wife takes him to a social gathering and asks for dues for an organization that is ostensibly *fighting for his rights,* because he sees his battles as essentially his alone. We lack details of how he articulates that battle, but we know that he feels an urgent need to change his family's pattern of interaction with the Willsons.

One site that makes that battle necessary is the name given to all the descendants of the African: Caliban. Dewitt Willson chose the name because he was reading Shakespeare's *The Tempest* at the time, and it apparently seemed an appropriate way to designate those presumed to have civilization from those presumed to be without civilization. Dewitt is the counterpart to Prospero in Shakespeare's play; he is the man with the power to name and to usurp land and the labor belonging to those he considers to be without civilization. The name becomes the demarcation of a dividing line between the so-called jungles of Africa and the enlightened territories of the West. More immediately, it labels all of the African's descendants as inherently inferior to the man who has named them. By breaking with the tradition of giving enslaved persons on his plantation his own last name, Dewitt Willson attempts to separate his humanity forever from the so-called savagery he has witnessed with the African. He is fascinated by that savagery, that chaos, but he wants to hold it at arm's distance, control it, contain it. Black and white designations, with their customarily assigned places, would surely have been enough to signal this division, but to add the name is to give all black persons working for the Willsons multiple dimensions of a burdensome history signaling their subjugation and inferiority. The very name Caliban thus aligns black people connected with the Willson family to the fate of ignorance and physical labor.

The irony inherent in that name is perhaps more intended for the likes of Mister Harper and Kelley's readers than for Tucker Caliban himself, for he is without formal education. For him, it is not the name, but the plantation, the land, the livestock, and the clock that are *all* reminders that there has been no appreciable change from eighteenth-century slavery to twentieth-century slavery. And since he does not wish to kill the perpetrators of his family's enslavement, he kills the symbols of it. For Tucker, who has spent most of his life with the Willsons as a chauffeur, the land does not represent money, or crops, or material advantage. For the generations of Calibans who have preceded him, the land did not presage opportunity or a future; it was simply a constant reminder of a status designated by persons who had the power to control other people's fates.

As the only adult Caliban left alive in the current action of the novel, Tucker centers upon *loss* as the representation of the Willson connection. Loss has been most recently indicated in his grandfather John's death. The old man had a heart attack and died in the back of a segregated bus on which the "colored" sign was the last thing he saw. Sadly, the Montgomery Bus Boycott did not have a chance to transform his life. With each generation of the Willsons inheriting the land and also inheriting the Calibans, Tucker comes to realize that he has lost any sustainable inheritance, for he is merely a part of the property that gets passed along. Another of his losses is self-determination, for until his fateful deed, he has not been able to control his life. Ultimately, he has lost, that is, *never experienced,* authority over himself or his world. Certainly he directs his wife, but they are both small cogs in the very large wheel of the white world they inhabit.

Descendants of the African, therefore, have been carved into little molds that suit other people's wishes and needs. Tucker believes that the only way they can become self-determining, the only way they can envision a future, is to dramatically sever themselves from the invisible chains tying them to Willson land and Willson heritage and all the limitations they represent in their lives. With Bethrah, Tucker's wife, having given birth to a child a few months earlier and now pregnant with a second one, those limitations become even clearer to Tucker. It seems that for each previous generation of Calibans, there was only one child, one person to carry on the carriage driver or chauffeur position with the Willsons; now Tucker has to worry about multiple future enslavement. All of the mentioned descendants have been male, and Tucker's first child is male, but there is the possibility that the second child could be female, which evokes an additional protective role in Tucker. The death of the last male elder, John Caliban, is the beginning of the process of freeing himself for which Tucker has hungered without perhaps having a precise plan of how to achieve his objective. With a wife who has given up her college education to become a cook in the Willson family, and with two children whose futures he does not want identified with the Willsons, Tucker has the incentive to move another step toward freeing himself and his family.

It is ironic that it takes so many generations for the Calibans to achieve what the African started. It is equally ironic that the petite Tucker (who is frequently described as looking like a tiny boy) is ultimately as strong in determination as the African had been in physical size and prowess. Tucker is strong enough to confront David Willson directly to ask to purchase the land and to challenge Willson when he briefly threatens Tucker for talking so directly and smartly to a white man. He is strong enough to endure the spectacle of whites and blacks watching him as he salts the land, shoots his animals, chops down the tree, chops up the clock, and sets his house afire. And he is strong enough to resist the questions of the formidable Mister Harper—to whom *everyone* in the town defers (the men who congregate on the front porch of the local store even leave when his daughter brings his lunch because he likes to eat alone).

Whereas the African rescued people physically, Tucker frees their *minds* and their imaginations, and they in turn take the *actions* that get them physically out of this unnamed southern state. By envisioning futures not tied to the land, the blacks in Sutton begin to revise history, reshape the patterns of which they have been a part. The extent to which their actions will have an impact can be measured in how the townspeople respond to their disappearance. Bobby-Joe, a young white hothead who leads the last lynching in Sutton, believes that "outside agitators" have caused the three-day exodus from Sutton. For him, Tucker Caliban is not smart enough to have started this trouble, to have liberated himself, so he blames the black Reverend Bradshaw, who has come south to study the migration phenomenon, and leads the furious violence against him. Bobby-Joe has nothing to hold on to when he must contemplate the idea of a "Negro-less world," so he reacts by leading a lynching ritual that is comfortably familiar to him. It amounts to a pathetic attempt to reinstate the status quo. Mister Harper, at times Kelley's spokesperson and certainly a more educated and enlightened person than most whites in Sutton, recognizes Tucker's actions for what they are—a signal that life could possibly never be the same in Sutton, that white people may never think of themselves in the same way.

David Willson sees Tucker's actions as the key to his own liberation. He was briefly radical about racial issues, then lost his resolve when he was fired from his newspaper job. Dymphna Willson, his daughter, remembers Tucker as having married the woman who kept her secrets and became her best friend. Camille Willson remembers Tucker as giving her advice that saved her marriage, and from the moment Tucker buys land from her husband, her long estrangement from her husband begins to be healed. Young Dewey Willson has difficulty remembering the sacrifice that Tucker made for him on the memorable day Tucker taught him to ride a bicycle, but Tucker's interaction with Dewey has nonetheless influenced him sufficiently for Dewey to try to save Rev. Bradshaw from lynching. In other words, Tucker Caliban is not a dramatic actor, but a quiet storm. Something fundamental in Sutton will not be the same once he is gone. His neighbors already treat Dewey Willson with less than the respect a Willson believes is due him, and even Mister Harper has executed the memorable act of rising from his wheelchair because there is finally something worth seeing in Sutton.

Indeed, what drew me to Kelley's novel when I first read it was the angle of vision from which he chose to present Tucker's story. By filtering it through the points of view of the white characters, and letting Tucker slip through their imaginations, Kelley reinforces an often-accepted adage: it was necessary for black people to know everything about whites in the South just to be able to survive. Whites, by contrast, perhaps in their belief that they were absolutely in control, felt less of a need to know blacks beyond stereotypes. While Tucker has an impact on most whites in the novel, that impact is filtered through their limited knowledge of blacks in general and a specific incident or two in connection with Tucker.

Tucker has been on the landscape of the Willson imagination for almost twenty-two years, yet no one really knows him. It is comforting, Kelley posits, for whites to be so blinded. Such blindness makes it easy not to disturb the imagined realities around them. Dewey barely remembers that Tucker received a severe beating that Dewey should have received; Dymphna can see Tucker only when Bethrah opens her eyes slightly; and both Willson parents filter their knowledge of Tucker through their own tortured private lives. Tucker is an enigma to them, a whiff of smoke, not a solid entity onto which they can hold. If whites know so little about people who linger intimately in their spaces, Kelley seems to argue, then how can they ever hope to grow into any true understanding of race relations? And, indeed, why should they even have such hope?

On the landscape of the Willson imagination, Tucker Caliban is invisible except for a few incidents over the years prior to his salting his farm. The Willsons have rolled the complexity and humanity of their tiny chauffeur into whatever comfort zone was convenient in their lives. His needs, dreams, and hopes are of no concern to them, because he is *in place* washing their cars, driving them to town, or performing whatever other errands and chores are necessary to them. After their contemplation of his "crazy" actions, and even as he changes them, they are not particularly more enlightened about *who* he is than they were before. He is as distanced from them as is the African, forever slippery as a complex, human entity.

The puzzle of Tucker Caliban is, in the minstrel tradition that Joseph Boskin describes in *Sambo: The Rise and Demise of an American Jester*, entertainment for the day. The audience in this novel may well be in a theatre watching a show. The black performer engages their attention, invites speculation about his actions, but finally they go home to what they know. They relate, very selectively, what they want of his performance to their own lives, then dismiss the rest as inconvenient worriation. Tucker Caliban is thus subjected to a faulty microscope, one that does not reveal the truth, but only what its viewers want to see. He moves from being "a good nigger" to being "an inexplicable nigger," a territory into which they cannot follow.

Until he disappears from view, Tucker Caliban literally hides in plain sight in the town of Sutton and in the home of the Willsons. It is questionable if any of the whites truly understands Tucker's message about black lives, labor, land, history, future, and the need for freedom. If landed labor and domestic chores are the only or just the primary bases for black-white interaction in the South, can there be a future? Hope lies with Mister Harper, the white intellectual patriarch, and Mister Leland, the little white boy to whom Tucker is compared in size. Yet Mister Harper seems to have lost his leadership role and is not on the scene to talk sense to his men when Bobby-Joe inspires the lynching fever. Mister Leland, lying in his bed on the night that Rev. Bradshaw is lynched on the nearby Caliban farm, mistakenly concludes that Tucker has returned and is having a party and that he will be invited to share the leftover goodies the next day. The truth is that the unenlightened, unprogressive white men are refertilizing Tucker's field with Bradshaw's blood, reinstating the cycle that may presage another four generations of limiting and violent interactions between blacks and whites in the South. Southern land, William Melvin Kelley suggests, will always have physical and psychological dimensions;

its possession and its products, both material and human, remain an inseparable part of the southern racial landscape. A Tucker Caliban may liberate himself, but he cannot finally change that overall pattern.

(1997)

Work Cited

Kelley, William Melvin. *A Different Drummer.* 1959, 1962. Reprint, New York: Anchor, 1969.

Ten Transformations of the
Land in Randall Kenan's
"The Foundations of
the Earth"

 Randall Kenan has made the tiny, imaginary town of Tims Creek, North Carolina,
the site for focus in *A Visitation of Spirits*
(1989) as well as in the short stories collected in *Let the Dead Bury
Their Dead* (1992). On the surface, Tims Creek is a very traditional
southern community in that the primary work activities are farming,
specifically tobacco farming, and other work connected with the land,
and the primary social activities are church and visiting. The rather
quiet and passive activities of the land reflect in some ways the rather
quiet patterns of the people's lives. Tims Creek, at a glance, is not
a territory on which unexpected or frightening things usually occur.
It is ostensibly a safe place where everyone knows everyone, where
lives go on pretty much as people planned them from early years of
marriage. People are born, they grow up, they work hard, they go to
church, and they die. The occasional aberration of an affair or a child
who does not turn out as expected is just that—an aberration. Mainly
the expected reigns.

Beneath that seemingly tranquil surface, however, is a smoldering
cauldron of human emotions, sexual violation/perversion, instances
of supernatural encounters with the natural, and bouts of insanity,
infidelity, and ghostly transgressions against the human world. A hog
speaks in "Clarence and the Dead," an angel falls from the sky in

"Things of This World," and a brother and sister fulfill their sexual desire for each other for two years in "Cornsilk." The mask of tranquility is merely that, for this small town offers human, animal, and extranatural drama that rivals anything created on a larger geographic landscape.

A case in point is "The Foundations of the Earth," in which familiar characters and settings change almost before our very eyes. In this story, Kenan shakes up the quiet land as well as the quiet patterns of living. Indeed, the very soil in this story, the earth itself, becomes the site on which Kenan disrupts the usual patterns in Tims Creek. Kenan sets the conflicts in his story on a front porch that looks out over fields, then in the very fields where one of the characters is plowing. By tying racism, hypocrisy, and sexuality to the land, Kenan raises questions about what is natural and what is not, who is religious and who is not. He also questions the nature of work and what should be judged to be sacred. His integration of human emotions, actions, and beliefs with the soil on which they are acted out furthers patterns of transformation of southern attitudes and possibilities that he explores in several of his works.

Maggie MacGowan Williams, the seventy-year-old African American grandmother in the story, from whose perspective the narrative is related, must confront crises in religion and transform her attitudes toward race and sexuality when she learns that her grandson Edward has been living in Boston with a white man, "like man and wife." Nothing in Maggie's staid traditional religious upbringing has prepared her for this set of circumstances. She is a comfortable merchant and matron in a small town where reputation is as important as going to church on Sunday morning. She practices a religion in which rituals are as important as substance, and in which the depths of one's emotional distresses remain hidden because one literally takes one's burdens to the Lord and leaves them there. Private pain is preferable to public confession, but emotions that must be expressed in public, such as those surrounding a funeral or those involved in offering religious testimony, are acceptable.

Maggie's reliance upon ritual is apparent when Gabriel, Edward's lover, shows up for Edward's funeral. Maggie is violently angry about this intrusion (religious, racial, and sexual), but her proper religious upbringing will not allow her to make a public fuss. Instead, she retreats to her bedroom, ostensibly in mourning but more in anger, and sleeps through the traumatic disturbance she cannot yet accept. When she emerges, she has garnered the strength necessary to follow through with the mourning rituals the community expects. She is able to assume "the mantle of one-who-comforts-more-than-needing-comfort,"[1] greet Gabriel warmly, and express superficial concern for his feelings. Her "How have you been?" addressed to Gabriel is in sharp contrast to how she truly feels when Gabriel tries to express his sorrow about Edward's death: "How dare he? This pathetic, stumbling, poor trashy white boy, to throw his sinful lust for her grandbaby in her face, as if to bury a grandchild weren't bad enough. Now this abomination had to be flaunted. —Sorry, indeed! The nerve! Who the hell did he think he was to parade their shame about?" (1994). Maggie is regal in acting out her superficial concern for Gabriel, but Kenan makes clear that form without substance does not offer resolution. Her performance is in the very vein of "form, fashion, and outside show to the world" that her fundamentalist religion condemns. Her traditional religion ultimately fails Maggie, and she must seek other options for how to resolve the turmoil of her feelings about Edward and toward Gabriel.

Given Kenan's project of transformation, of dislodging the comfortable, it is ironically appropriate that Edward's white lover bears the name of Gabriel. One of the archangels, Gabriel is revered in African American folk religious tradition; indeed, he carries the assignment to waken "the quick and the dead" on Judgment Day. God will call him to blow his horn, and as James Weldon Johnson portrays him in *God's Trombones,* he will put one foot on the mountaintop and the other in the middle of the sea and do God's bidding.[2] Gabriel is therefore a disturber of superficial tranquility, a transformer of the states of life and death, and a cherished representative of a beloved

God. For Maggie to have to confront the name so well known to her in the figure of a northern, white, gay male who loved her grandson is, to put it mildly, a bit much for her to bear. The Gabriel before her is presumably antithetical to everything her religion has taught her, but she is not allowed to escape or ignore what this flesh-and-blood Gabriel forces her to confront about life, sexuality, and religion. In Gabriel, gayness and religion, from Maggie's perspective, are inextricably entangled. At this crucial moment in her life, she cannot deal with one without dealing with the other.

Kenan uses the relationship between Edward and Gabriel, and the situation with Maggie and Gabriel, to satirize and thereby unseat religious authority in Tims Creek. Once that authority is deposed, there is room for alternative ways of viewing and evaluating the world. Maggie begins the process by inviting Gabriel to return to Tims Creek six months after Edward's funeral. Perhaps out of guilt for how she treated him initially, but perhaps more out of a genuine need to forgive and go forward, Maggie hopes that conversations and interactions with Gabriel will give her a new perspective from which to understand Edward as well as to understand herself. She begins this journey by taking Gabriel to church, that center of religious and social activity in such small communities, and by inviting the minister and another parishioner to her home for the ubiquitous Sunday dinner.

Kenan exhibits little tolerance for intolerant Christians as he proceeds to unmask the pompous Reverend Hezekiah Barden and to show Maggie's "friend," Henrietta Fuchee, as the hypocrite she is. These unmaskings, against the background of southern landscape, rituals, and beliefs, serve as the surface actions for the more important question: how does a traditional southern grandmother learn to accept the fact that her grandson was gay and that he essentially ran away from home and died rather than trust her to accept that knowledge? The unseating of religious authority in the surface actions, then, has this secondary plot underlying everything that occurs at the upper depth.

Reverend Barden and Henrietta are self-righteous and hypocritical in how they respond to Gabriel as well as how they respond to
Morton Henry, the white man who has rented land from Maggie and
who, from their perspective, *dares* to be so heathenish as to plow on
Sunday. The unmasking of hypocrisy begins with public claims versus private actions. In something as simple as confirming whether or
not she watches soap operas, Henrietta refuses to admit her interest
in such shows in front of the Reverend Barden. When Emma Lewis,
Maggie's "sometimes housekeeper," tries to talk about the soap opera
that they both watch, Henrietta refuses this leisurely kinship. She becomes agitated in her effort not to lie, but she hedges enough to make
it clear to Emma that she does not wish to pursue this discussion in
the presence of the Reverend Barden. Perhaps, in her mind, to admit
watching soap operas would be a confirmation of her succumbing to
the adage "an idle mind is the devil's workshop," for watching television in the middle of the day could surely be judged as being idle. To
the world at large, and in the face of Maggie's recent loss, watching
soap operas is a minor offense at best. The significance Henrietta
gives to it indicates the distorted view of the world and religious gov-
ernance that will inform her other actions in the narrative.

The Reverend Barden and Henrietta's hypocrisy is noticeable in
how they interpret and respond to notions of work. As fundamentalist, traditional Christians, they firmly believe that God made the
world in six days and rested on the seventh; therefore, human beings
should follow the same pattern. After all, what business could hu-
mans possibly have that could be more important than God's creation
of the world? But the question becomes, what is work? And what determines when work is necessary or not? Kenan begins his story by
cataloging items in the huge meal that all the characters have just enjoyed. As the Reverend Barden lounges sipping Coca-Cola and bitter
lemonade afterward, he has clearly committed one of the seven deadly
sins, that of gluttony. And his gluttony has been fueled by someone's
work. Emma has obviously prepared the meal, which means that she
has spent hours *on this Sunday* either cooking or, if she has cooked

on Saturday, laying out the feast. She has set the table, brought out the food, served the guests, cleared the table, and is in the process of washing dishes. Her work is obvious in their bellies, their contented sighs, and their relaxed postures.

It is also ironic that fundamentalist Christians would place so much emphasis on *not* working on Sunday when the basis of their belief involves work. What else has the Reverend Barden been doing in the pulpit preaching this Sunday morning if not work? It certainly involves physical exertion comparable to that which the Reverend will shortly criticize. It involves mental exertion as well, certainly comparable to what most employed human beings do between Monday morning and Friday afternoon every week. This inherently flawed notion of *work,* which inevitably informs the notion of *worship,* is one in which the Reverend Barden is incapable of teasing out the nuances; he compartmentalizes the idea and reacts arbitrarily and judgmentally by some Procrustean yardstick that can be shortened or lengthened according to his desires and needs. He consistently fails to see the potential hypocrisy in such arbitrary compartmentalization.

Maggie's response to the Reverend Barden and Henrietta's contentment following the meal provides another angle from which to view their hypocrisy. Maggie thinks that Henrietta is a "buck-toothed hypocrite" for denying her interest in soap operas, and Maggie considers Henrietta and the Reverend "self-important fools" (1992) for their cool treatment of Gabriel. By allowing Maggie the questionable middle position, the one in which she is willing to embrace Gabriel and feel protective toward him when the others are merely curious and dismissive, Kenan cracks the solidity of the religiously judgmental small southern black town's wall of belief. As the outsider/skeptic in her own community—exhibited by her willingness to embrace Gabriel—Maggie is aligned with potential positive reader reaction to the story. Her registering of problematic responses to the Reverend Barden and Henrietta mirrors the reader's registering of similar responses and makes both receptive to the changes Kenan effects on this territory.

When the Reverend Barden and Henrietta respond so vehemently to Morton Henry's Sunday plowing, therefore, readers already have multiple contexts in which to analyze and react to their disapproval. As they sit contentedly on the porch gazing off into the distance, the Reverend and Henrietta find their challenge for the day (Henrietta noticeably uses Morton Henry to divert attention from her having to respond to questions about the soap opera). They see Morton Henry plowing his fields, and they are insistent that something be done about it, because " . . . that man should know better than to be plowing on a Sunday. Sunday! Why, the Lord said . . ." (1996; Kenan's ellipses). Henrietta remarks that Maggie's soul is in danger because Morton Henry is renting land from her, therefore Maggie should be compelled to tell him to stop working. The Reverend Barden, however, cannot remember the exact scripture to support what Henrietta asserts that the Lord said, which raises questions again about his mastery—or not—of his chosen profession and his implicit and absurd inadequacy in it.

Using scripture—recountable or not—as their armor, the Reverend Barden and Henrietta march off ("like old Nathan on his way to confront King David," 1996) to set Morton Henry straight and reclaim his heathen soul for the Lord. Maggie and a now-smiling Gabriel trail behind, which leads her to muse about his relationship with Edward. Although she cannot imagine them together, "at that moment she understood that she was being called on to realign her thinking about men and women, and men and men, and even women and women. Together . . . the way Adam and Eve were meant to be together" (1996). This epiphanic revelation is crucial to paving the way for her to realign her sense of religion when the Reverend Barden and Henrietta confront Morton Henry. The Reverend and Henrietta are guided by the superficial injunction to remember the Sabbath day, to keep it holy. On a much more mundane level, however, they are self-righteously intent upon pointing out Morton Henry's wrongs and triumphing in a virtue that they can showcase to Maggie's unbelieving white guest. When they ask Gabriel about his religious practices and church attendance, they are appalled that he is not as regular a communicant as they. If they can confront Morton Henry, make him quit his plowing on Sunday, or at least make him feel sufficiently guilty about it, then they can show Gabriel the gap he needs to close between skepticism and belief. It will be not only a triumph for religion but also a triumph for race and their version of southern hospitality. Through chastising Henry, they can show this puny, unbelieving, and somewhat suspect white northerner the superiority of southern ways and southern religious traditions as well as the superiority of black morality and virtue over heathen whiteness. The moral and color dynamics thus make for an interesting confrontation in Maggie's fields.

With this stage setting, Kenan succeeds in making the Reverend Barden and Henrietta look like buffoons when Morton Henry not only resists their insistent self-righteousness, but laughs in their faces. The fact that Kenan dares to attack ingrained black southern religious practices and their practitioners is itself a transformation, a willingness to challenge what readers might usually expect of a black southern writer. By further showing the Reverend Barden and Henrietta to be pathetic and almost silly in how they "witness" to a "heathen," Kenan effectively destroys the idea of missionary work. The Reverend and Henrietta would be disastrous candidates for going out into the world and baptizing people in the name of the Father, the Son, and the Holy Ghost, for they cannot even successfully go out into Maggie's fields and claim a convert without alienating him beyond reclamation. Their attitudes are the most striking hindrance to what they hope to accomplish, for they are too busy judging Morton Henry and expressing anger to have any hope of changing his mind about his plowing.

The Reverend Barden and Henrietta, but especially Henrietta, are portrayed as angry children who are pouting because they cannot get other children to play the game they prefer. A brief section of the conversation will serve to make the point. After the Reverend Barden asks Morton Henry about his church and his preacher,

Henrietta piped up. "It's Sunday! You ain't supposed to be working and plowing fields on a Sunday!"

Morton Henry looked over to Maggie, who stood there in the bright sun, then to Gabriel, as if to beg him to speak, make some sense of this curious event. He scratched his head. "You mean to tell me you all come out here to tell me I ain't suppose to plow this here field?"

"Not on Sunday you ain't. It's the Lord's Day."

"'The Lord's Day?'" Morton Henry was visibly amused. He tongued at the wad of tobacco in his jaw. "The Lord's Day." He chuckled out loud.

"Now it ain't no laughing matter, young man." The Reverend's voice took on a dark tone.

Morton seemed to be trying to figure out who Gabriel was. He spat. "Well, I tell you, Reverend. If the Lord wants to come plow these fields I'd be happy to let him."

"You . . ." Henrietta stomped her foot, causing dust to rise. "You can't talk about the Lord like that. You're using His name in vain."

"I'll talk about Him any way I please to." Morton Henry's face became redder by the minute. "I got two jobs, five head of children, and a sick wife, and the Lord don't seem too worried about that. I spect I ain't gone worry to [sic] much about plowing this here field on His day none neither."

"Young man, you can't—" (1999–2000)

The conversation ends when Morton Henry demands that Maggie either let him do his work or give him back his money for leasing the field. Maggie's "You do what you got to do. Just like the rest of us"—her short but emphatic sermon of acceptance—signals further her transformation away from the Reverend Barden, Henrietta, and their brand of religion, a stagnant, seriously flawed one that ignores the practicalities of the day—such as Henry's acute family situation—for the pie in the sky. Maggie labels them "childish, hypocritical idiots and fools" who "fuss and bother about other folk's business while their own houses are burning down" (2000). Kenan's narrator adds his note of condemnation to the two in earlier passages when he describes the Reverend as "round and pompous" while Henrietta is "prim and priggish" and has "sagging breasts" on which she rests her glasses (1991, 1992).

As far as Henrietta is concerned, all she need do is stamp her feet and Morton Henry will/should obey her desire. She cannot possibly conceive of someone not thinking of God in the same terms in which she thinks of Him. The Reverend Barden similarly cannot conceive of someone who would not respect or not believe in God, and his quoting of scripture reinforces the narrow slot of distorted Christian belief into which he has led himself and his parishioners. Through these antics, the Reverend and Henrietta reduce religion to a minstrel show or a circus act. By recognizing their poisonous, insensitive, and restricting attitudes, and by distancing herself from them, Maggie once again becomes the character through whom Kenan can effect change. Maggie, after all, is cut from the same cloth as these characters. If she can see fading or tears in the garment, then there is hope for transformed and thereby true Christian attitudes on this small bit of southern soil.

The surface action of the story—that is, the confrontation with Morton Henry and the Reverend Barden and Henrietta's reaction to him—continues to inform the deeper level of the narrative, the one in which Kenan entertains the possibility—or not—of persons who are raised in rather restricting environments to grow beyond those environments. The Reverend and Henrietta are incapable of growth; thus they consign their practice of Christianity to a realm that Kenan rejects. Maggie is willing to allow for new fields of Christian belief to be planted, ones in which racial and sexual diversity are as embraced as the concept of baptism.

The field that Morton Henry has rented from Maggie is thus the symbolic ground of transformative southern space in the text. This field and ones like it have enabled Maggie and her husband to earn some of the money that has made them prominent citizens in Tims Creek. With its ties to repressive sexual attitudes, it is a contrast to the freedom of Boston. By placing Maggie and Gabriel physically on that space, together and united against the Reverend Barden and Henrietta, Kenan sets the stage for Maggie and Gabriel to achieve a new understanding of each other and of themselves; this is especially the case with Maggie. The field is emblematic of the biblical injunction to go out into all the world, baptizing in the name of the Father, the Son, and the Holy Ghost, as well as the general injunction for Christians to go into the "fields" of the world and reap converts for Christ. It also evokes the biblical notions of working in God's vineyard, or generally laboring in the fields of the world (with all its trials and tribulations for Christians). Literarily, it evokes the transformation suggested by Baby Suggs's clearing in Toni Morrison's *Beloved* (1987), in which a new kind of sermon is preached. The Reverend Barden and Henrietta go out as the intended transformers of morality, the intended gatherers of sinners into the fold. However, Maggie emerges as the true preacher and Gabriel as her silent convert. Morton Henry is the medium through whom this whole process occurs, which makes him holier, in a way, than either the Reverend or Henrietta. In this connection, Henry's first name, "Morton," is also worthy of note. Since Morton is a well-known American brand of salt, it further links Henry to the land as "the salt of the earth," a hardworking, hard-sweating man. He is consequently in a more natural relationship to God and to the land than are his accusers.

With all its connotations of religion and conversion, plowing and reaping in the fields of sin to bring forth converts to Christ, Maggie's field becomes the site on which Maggie is finally converted into believing in her own path, her own heartfelt divergence from her traditional teachings, and, by her example, she signals Gabriel that she *will* finally be reconciled about Edward and his homosexuality as well as about her unorthodox decision to cultivate a relationship with Gabriel. In the open space of the field, where all the characters stand puny in the face of the land and the sky, Kenan can effect profound attitude changes with Maggie and essentially consign the Reverend Barden and his ilk to the outer reaches of disregard.

On this southern soil, Maggie moves toward the symbolic freedom represented by Boston in her attitude toward homosexuality, and Gabriel learns a bit more of the religious world that has informed her life. Yet these significant transformations are not the only ones Kenan brings about in the story. A series of reversals informs these larger transformations. First of all, Maggie is a very successful *black* business*woman* in a world where that is not the norm. Second, in a reversal of the usual expectations for sharecropping or renting of farmland, Morton Henry, a white man, rents the land that Maggie, a black woman, owns. Third, the relationship between Morton Henry and Maggie is based on mutual respect (Morton Henry refers to her as "Miss Maggie" and "Ma'am") and fair exchange, not on exploitation. Maggie thus has inherent—though perhaps dormant—in her character the traits that are fully drawn out during the scene in the fields; she has already reached across racial lines, and she has already been set apart as a woman who, with her husband, was willing to dream big and work hard to achieve those dreams. Though her husband did not turn out to be as altruistic as she anticipated, he has nonetheless given Maggie the opportunity to envision life somewhat differently from most of her neighbors. This setting apart is yet another part of the puzzle forming her ability to change.

The "foundations of the earth," then, point in several transformative directions in the story. The land is the foundation of Maggie's wealth, the source of her success as a businesswoman in her dry-goods and hardware stores in Tims Creek as well as the source of rental income from Morton Henry. In this traditional sense of financial "foundation," Maggie is on solid ground. She and her husband have not followed a quick path to success. They have been willing to work just as hard and as long as Morton Henry and other persons in the town who earn their livings by the sweat of their brows.

The "foundations of the earth" also point to the rock of religion on which the Reverend Barden, Henrietta, and Maggie have based most

of their lives. Those foundations are shown to be very shaky. The rock
upon which Christ might have built His church has become, in the
hands of the Reverend, a rock with which he beats people over the
head in his efforts to force them to see the world as he does. Kenan
depicts that rock as shattering into little pieces in the face of the Reverend Barden's buffoonery and hypocrisy. His absurd renditions of
professed biblical injunctions and his absolutely insensitive method
of trying to bring "sinners" to Christ turn the rock of his religion
from diamond to coal. His close-minded, simplistic interpretation of
the Bible and his narrow-minded practice of what he believes to be
religious ultimately consign him to dismissal. While Maggie remarks
on the peculiar position into which she is placed by being "a black
woman defending a white man against a black minister" (2000), her
instincts are nonetheless correct and admirable, for she is ultimately
on the side of exploration and embracing, which are truer representations of Christian teachings than those practiced by the minister she
implicitly rejects.

From Maggie's perspective and the way she has viewed the world
all of her conscious life, "the foundations of the earth" also refer to
the presumed rock-solid base of her personal and religious belief. For
her to accept her grandson's homosexuality is comparable to blasting
out from under her the foundation of her world of belief, her personal worldview, and the rock of her religion within that larger body
of religious practice of which she is a part. Maggie has been content
to have her world in place, to have her children and grandchildren be
merely that, without any undue disturbances. If she can accept Edward and Gabriel's homosexual liaison, she would literally have up-
ended the foundations of her world, disturbing all that she believes in.
Kenan implicitly suggests that this disturbance is not only profoundly
to be desired, but it is ultimately profoundly good, for homosexuals,
as represented by Gabriel, are infinitely preferable character types to
the likes of the Reverend Barden and Henrietta.

Maggie comes to that understanding when she recounts, from a
dream, another biblical story, that of God asking her, in response to

her presumptuous questioning of Him about Edward's death, "*Where wast thou when I laid the foundations of the earth?*" (1995). Man, and particularly Maggie, was nowhere in sight. How, then, can man or woman presume to question God's ways, in this case, either about Edward's death or about Edward and Gabriel's love? And the fact that Edward and Gabriel are both creations of God urges Maggie to try to come to some understanding of the relationship that existed between them. How can she question or ultimately reject it when it was a part of intended creation long before she arrived on the scene? Maggie's dream suggests to her that to reject Edward and Gabriel is somehow to reject God. Though she struggles with the prospect, she cannot finally bring herself to reject her own flesh and blood or the man who simply loved him.

It is important that Edward never appears as a character in the story and only as a body we never see at the funeral. His physical invisibility but pervasive occupation of Maggie's mind mirrors unspoken desire throughout the story. Maggie would prefer that Gabriel not "parade" the desire she names "shame" at Edward's funeral. She would also initially prefer that Gabriel be "normal" rather than naming homosexuality. In relation to the Reverend Barden, Maggie prefers that he leave his desire for her unnamed. Similarly, she recognizes the unnamed desire that Henrietta has for the Reverend. The story is thus one in which most of the characters cannot or do not want to name/acknowledge sexuality (Gabriel is the conspicuous exception). That repression, Kenan posits, is a core of emotional dislocation; true emotional health can evolve only by rectifying that dislocation. When Maggie begins to accept Gabriel's homosexuality as normal, she moves toward the position the story implicitly and explicitly advocates. While Maggie is certainly presented as an individual, she also becomes representative of small-town black southern morality arrayed against alternative sexualities. From this perspective, therefore, and with Maggie's transformation, the story can be read as an exemplar.

"The Foundations of the Earth," finally, is a story about striking out from the ark of safety—in spite of age and comfort and perhaps with only the self as guide—and discovering and rediscovering what it means to love and forgive. If that means discarding traditional religious guides, whether human or doctrinal, then so be it. It is significant throughout the story that Maggie has "Questions. Questions. Questions" (1995), not the answers that come so readily to the Reverend Barden and Henrietta Fuchee. A willingness to ask and to learn, to explore and to accept leads Maggie to a state of calm; instead of rejecting the shaking of her foundations, she seeks the time and a quiet place to contemplate all the newness that she must accept and absorb if she is to continue to label herself a sensitive and caring human being.

(1998, 2001)

Notes

1. Kenan, "The Foundations of the Earth," in *Let the Dead Bury Their Dead,* 49–72. Reprinted in Hill et al., *Call and Response,* 1991–2000 and Andrews et al., *The Literature of the American South,* 1081–1093. Quotations throughout this chapter are from *Call and Response.*

2. In August Wilson's *Fences,* the character Gabriel is a shell-shocked veteran of World War II who blows on a nonfunctional trumpet. His role is nonetheless significant, for upon his brother's death at the end of the play, he is finally able to execute the blowing vision for which he has been striving throughout the play.

Works Cited

Andrews, William, et al. *The Literature of the American South: A Norton Anthology.* New York: Norton, 1996.

Hill, Patricia Liggins, et al. *Call and Response: The Riverside Anthology of the African American Literary Tradition.* Boston: Houghton Mifflin, 1998.

Kenan, Randall. *Let the Dead Bury Their Dead.* New York: Harcourt Brace Jovanovich, 1992.

———. *A Visitation of Spirits.* New York: Grove Press, 1989.

Wilson, August. *Fences.* New York: Plume, 1986.

Eleven

Expectations Too Great

The Failure of Racial Calling
in Ralph Ellison's *Juneteenth*

 In a television documentary about George Wallace, aired in 2000, several interviewees commented on the fact that Wallace was a reasonably progressive man before he first ran for public office in Alabama. Upon his first attempt to get elected, when he was beaten soundly, he realized that the way to the hearts of the good white citizens of Alabama was through their racist beliefs. He therefore transformed himself into the racist politician whom millions of people throughout Alabama and the United States grew either to love or to hate. While it is doubtful that Ralph Ellison even thought of George Wallace while he was composing *Juneteenth* (1999), the immediate comparisons between his Senator Adam Sunraider and George Wallace are striking. Noticeably, Sunraider, like Wallace, held to a different course before he fixed onto the pattern that determined his major courses of political action.

Reflections upon Wallace provide an interesting point of departure for considering the character Ellison creates in his posthumously published novel. *Juneteenth* takes its title from the date in June 1865 when some African Americans (particularly in Texas, but in other parts of the South as well) learned that they had been freed and began the process of celebrating. Juneteenth celebrations are still held in various southern locations.

With its implications of enslavement and freedom, both spiritual and physical, of this world as well as the one beyond, Ellison's novel overlays the familial relationship between Daddy Hickman, a traditional black preacher, and his adopted son, Bliss (Adam Sunraider), with American history, Christianity, race and racism, identity, politics, troubled parent-child relations, forbidden love, the fulfillment (or not) of dreams, and a host of other concerns. Much of the discussion about the novel, ostensibly set "around 1955," has centered—and will center—upon its posthumous editing and publication and the intricacies thereof. Issues surrounding scholarly intervention in and interpretation of authorial intention will reign, as will concerns about the cross-racial choice Ellison made for his literary executor and editor in naming John F. Callahan to take over the future of Ellison's mountains of notes, papers, and partial manuscript segments. There will be many reams of paper used up to comment on the choices the editor made in splicing the final manuscript together, controversies that will expand once the scholarly edition of the novel appears and scholars have the opportunity to peruse for themselves the choices Callahan made. And we can anticipate that much second-guessing will go on. Rather than enter that sea of troubled waters at this moment, I prefer instead to focus on what Ellison has done with his characters. After all, no matter the editorial selections and placements, the words and the creations are finally Ellison's.

In the creation of the character Bliss, who morphs into the abhorrent Senator Sunraider, Ellison echoes/anticipates other African American novelists who in turn have relied upon the folk tradition to shape the development of their fictional persona. Bliss's white mother gives Bliss to Hickman in partial expiation of the guilt she feels for the death of Hickman's brother and mother. Both were victims of racial violence, which the woman has caused by lying and naming Hickman's brother, Robert, as her assailant. As expected, Robert was lynched. The nature of Hickman and Robert's mother's death is not disclosed, but it is clear that it, also, resulted from the deliberately erroneous accusation of rape. To counter a life with a life, Bliss's mother gives Bliss to Hickman in exchange for Robert's life—and, of course, to salve a reputation that would be destroyed if it becomes known that she has given birth to a child out of wedlock. Hickman names the child "Bliss" ("ignorance is bliss") in the hope that he will indeed remain ignorant of the circumstances of his origins and how he came to reside with Hickman; he is successful in his intent, for Bliss never learns that his pregnant white mother had come to Hickman's cabin and that Hickman himself had played the role of midwife in Bliss's birth (which means that Hickman has been *invited* to view all the private parts of the white woman in whose name his mother and brother were killed; though the text depicts Hickman drinking after the baby's birth and trying to resolve to abandon the baby, it never deals fully with the emotional impact of this complex set of circumstances upon Hickman).

While it is unclear if the child's father is actually black, it *is* clear that Bliss has no visible Negroid racial markers. That condition enables Hickman to use Bliss in the experiment that heaps psychological destruction upon both of them. With so much racial violence and hatred in his past, Hickman believes that if he can instill in Bliss a love for African American people and culture, then position him so that he can be a spokesperson for African Americans, then somehow the racial climate—in their small part of the southwestern world as well as the nation—will be transformed. Hickman articulates his hope and his mistake:

> *Blood spilled in violence doesn't just dry and drift away in the wind, no! It cries out for restitution, redemption; and we (or at least I—because it was only me in the beginning), but we took the child and tried to seek the end of the old brutal dispensation in the hope that a little gifted child would speak for our condition from inside the only acceptable mask. That he would embody our spirit in the councils of our enemies—but, oh, what a foolish miscalculation! Way back there . . . I'm no wise man now, but then, Lord, how mixed-up and naïve I was!* (271)

This hindsight in Bliss's hospital room, however, is much too late to have an impact upon the circumstances that have led Hickman and Bliss/Sunraider from potential father and son to almost total strangers.

So brief a synopsis barely begins to provide a glimpse of Ellison's more than two thousand pages of meditations upon history, race, politics, and human relations (a mere 348 of which are included in the novel), but it does position us to begin to understand some of the things that happen in the text. As Ellison makes clear in his notes to the novel, it is less about actions (though the few that occur are significant) than about *reflections upon actions*. Part of the frustration of reading the text is that so much happens in the heads of the characters. A key action at the beginning is the impetus to hundreds of pages of reflections. A few pages into the text, after Hickman and a delegation of his elderly black parishioners have not been allowed to see the senator in an effort to warn him, Senator Sunraider is gunned down as he is giving a speech in the Senate (Hickman and his group are in the Senate balcony and witness the horror). The fatally wounded senator calls Hickman to his hospital bedside where, in alternating reflections and some brief snatches of conversation interrupted by the senator's drug haze, the two bare their lives for readers. Actions recounted within reflections appear less important at times than the reflections themselves; the exception, of course, is the explanation of Bliss's birth near the end of the text. That action makes clear many of the reflections that have come before.

Informing all these reflections is *desire*—desire to bring folkloristic and racial myth to life, desire to shape a communal, missionary calling in a young man who rejects being chosen. When the Reverend Hickman, in the process of being called to preach, is finally able to transcend his hatred of Bliss's mother, he lapses into a plan to make Bliss "the one" (I use the phrase "lapses into," with its pejorative connotations, because I hope to show the error of his decision). By so doing, he anticipates/echoes writers such as Ernest Gaines. In *The Autobiography of Miss Jane Pittman* (1971), Gaines articulates the problems inherent in a black community placing its racial future in a single individual. Jimmy, the young man who is believed to be "the one," is trained from an early age in knowledge of the expectations that are being held out for him. While other young men in the community are out playing, Jimmy is reading to or writing letters for the elderly black people in the neighborhood. When other young black men make low grades in school or become interested in dating, Jimmy is held to the straight and narrow path of what his future should be in terms of *community, racial advancement.* Jimmy is chosen by Miss Jane and other members of the community; he must simply recognize and accept the role for which he has been selected. The training Jimmy receives makes him an exceptional young man, and he is willing to accept that status. Unfortunately, almost as soon as he begins the race work for which he has been chosen and trained, he is shot and killed by racists during a demonstration.

Jimmy's selection reflects the desire of downtrodden black communities to find saviors. More often than not, what they end up finding are martyrs, whether those martyrs exist in literary texts, as Jimmy does, or in life, as does Dr. Martin Luther King Jr. The constant failure to locate "the one" and to position him within the society at large has not in any way diminished the desire to find "the one." That desire is so strong that it could reasonably be understood within the context of an African American folk tradition, a belief to which folks adhere in spite of a wealth of historical failures in such attempts. The desire to locate such a figure, one who can confront whites and make a difference, takes on mythical proportions in African American communities. The phenomenon can be understood simply by contemplating what Jack Johnson meant to blacks at the turn of the twentieth century or what Joe Louis meant when he defeated Max Schmeling. Communal desires, identifications, and hopes become so entangled with the chosen person that disappointment reigns supreme if that person fails to live up to expectations, or if that person, like Jimmy or Medgar Evers, is cut down by an assassin's bullet before his work is complete.

Persons so chosen are expected to respond to their calling in ways comparable to black ministers responding to the higher calling to preach the Word of God. Seldom would anyone dare to reject such expectations, and, if they do, they suffer greatly for the rejection. For example, a minister in the video *Two Black Churches,* which Bill Ferris made in 1975, discusses the consequences to him of having rejected God's calling. He suffers a number of physical ailments (back pain, gum disease) and can find no peace of mind until he agrees to preach God's Word. Sufficiently frightened of the Being he serves, the minister maintains that he could never go back into the world. Other black preachers recount similar sufferings when they initially rejected God's calling. Their final decisions to be "in the Word" thus become irrevocable. Since Bliss is initially called to preach (though that calling is suspect), the sacred context for the concept of being chosen is not an inappropriate one to apply here.

As a young minister, Bliss has been taught and has come to understand the power to influence others, the power of the Word upon those in Hickman's and other congregations in which he has appeared or preached. Hickman has tried to instill in Bliss the values that he hopes will sustain Bliss in a secular commitment to transforming people's hearts, in this case, the white people who have power over African Americans. Hickman believes—and hopes, for hope is at the center of all these African American expressions of desire for "the one"—that Bliss will identify so thoroughly with black people that, once he is educated and living/working freely among whites, he will be able to influence positively their thinking about blacks. The problem is that the moldable *sacred* vision into which Hickman is able to guide Bliss—or forcibly encourage him to participate—does not operate as effectively in the *secular* realm.

It is important to note that Hickman's shaping of Bliss in the church occurs from the time Bliss is a baby until he is a teenager; thus age is definitely a factor in the young Bliss's inability to resist the early sacred path carved out for him. That is strikingly demonstrated in the scheme Hickman has designed to convince sinners of the need to come to God. He devises a plan in which the child Bliss, dressed all in white, rises out of a coffin and begins *responding* to Hickman's various *calls* in the African American folk sermonic tradition. The specter of the child rising from the "dead" is supposed to make clear to observers the immediacy of death, hell, and damnation; the plan is effective enough to bring many sinners to God. What Hickman fails to realize is that Bliss (who enters this scheme when he is around six years old) is horribly frightened of the coffin, its enclosing nature, and the tube through which he is forced to breathe for the long minutes before Hickman calls him forth to make his existential point. This birth, death, rebirth cycle will finally only point to the womblike connotations of the coffin and Bliss's inability to know the mother on whom he becomes fixated (in a form of displacement, he eventually sneaks to the movies to which Hickman has forbidden him to go and fantasizes that one of the white movie stars is his mother).

What Hickman is able to force—politely so—when Bliss is a child, therefore, does not work by the time Bliss is a teenager. He runs away from home and never looks back.[1] In superimposing a calling upon Bliss, Hickman has disallowed the child's own basic desires. In shaping a human being into a role that he himself has not willingly accepted, Hickman has unwittingly warped Bliss out of ever becoming "the one." What chosen saviors have in common, finally, is the choice they make in the right direction; Bliss is not allowed to nor can he make such an altruistic choice. His desires, his needs are, to his mind, greater than the desires and needs of the community that has embraced and, in many ways, saved him.

What Hickman fails to take into consideration in selecting an ultimate life path for Bliss is that, though Bliss's mother may have given him up without a backward glance, Bliss is not equally able to function well without the maternal parental bond. He is content in Hickman's world until a famed Juneteenth celebration (the specific incident that gives title to the novel) in which a crazed white woman bursts into the church where Hickman is preaching and where Bliss is just rising out of the coffin to claim that Bliss is really her child. She yells, screams, cries, and holds on to his upper body, while black church sisters try to take him from her by holding on to whatever parts they can grab. The scene is enough to traumatize any remotely healthy child; one who has no visible mother figure is perhaps even more susceptible to the emotional trauma of being claimed in such a physical, dramatic fashion. Although the confusion is eventually cleared up (though not without Hickman suffering a beating at the hands of local authorities), the event becomes as dramatic (and traumatic) for Bliss as the drowning of his friend Lem becomes for Thomas in Rita Dove's *Thomas and Beulah* (1986). Like Thomas, Bliss can never return to the complacence of his former existence; almost every incident for the remainder of his life is shaped by that particular Juneteenth night. The woman's claim raises the issue of motherhood that will haunt him for the rest of his life.

That evening is also the occasion on which Bliss is taken home by a young, single church sister (a part of the rescue effort from the white woman) and finds himself irresistibly drawn to uncovering her and viewing her nakedness when she innocently allows him to sleep in her bed. The sexual curiosity, combined with the questions about his mother, sets Bliss on a course away from Hickman, away from the church, and away from altruistic concern about the black community in which he has grown up and with which Hickman hoped he would identify. Bliss trades community interest (if indeed he ever truly experienced such) for individual interest and elects the pleasure of movies over the sacrifice of becoming an object lesson through his coffin ventures.

Bliss's desire for a mother, which Hickman acutely underestimates, is stronger than racial memory or racial mission. When Bliss encounters a woman who gives a name (mother) to his lack, the coffin from which she pulls him severs him forever from Hickman. Although the physical separation takes several more years to effect, the birth into another way of perceiving the world has begun. This is the moment at which Bliss rejects the path of becoming "the one," and his rejection reveals the great gap between Hickman's expectations and the actual desires of the child for whom he has assumed child-rearing responsibilities. For Bliss, there is little more important than identifying with some white female who could possibly be his mother. He therefore goes from the redheaded white woman who has violently disrupted the Juneteenth church celebration to a star in one of the forbidden movies. He fantasizes that he can actually enter the celluloid movie screen and interact with the actress, connect with her on some hyper-spiritual level at which she will know instinctively that he has a bio-logical connection with her. His desire is a desperation that Hickman does not recognize or does not have the words to articulate. What is clear is that Bliss's desire for a mother is stronger than his church affiliation and that it thus breaks the bond that Hickman so easily assumed to be Bliss's true calling.

The bond that Bliss breaks with Hickman and the church also high-lights the breakdown in the secular calling that Hickman tried to im-pose upon Bliss. That breakdown is tied to color. Hickman's hope that the visibly white Bliss would become so immersed in African Ameri-can culture that he would opt for it instead of white culture is under-mined when Bliss moves, as Toni Morrison's Pauline Breedlove does in *The Bluest Eye* (1970), into total identification with the white world. He therefore can never be a spokesperson for African Americans. Bliss's rejection of the calling superimposed upon him opens the door for him to become the most virulent of racists, which he proceeds to do many years later when he is elected to the United States Sen-ate. In fact, he out-Herods Herod, becoming so ugly in his negative racial pronouncements that even "regular" racists want to steer clear of him. One of Bliss's cohorts tells him: " 'Dam' it, Senator, we're losing your state and my state and even New York seems doubtful [Sunraider represents an unnamed New England state]. You'll have to lay off the nigger issue because the niggers and the New York Jews are out to get us this year. They don't have to take it and they won't. . . . But you restrain yourself, you hear? We want you to curb that mouth of yours or else" (56). Yet Bliss/Sunraider persists in his course of *not* being "the one."

The mythology of selecting an earthly savior into which Hickman has bought, therefore, backfires horribly. Why it backfires is tied to a failure of parenting as well as a failure of language. The failure in parenting is ironic because Hickman has bought into the idea so thoroughly once he agreed to take the baby. Almost in part to make up for his earlier anger at Bliss's mother and his reluctance to assume the burden she wants to impose upon him, Hickman has become, in many ways, an exceptional parent. He has given up his bluesman career (he is a saxophonist who now uses his saxophone in church services), and he has given up the one true opportunity he had to get married (the woman thought Bliss was the result of a liaison between Hickman and a white woman). He also has given up an impressive measure of freedom by taking on Bliss. He thus prepares well the life space necessary to caring for a baby. That space is created in part also because Hickman's call to the ministry, so he believes, begins during the time he has to transcend his hatred of Bliss's white mother and begin to accept responsibility for the child. The irony is that he has very little clue as to what raising a child entails; therefore, the women in the churches in which he preaches play a large role in taking care of Bliss. Of course, Hickman could learn from their example; the sad part is that he does not seem to learn terribly much about the intangible needs of a child/adolescent/teenager.

Most important to his larger project, both sacred and secular, Hickman fails to realize the traumatic effect upon Bliss of the exemplar into which Hickman casts him. A series of snippets from Bliss's memories makes the trauma clear:

No, please. Please, Daddy Hickman. PLEASE! . . . But I'm scaird. In all that darkness and with that silk cloth around my mouth and eyes. . . .

Daddy Hickman, I said, can I take Teddy too? . . . But it's dark in there and I feel braver with Teddy. Because you see, Teddy's a bear and bears ain't afraid of the dark. . . .

Why don't they hurry and open the light? Please. Please, Please Daddy! . . .

Teddy, Teddy! Where's my bear? Daddy! (43, 47, 56, 57)

Lack of understanding of a child's fear of enclosing, dark spaces leads Hickman to pursue his course of action in spite of Bliss's reluctance. That reluctance can be measured in Bliss's desire to have his Teddy Bear and his water pistol in the coffin with him. Toys thus substitute for parental understanding, or at least the child turns to the toys as a balm from the parent's insistence that he do something he finds unpleasant.

It is also noteworthy that Bliss's repeated cries of "Daddy" and "Please" evoke comparison to pimps and the women in their "stables." Such women are just as helpless in resisting "Daddy" Pimp as Bliss is in resisting Daddy Hickman. In between each of the quoted passages, Hickman soothingly cajoles Bliss to do his bidding. For each objection, Hickman has a rejoinder, and Bliss finally has no choice. Whereas the pimp achieves his objective through violence, Hickman achieves his through "whipping" Bliss with the Bible, with the higher purpose of the need to convert sinners. Against that rhetoric, those words, Bliss has no defense. He must suppress his fear (just as a prostitute must suppress her bruises and squelch her desire not to work) and follow Hickman's directives. Bliss is finally "seduced" into being an object religious lesson. It is clear in some of the passages that Hickman's scheme is motivated as much by pride in what he has devised as it is by the need to bring people to God and into the church. Consider the following passage in which he recounts a sermon that he preached in the presence of seven other ministers, a scenario not unlike that of James Baldwin's Gabriel Grimes in *Go Tell It on the Mountain,* preaching among twenty-four elders who are presumably better speakers than he is:

> "I preached them down into silence that night. True, there was preacher pride in it, there always is. Because Eatmore had set such a pace that I had to accept his challenge, but there was more to it too. We had mourned and rejoiced and rejoiced and moaned and he had released the pure agony and raised it to the skies. So I had to give them transcendence. Wasn't anything left to do but shift to

a higher gear. I had to go beyond the singing and the shouting and reach into the territory of the pure unblemished Word. I had to climb up there where fire is so hot it's ice, and ice so cold it burns like fire. Where the Word was so loud that it was silent, and so silent that it rang like a timeless gong. I had to reach the Word within the Word that was both song and scream and whisper. The Word that was beyond sense but leaping like a tree of flittering birds with its *own* dictionary of light and meaning." (138–39)

The twists and turns of language in this passage—as throughout the text—make clear Hickman's pride in his ability to master the language and compete with his elders, as well as his pride in his ability to bring sinners to Christ. Because he understands so well the usage of language, it finally could be argued, therefore, that Hickman's lack of substantive response to the word "Daddy" is another of the motivating forces that drives Bliss so desperately in search of a mother (Bliss even eavesdrops on a couple of gossiping neighbor women in an effort to learn if the white woman who has snatched him out of the coffin is indeed his mother).

Hickman is on a mission, initially a religious one, and he is so self-centered in his ultimate objective of bringing souls to Christ that he downplays the wants of the child being used in that scenario. This is certainly not to suggest that Hickman does not love Bliss, for there is abundant evidence to suggest that he does; it is nonetheless a tough love, one in which father is literally presented as knowing best. He especially knows best when the prize involves striving for a heavenly reward. And Bliss in turn loves Hickman; it is a love mixed, however, with questions: "Ah yes, yes, I loved him. Everyone did, deep down. Like a great, kindly daddy bear along the streets, my hand lost in his huge paw. Carrying me on his shoulder so that I could touch the leaves of the trees as we passed. The true father, but black, black. Was he a charlatan? Am I—or simply as resourceful in my fashion? Did he know himself, or care?" (117).

Hickman's flaw as he is attempting to raise the young child is that he expects too much of Bliss, perhaps treats him as if he has too much adult—or at least beyond childhood—understanding of what Hickman wants. That flaw at the level of parent-child relationship carries over into the flaw of expecting too much of Bliss in the social world. The gaps in both expectations reveal a gap in communication between the man and the child (later revealed in the gap in communication between the two men). Hickman contains and structures emotion (most of the time) to use it for the benefit of his ministry; Bliss imitates that as best he can. It becomes clear after the fatal shooting just how wide the gap is between the two men. Although the two men have not seen each other for more than twenty-five years, when Hickman arrives at the hospital, he does not undergo the usual pattern of expressing emotion that might seem appropriate (a pat on the prostrate head of the senator, some affectionate greeting). Instead, when the senator awakens briefly, Hickman immediately launches into a story he has heard about Bliss in a church after he left home, then he comments about their glory days as ministers together. He wants to take Bliss back, have him relive and hopefully reclaim what he was before he rejected the black community and black people. That process, while ostensibly admirable, nonetheless places Hickman in the same "my vision of the world is right" mode that he was in when Bliss was a child. The language he uses to reminisce about the early days could arguably be considered a form of erasure (erasing what Bliss has become), but it could also be looked upon as continuing the distance between the man who was once a parent and the man who was once a child.

Hickman's entry into Bliss's hospital room is a mixture of sadness and excitement. The sadness obviously originates from the shooting. The excitement, however, is noteworthy. It originates less from a father's reconnection with his son than from the pleasure of shared remembrances of religious escapades. In other words, Hickman is excited about what he and Bliss were together as ministers more than about what they meant to each other as father/son. That separation of emotion can be made on the basis of the events on which Hickman chooses to focus. They do not entail, "Oh, you were so cute when you made your first step" or "Remember how you used to eat blackberry pie by nibbling the crust first?" They are still all about issues of this world and the next, which means that Hickman is still using Bliss as a man in the same ways that he wanted to use him as a child.

Hickman's ultimate failing as a parent, therefore, is in his assuming godhead over his offspring. By attempting to pattern his treatment of Bliss after God's treatment of His people, Hickman sins without recognizing the nature of his violation. In the matter of the biblical word being brought to life, Hickman hopes that by naming the child "Bliss," he will shape a particular future for him. That future involves, first of all, an interdiction against remembering the past (another irony is that Hickman is now specifically trying to get Bliss to remember the past). In that early naming process, Hickman assumes that he has the *power* to control the future, the destiny of another human being. Bliss's early years can thus be viewed as an extended creation myth in which Hickman attempts to mold and shape Bliss culturally, racially, and spiritually. Of course, all human beings experience some kind of shaping; the problem here is that Hickman turns Bliss into a *project,* an elaborate experiment that has arrogance as its basis. He is proud enough to believe that he knows the problems of the world around him, and he is determined to forge Bliss into the instrument to correct them. This total denial of what Bliss might want marks one of the points at which Hickman crosses the line from father to creator.

Hickman reminisces in Bliss's hospital room about the plans he had for his human project. He remembers one of his parishioners' response to seeing the statue of Lincoln at the Lincoln Memorial and reflects: *"And to think . . . we had hoped to raise ourselves that kind of man"* (283). He thinks of the "craziness" that has brought him to the hospital room as well as the "craziness" that inspired his hopes for Bliss: *"—and yet part of that craziness contains the hope that has sustained us for all these many years. . . . We just couldn't get around the hard fact that for a hope or an idea to become real it has to be embodied in a man, and men change and have wills and wear masks"* (283–84). Hickman remembers as well that he "lied and denied so he [Bliss] could climb higher into the hills of power hoping that he'd find security and in his security and power he'd find his memory and with memory use his power for the good of everyone" (316). Mask wearing, however, has reigned over memory, and Hickman's creative efforts have fallen far, far short of his expectations.

As Ellison has constructed his two major characters, it is reasonable to assume that Hickman is offered as the more admirable of the two. Significantly, Hickman—as the comments above suggest—does not escape unscathed. He is as flawed in his humanized complexity as is Sunraider in his racism. The path that Bliss follows to become Sunraider is one in which it becomes clear that he has learned some of Daddy Hickman's lessons much too well; the problem is the purpose to which he puts them. For example, naming Bliss is about changing reality, and the coffin scheme borders on con artistry in the way that it is used to convert sinners. Bliss initially turns to the movies as a way of changing reality; this process begins the very first time Hickman takes him to a movie (with the intention of showing him how fantasy is manipulated so that he will be discouraged from going in the future—an objective that obviously backfires). Through his imagination, Bliss has an out-of-body experience in which he penetrates the screen ("I went out of me, up and around like a butterfly in a curve of flight and there was moss in the trees and a single bird flipped its tail and flew up and away, and I was drawn through the wall and into the action," 238), enters the same room in which the characters are acting, and anxiously waits for them to engage him.

That experience is one of the most transforming of his life. He returns to the movies without Hickman to try to recapture it, and it is the motivation for him becoming "Mr. Movie Man," the con artist who travels with two white partners and pretends to make movies about everyday folks in small southern and southwestern towns (he gets the folks to raise money for the filmmaking, with which he and his partners then abscond). The idea of changing reality is at the heart of all those adventures: *"So now when I changed places I changed me, and when I entered a place that place changed imperceptibly. The mystery went with me, entered with me, realigning time and place and personality. When I entered all was changed, as by an odorless gas. So the mystery pursued me, shifting and changing faces"* (266). His reflections here will expand to his perception of history, which he incorporates as part of his Senate speech: " 'So again, my friends, we become victims of history only if we fail to evolve ways of life that are more free, more youthful, more human. We are defeated only if we fail in the task of creating a total way of life which will allow each and every one of us to rise high above the site of his origins, and to soar released and ever reinvigorated in human space!' " (19). His text, with its multiple national and personal meanings, combined with his history, makes clear that he has become the living example of the evolution he espouses. He has reshaped himself, and he shapes others.

Bliss thus shares with Hickman a desire to alter humanity around him; before he reaches the Senate and relies totally on words, film is his Bible, his medium for trying to achieve that objective in reality. He seduces any number of black country girls by claiming that he will make them movie stars (one of these is the mother of Severen, the young man who shoots Sunraider and about whom little else is offered in the text beyond the fact that Bliss seduced his mother). Thus it is that film becomes Bliss's power to name, power to create, power to imitate Daddy Hickman. He is fascinated by the editing process, the splicing together of film, for it is in the black spaces between frames that his creative power lies, the power to manipulate time and perception (265). Those junctures enable him to make the people he has filmed as attractive or as unattractive as he desires. Those seconds of blackness also come to represent who/what he is or has run away from.

Bliss's rejection of Hickman thus leads him to prey upon black people financially and sexually; it is a short distance to spouting racial hatred. The most extended view of Bliss preying upon the locals is contained in his reflections about a young "teasing brown" with whom he went on a picnic (65–94) in one hick town (it is not clear if this is Severen's mother). Although the girl seems wiser and more engaging than many of the women he has seduced, she is ultimately no match for him. Strikingly, in the manner of Jean Toomer's poet/narrator in *Cane* (1923), Bliss contemplates taking the young woman out of her environment and reshaping her elsewhere.

> I watched her, thinking wildly, What would happen to this natural grace under coaching? With a formal veil placed between it and the sharp world and all the lessons learned and carried out with this native graciousness to warm the social skills? Not a light against a screen for keeps, Newport in July, Antibes with the proper costumes. Saratoga. Could she fly right? With a sari, say, enfolding her girlish charm? What if I taught her to speak and not to speak, to parry in polished tone the innuendoes dropped over cocktail crystal? To master the smile in time that saves lines? With a diamond of a certain size on that slender hand. Or an emerald, its watery green in platinum against that peach-brown skin. Who blushed this peach? (71)

But Bliss does not remove her from her environment; he simply ruins her in it.

The pattern Bliss pursues finally amounts to an elaborate form of self-hatred, or at least an inability to reconcile the possibility that he may indeed be related to black people. Identity issues emerge for him early in his life, and they are highlighted when the redheaded woman tries to snatch him out of his coffin. He begins to ply Hickman with questions about his skin coloring in comparison to those around him, as well as about his parentage. In response, Hickman makes unsatisfactory comments about sameness in spite of difference, and he weaves elaborate stories about the "crazy" redheaded woman (203–8) in an effort to turn Bliss away from asking questions. Again, Hickman's failure as a parent is in large part responsible for what and who Bliss becomes. Set adrift somewhere between tales and fear, Bliss is unable to forge a solid racial identity. Therefore, like James Weldon

Johnson's narrator in *The Autobiography of an Ex–Coloured Man* (1912), he elects to adopt a mask and identify with the powerful oppressor rather than with the downtrodden victim. He can have only contempt for people who do not have the power to speak up and defend themselves. Consequently, his choice makes him into another of the victimizers. Because Bliss had choices, many of them good ones, the path he chooses to follow damns him even more.

It is a short step for Bliss to move from the manipulation of reality in film images to becoming one of those images. As Adam Sunraider, he draws upon his early preacher career as well as filmmaking to become a consummate master of reality, shaper of words and ideas that influence his politician colleagues in their policies toward African Americans. He knows and feels no shame for his actions; in fact, he is comfortable enough in his racist attitudes to resort to easy stereotypes even on the Senate floor. At one point, he asserts: " 'I say that even the wildest black man rampaging the streets of our cities in a Fleetwood knows that it is not our fate to be mere victims of history but to be courageous and insightful before its assaults and riddles' " (22). He suggests that the Fleetwood should be renamed "the 'Coon Cage Eight' " (23) because of its prevalence in Harlem. Hickman and his parishioners are among the hearers of this speech and can witness for themselves the failure of their desire to make Bliss "the one."

For Hickman's experiment with Bliss to have failed so horribly mirrors the second great failure in the text: that of language. The failure is less in the public arena than in the interpersonal sphere. Ellison is obviously a lover of words, as anyone who has read *Invisible Man* (1952), his short stories, or any of his essays can attest. In *Juneteenth,* language flies, swoops, curves, and turns somersaults. There are countless paradoxes, turns of phrases, and plays on words, such as "It was, as I understand it, a cruel calamity laced up with a blessing—or maybe a blessing laced up with a calamity" (118); "realizing in that second of His anguished cry that life in this world is but a zoom between the warm womb and the lonely tomb" (152); and *"With them going from pondering to pandering the nation's secret to pandering their pondering?"* (259).

The prose sings, shouts, transforms itself, moves easily between the surreal and the mundane, and twists and turns back on itself, which means that it ultimately becomes unreliable as a medium of explanation or communication at the minimalist level of two human beings interacting with each other.

In the space where Bliss wants explanation, understanding, and human contact, Hickman puts words, loads upon loads of words, whether he is justifying the need for the coffin, or describing the "crazy" white woman, or telling Bliss that he cannot go to the movies again after their first trip. In this last instance, Bliss recognizes the limits of language when he wants to tell Hickman that he would rather not go to the movie in the first place if he has to forgo future pleasure in viewing, but he cannot: "But I could not say it, nor could I refuse; for no language existed between child and man" (235). There are many, many words between the child and the man, but these words do not ultimately shape a coherent, understandable language. That is especially clear in the tale upon tale that Hickman tells Bliss about the redheaded woman to distract him from curiosity. The storytelling cannot work beyond the merest superficial level in this instance, but it is all that Bliss gets from Hickman.

Perhaps the language problem begins when Hickman cannot bring himself to tell Bliss about his mother. It is never revealed exactly why Hickman does not tell Bliss the story of his birth; perhaps it is as simple as not wanting him to feel any more orphaned than he maybe already does. Ironically, the more words Hickman can master through preaching, the fewer words he can master in his role as father. Indeed, Ellison runs the risk with Hickman of suggesting, stereotypically, that men cannot talk about matters of the heart. There is consistently a great gap between whatever Hickman feels and the words that actually come out of his mouth. He hides behind the rhetoric of the Bible, allowing it to conceal and conceal rather than reveal. Beyond that concealment, he has no words to reach out to Bliss. Even when Hickman is in the hospital and wants to hold on to Bliss/Sunraider, he can rely only on the old words, derived from biblical texts and associated with people who preach them. Beyond his initial anger with Bliss's pregnant mother, he never takes an independent plunge into the emotional depths of any language that will reveal the pain of his loss of his mother and brother or the love he has developed for Bliss in spite of himself. Language allows him a separate, bearable dignity, one that distances him forever from the child who grew up to be the man who would steal the sun from the very people who gave him life and light.

Juneteenth is finally not just a meditation upon history, as Ellison asserts in one of his notes, but a meditation upon meditation, a meditation upon the impossibility of forging relationships in which people use words to bar the doors to their hearts. Personal relationships as well as interracial liaisons can be established only when individuals are willing to bare themselves, to risk something—as Bliss's mother did when she came to Hickman's cabin and essentially put her destiny and reputation in Hickman's hands. Unfortunately, Hickman has never been able to duplicate that baring (remember that he remains single because he cannot deal with the accusation leveled against him by the woman he wants to marry). He therefore cannot pass on to Bliss what he himself has not learned or experienced. Both Hickman and Bliss remain awash in language, tons upon tons of words that do very little to bring them to some understanding of what has happened *in* and *to* their lives and to each other. It is no wonder, then, that Ellison never put the final, finishing touches on the novel. That would simply mean more words, and more words beget more words, until relationships sink under their weight. Nonetheless, though the fictional interpersonal relationships may suffer, Ellison has given teachers, scholars, and students a richly textured enigma to contemplate for generations.

(2000, 2001)

Note

1. In the notes Callahan includes at the end of the text, Ellison comments on Bliss running away at least three times. In the published text, however, only one dramatic depiction of running away occurs.

Works Cited

Baldwin, James. *Go Tell It on the Mountain*. New York: Dell Publishing, 1953.

Dove, Rita. *Thomas and Beulah*. Pittsburgh: Carnegie-Mellon University Press, 1986.

Ellison, Ralph. *Juneteenth*. Ed. John F. Callahan. New York: Random House, 1999.

Ferris, William. *Two Black Churches*. 1975. Videocassette.

Gaines, Ernest. *The Autobiography of Miss Jane Pittman*. New York: Dial Press, 1971.

Johnson, James Weldon. *The Autobiography of an Ex–Coloured Man*. New York: Knopf, 1912.

Morrison, Toni. *The Bluest Eye*. New York: Holt Rinehart Winston, 1970.

Toomer, Jean. *Cane*. New York: Boni and Liveright, 1923.

Twelve

Ugly Legacies of the Harlem Renaissance and Earlier

Soul Food and New Negroes

 Soul Food is a movie much praised by a variety of viewers, especially African Americans. When it was released in 1997, I discovered that my reaction to it was strikingly unlike that of many of my African American friends and colleagues. They countered my objections with the admonition that I should celebrate *Soul Food* for the wonderful ritual of family interaction that it preserves, as well as for its diversity in presentation of African American images. That diversity includes the working class, the middle class, a creative artist, an entrepreneur, a devoted black husband and father, and a precocious black kid—who just happens to be male—all of which are presumably progressions from earlier monolithic screen depictions of blacks. While I can understand the points my friends and colleagues make, I also saw other things in the movie, things, surprisingly, that some of them almost totally ignored.

In its presentation of the women, but especially in its depiction of the men, the movie is a throwback to stereotypical images that populated literary, stage, and visual media in the late nineteenth and early twentieth centuries, particularly during the Harlem Renaissance. From the domineering grandmother figure to the angry young black man, *Soul Food* posits black life as a window for voyeurs, whether they want to see intrafamilial anger and violence, black female undercutting of black males, or black males who cannot control their sexual appetites.

First and foremost is the problematic image of the mother/grand-mother. Strong and domineering, she fits easily the paradigm of the book project that I completed in 2001. Titled *Saints, Sinners, Saviors: Strong Black Women in African American Literature,* the project centers upon black female characters, whose origins lie in slavery and Reconstruction, that have pervaded visual media and African American literature throughout its history. As Donald Bogle documents in *Toms, Coons, Mulattoes, Mammies, and Bucks* (1994), America was in love with the likes of Hattie McDaniel and Louise Beavers as they were cast in such stalwart films as *Gone with the Wind.* These large, bossy black women became the stereotypical norm for the representation of black female character.

The height of that particular representation in literature is Lorraine Hansberry's Mama Lena Younger in *A Raisin in the Sun* (1959); the stage production featuring full-figured, full-bosomed Claudia McNeil echoed the size-type of African American women that had previously appeared on stage as well as in the movies. From Charles Chesnutt's Mammy Jane Letlow in *The Marrow of Tradition* (1901), to Zora Neale Hurston's Nanny in *Their Eyes Were Watching God* (1937), to Mama Lena, to the two elderly women in Ernest Gaines's *A Lesson before Dying* (1993), a dominant strand of black female representation is that of the strong black woman who manages everybody's life. Stage and movie images portray black women as prominently in these roles as does the literature. Another recent movie counterpart and representative sister to the grandmother in *Soul Food* is the woman who plays Martin Lawrence's mother in *Nothing to Lose.*[1] She smacks him upside the head when he comes in at two o'clock in the morning—although he is old enough to be married and have two children—and she similarly slaps his white friend, played by Tim Robbins, for being out with Lawrence's character. The creators of such women characters and their families—whether on stage, in the movies, or in literature—ignore the prices these women pay for their management of the lives of their families, effects that include emotional isolation, the absence of peers, an unquestioning immersion in fundamentalist religious practices, and an implicit self-destructive tendency.

The grandmother in *Soul Food* is no exception. She gives *all* to her family—indeed, she maintains in a conversation with her three daughters that "you do what you have to do to stay strong, to save the family"—and they in turn keep taking until she is dead. Viewers do not focus overly long on the fact that she dies of diabetes, which is one of the primary killers of black people and which is assuredly caused by the very soul food touted as keeping the family together through its forty-year ritual of Sunday dinners (and the weekly eating contests, which the minister usually wins, do not help matters). The representation of this black grandmother as a woman of strong folk origins, who is described as "always knowing what to do to set things right" and "the rock of the family," extends one of the legacies of the Harlem Renaissance. In her, we see the descendants of Jean Toomer's women characters who sing their supper-getting-ready songs and of Langston Hughes's protagonist in "Aunt Sue's Stories" (1921)—the romantic, self-sacrificial women who have the potential to pay with their lives for the nurturing they provide for their families.

It is striking that the mother/grandmother is identified simply as "Big Mama Joe" (spelled J-o-e). This appellation reinforces her role in the family as husband, father, "masculine" provider. She emphasizes strength as her most important trait, and her daughter Maxine (called Max), with a comparable masculine-identified name, is similarly touted as "the strongest" of the next generation of women; Max is the one Mama Joe has selected to take her place.[2] The grandmother image, whether in the current generation or planned for the next generation, is therefore a cause for celebration as well as a cause for reflection upon the direction in which such representation has moved—or has *failed* to move.

Soul Food is also striking for its representation of what one of my colleagues refers to as "bourgeois realism" in the character of Vanessa L. Williams. Light-skinned, green-eyed, perfectly dressed Terry is the 1990s version of James Weldon Johnson's and W. E. B. Du Bois's "best foot forward" portrayal of African American aspiration. If she were just a tad lighter, she might even pass for white. She has earned her law degree, is supportive of her family, and resides in a home that could be the envy of a large portion of African Americans in particular and Americans in general. In making her successful and *clean* (to use James Baldwin's concept of black middle class upward mobility, no flies would light on her), the filmmaker has also made her cold, hard, incapable of sustaining a romantic relationship, and carping toward her family about the financial support she is forced to provide for them. She is a failed success, or a successful failure, depending on an upward mobility or an emotional health perspective.

Perhaps the most striking leftover from earlier representations of African Americans and of stereotypes in the popular imagination is that of black males and their sexual appetites. Think of Miles, Vanessa L. Williams's screen husband. He lives in a fashionable neighborhood, has a beautiful and successful wife, and is himself a successful lawyer and aspiring musician. Presumably there are no flies here. Ah, but the jungle lurks in the background. There are echoes of primitivism, one of the issues that pervaded literature of the Harlem Renaissance, in Miles giving in to the jungle rhythms that beat in his blood and having sex with Terry's cousin Faith in his rooftop studio. The drive is so strong that they "do it" standing up, with her hanging against the wall, and with their clothes only partially removed—we see only her legs and a part of his naked butt. The implication is that you can take the man out of the jungle, dress him up, get him to play soulful music, and marry him off to a beautiful lawyer, but you can't take the jungle out of the man. As Countee Cullen's narrator asserts in "Heritage," the calls of the jungle encourage Miles to "Strip! / Doff this new exuberance"—that is, the cloak of civilization—and remember the jungle beats of African rhythms as he performs "the lover's dance" (912).

The clash between primitivism and civilization is reinforced in the way the director chose to shoot the rooftop scene. Terry and her nephew Ahmad, who is the adolescent narrator of the film, enter

Terry and Miles's fabulous house as the fornication scene is about
to take place on the roof. The camera alternates between shots of the
innocent actions of Terry and her nephew downstairs and Miles and
Faith upstairs beginning their "lover's dance." The scenes cut back
and forth between innocence and infidelity as Terry and Ahmad make
their way upstairs so that Ahmad can visit with his Uncle Miles. Ahmad's pause to admire the beautiful scenery from the rooftop conveniently puts Terry ahead of him. She peers through the extensive glass
paneling that her class status has reaped and watches that very class
status or superior civilization being undermined by the jungle eruption of Miles and Faith screwing standing up against the wall. Terry,
the height of cool, quickly insists that her nephew return downstairs
before he can witness the scene. Terry does not herself resort to the
jungle by bursting into the room and yelling, screaming, or cursing at
Miles and Faith—at least not at this point; rather calmly, she simply
retreats to civilization. Indeed, Terry's response to this striking marital
violation suggests that Terry finds this jungle quality in Miles not at
all unexpected.

However, Terry's cool pose is merely veneer, for at a family gathering later that evening, Terry cries and attempts to attack Miles with
a large kitchen knife. It is noteworthy that she is at Max's house—in
the ghetto, so to speak—when this eruption occurs, so the filmmaker
is able to play upon stereotypes of black violence that are connected
with that space. Raw emotions such as anger can be contained only
for a short while under the cover of civilization. Finally, Terry resorts
to the same cuttin' and slashin' stereotype of black female jealousy to
which working-class black women who never set foot in college are
heir. In giving in to violent anger, Terry parallels in intensity Miles's
inability to contain his sexual appetite. Primitivism will out—just wait
long enough and give it the right stimulation.

The same is true with Lem, called Boo (and note that nickname),
the husband of the youngest sister in the film. Having served one
prison sentence, it is only a matter of time before Boo explodes in
some way and repeats the offense, which he does when he becomes

so frustrated about not finding a job that he is goaded into a fight and brandishes a gun, which he should not possess while on parole from the first offense. While Miles is the contained jungle, Boo is rawness, ever ready to return to his natural element—or so he is depicted. His bald head and dark skin, together with his basically unsmiling face, signal to viewing audiences that he is a dangerous black man, not exactly Chesnutt's Josh Green in size, but close to that image in his potential to explode. He, like Miles, has a scene in the movie in which he has rather rough, lusty, uncontrollable sex, but he has it with his new wife. They merely look at each other during one of those Sunday dinner gatherings, decide that they must indulge, and retire to the bathroom, where they bump and grind their passion out while partly hanging over the bathroom sink. Bird puts one of her hands over Boo's mouth to contain his profanity and passionate cries so that her family members—who continue the preparation of Sunday dinner—will not hear him rising to the moment of sexual ecstasy.

It does not matter that this is a newly married couple. This is a question of quenching thirst, satiating desire, and it has no limits. Lack of restraint is what governed the family's weekly eating contests, and that is the imperative that holds sway with Bird and Boo. The emphasis is upon uncontrollable passion, jungle lustfulness that comes to the fore in spite of the veneer of a Sunday dinner gathering—in other words, in spite of the veneer of civilization. Sex is another brand of "soul food," and neither Boo nor Miles will be denied access to it. Appetites—whether of hunger or sex—are satisfied in each case. Gratification is the most important thing.

The places in which they engage in sex are also noteworthy: a bathroom in one instance and standing up in a loft studio in the other. The filmmaker makes clear that these men do not respect the usual decorum that might confine such practices to the bedroom—or at least to a comfortable space—and he, in turn, does not respect them. From lower class to middle class, from sex within marriage to illicit sex, the filmmaker does not make a distinction in the lust of the men. Class and education cannot contain Miles, and a mother-in-law and family members just beyond a thin wall cannot contain Boo. An irresistible urge controls both of them. Reductionist treatment renders the men the same while the women are distinguished by personality, education, and skin color.

Even Kenny, the stable black husband and father figure in the movie, has arrived at that status only through a process of evolution. Max, his wife, is actually the sister of Terry, the woman Kenny was dating when he met Max. He was whorish enough not to resist when Maxine flirted with him during a skating outing with Terry. Certainly he loves Max, and certainly he is a good father, but he, like the other black men in the movie, could not, at that significant moment in his life, resist the urge of the jungle. No negative comment is offered about his dating infidelity (or his ignoring Terry's fall at the skating rink) and how he came to be husband and father. He is depicted in the current action of the film as a lusty sexual performer—by the number of children he has, including the film's narrator, and by his obvious sexual attraction to his wife mere days after she has delivered their most recent child. His actions are presented as good, healthy, acceptable, and *normal* for black men.

I have focused on *Soul Food* to this extent because the movies are one of the major sites on which representation of African Americans occurred in the post-1970 twentieth century. And those representations return to, update, expand, or devolve from many of the considerations that faced writers and artists of the Harlem Renaissance and decades before that. The numbers of African American filmmakers and black persons starring in films in the late twentieth and early twenty-first centuries have made that genre perhaps more persuasive than literature in keeping before the public certain images of black people. Those images, more often than not, are unflattering ones. Yet African American filmmakers frequently command the roles, and African American actors and actresses willingly play these roles.

An urge to perform is certainly understandable, but it is more often than not controlled by the plantation mentality of persons with enough money to produce the films, even when those persons are black. In turn, African American actors and actresses play roles that they may or may not prefer to play if they are to reap the financial rewards of their chosen professions. If such roles degrade or present stereotypical depictions of black people, the actors and actresses seem to impose little censorship upon themselves or upon the movie industry for which they work. Their acquiescence in this process ensures the continuation of these jungle-derived images.[3]

The same might be said of those traveling stage shows, such as *Mama, I Wanna Sing,* in which black people play the buffoon in broadly slapsticked images and in which little of African American culture or African American selfhood is considered sacred. Everything is subjected to laughter, and the more broadly based the laughter, the better. Audiences trained on such pathetic representations of drama, in which they see some of their everyday lives—as in those dramas focusing on barber shops and beauty parlors—do not develop the viewing skills necessary to appreciate the works of August Wilson or Lorraine Hansberry. In 1995, for example, the Alliance Theater in Atlanta produced *A Raisin in the Sun.* The producers were successful in getting Esther Rolle to play the part of Mama Lena Younger. Kenny Leon, the artistic director, however, played the role of Walter Lee Younger. He was miscast as a skinny, over-six-feet-tall, bald-headed Walter Lee, and that was problematic enough. But when he crawled around on the floor illustrating the speech he planned to deliver to Mr. Lindner when he proposed to accept the money *not* to move into the white neighborhood, the audience laughed—great guffawing laughter. For laughter to have been the response at that most powerful moment of the play was a testament to what the black Atlanta audience had been seasoned on in so-called theater and to its inability to appreciate its own suffering. Unless black actors were laughing and playing the clown on stage, this kind of audience had little understanding of—or perhaps even patience for—what it was watching.

Alain Locke declared in the introductory essay to *The New Negro* in 1925 that "the day of 'aunties,' 'uncles' and 'mammies' [was] . . . gone. Uncle Tom and Sambo have passed on, and even the 'Colonel' and 'George' play barnstorm roles from which they escape with relief when the public spotlight is off. The popular melodrama has about played itself out, and it is time to scrap the fictions, garret the bogeys and settle down to a realistic facing of facts" (Mitchell, 23). Locke's dust would probably swirl into a tornado if he could glimpse the extent to which the efforts of Harlem Renaissance writers to represent with dignity the black folk population have been perverted by contemporary producers who are motivated only by dollar signs. In 1986, Joseph Boskin published *Sambo: The Rise and Demise of an American Jester.* In this scholarly study, Boskin argued that Sambo is dead. He/she/it was killed by the civil rights movement. In spite of Locke's claims and Boskin's assertion, Sambo is alive and well in practically every visual medium through which African Americans are presented after 1970; that was especially the case in the 1990s.

This is no less true of television. Whether we consider popular 1970s shows with all those excessively large black women—such as Esther Rolle on *Good Times* or Theresa Merritt on *That's My Mama* or Nell Carter on *Gimme a Break*—or more contemporary shows such as *Living Single, Family Matters,* or *Martin*, black Sambos and clowns abound. It is no matter that they are not Bert Williams performing in blackface. These so-called comedians still convey to viewing audiences that black people are only a few steps removed from the characters portrayed in Paul Laurence Dunbar's "The Party" in 1896. They may suffer minor setbacks, but their problems are easily solvable, and they excel above all else in laughing, singing, and dancing. It's the plantation tradition revisited, a voluntary imposition that would please Thomas Dixon immeasurably.

On occasion, these characters take the primitive reflected in Carl Van Vechten's *Nigger Heaven* (1926) or Claude McKay's *Home to Harlem* (1928) to new depths of licentious excess. This is certainly the case with most of the *Def Comedy Jam* shows, in which the word "motherfucker" is as essential as breathing. Black people deride themselves and their institutions. I heard a comedian do a routine once in which he celebrated being a crackhead and going out and robbing people.

He mistakenly robbed his own mother one night, yet he presented that violation in such a way that his audience roared—it was unclear if it was roaring from the humor or from the actions.

The primitive in the literature might be reflected in the opening up of new arenas of representation in terms of sexuality, especially same-sex sexuality. E. Lynn Harris's works focusing on gay men are tremendously popular, especially among black women. Some gay black men assert that straight and gay black men are less inclined to read Harris's novels for fear of being thought to be gay or of actually being "outed." So black women, I am told, are the mainstay for sales of Harris's books. In the absence of an open society where discussions of sexuality could be commonplace and enlightening, readers go to fiction for their knowledge and obviously come away with a distorted or exaggerated sense of what actually occurs in same-sex relationships, both romantic and sexual. So instead of white folks going to Harlem and slumming, we have black readers looking for the primitive and serving the voyeuristic roles toward black subject matter that whites did in the 1920s.

Bruce Nugent's timidity about writing about homosexuality in "Smoke Lilies and Jade" and Wallace Thurman's reluctance to depict prostitution in "Cordelia the Crude," both of which appeared in *Fire!!* in 1926, find no contemporary counterpart discussions of self-censure. The more outrageous the sexual representation, it seems, the better. Harris's *Invisible Life* (1991) was so popular that his publisher contracted him to produce two more such books—*Just As I Am* (1994) and *And This Too Shall Pass* (1996)—and he has now become a one-man industry; he is further distinguished by being the best-selling African American male novelist writing today. Voyeurism, specifically the expectation that Harris will reveal graphic details about the sex lives of homosexual males, guides much of the response to his work. Shay Youngblood, a graduate of Spelman College, has published *Soul Kiss* (1997), a novel in which she eroticizes the relationship between a seven-year-old girl and her mother. Youngblood's description of the child's pleasure in taking baths with the mother borders on the pornographic. After Jean Toomer published *Cane* in 1923, W. E. B. Du Bois and Alain Locke collaborated on an article published in *Crisis* in 1924 in which they asserted that "the world of black folk will some day arise and point to Jean Toomer as a writer who first dared to emancipate the colored world from the conventions of sex" (161–62). They could not remotely have anticipated what that liberation would look like almost eighty years later, when a movie like *Soul Food* reclassifies sex as mere lust or perversion. While Gloria Akasha Hull had to search through the diaries and letters, as well as the poetry and other literary works, of Angelina Grimke, Georgia Douglas Johnson, and Alice Dunbar Nelson looking for veiled messages of their sexual and/or romantic interest in other women, contemporary black writers such as Carolivia Herron, Michelle Cliff, Jewelle Gomez, and Alexis De Veaux make such references blatant and unapologetic. What Harlem Renaissance writers pondered and worried about, black writers in the past two decades have presented in the extreme, have saturated themselves and their readers with no-holds-barred approaches to just about everything. And yet these apparent freedoms are troubling.

Whether in the movies, on television, on stage, or in the literature, the *newest* version of the New Negro is represented—and he or she represents himself or herself—as one who pimps or prostitutes African American culture, who sells his or her soul for the almighty American dollar, and who occasionally—but only occasionally—might be a serious literary presence. As Ralph Ellison's *Invisible Man* asserts, history is not a circle, it is a boomerang, and those arbiters of contemporary representations of black people are willing to have them boomeranged over the head forever if it means being paid well for their hatchet jobs.

Consider some of the biggest issues of the Harlem Renaissance and how they are currently manifested. Toomer went to Georgia to try to salvage something of the rich black folk culture there, and Hughes eventually became poet laureate of Harlem, digging and being dug in return by the black folk populations there. Hurston depicted working-class black people who kept on keeping on in spite of the threats to their culture, persons, and sanity from outside as well as from inside black communities. When we think of folk representation, or the pastoral in African American literature—as Ted Mason refers to it—we see Alice Walker's *The Color Purple* (1982) with all its entangled reader responses and, more recently, Shay Youngblood's *The Big Mama Stories* (1989). Walker certainly had no preservative intention in mind for her novel; she was more concerned about exposé. She wanted the world to know that perversity was just as pervasive in black communities as it was presumed to be in white communities, so she could present an ignorant black girl in Georgia impregnated twice by her stepfather, beaten repeatedly by a husband who does not value her, and eventually finding a way of saving herself. Her mostly individualistic quest, not unlike Frederick Douglass's in *Narrative of the Life of Frederick Douglass,* does not change the way her community is perceived. Nor does it hold out much hope that violators of young black girls can change. Celie's stepfather dies, but he dies in bed, sexually violating another young black girl; it does not matter that she is his wife.

Youngblood's stories glorify ancient and not-so-ancient African American women in southern communities and in settings not unlike those Toomer uncovered in Georgia. Big Mama, the central figure in the composite novel, shares kinship with Mama Lena Younger and with Big Mama in *Soul Food.* She is a good-hearted person whose strength comes from God and the church. Her repertoire of stories keeps the young narrator entertained when she is sent to live with Big Mama. Other women in the neighborhood are not appreciably unlike Big Mama, and there is ultimately romanticization—if only slightly so—of their places in society, their relationships to each other, and their roles in the life of the protagonist. Youngblood overlays these traditional images with some slight modification—for example, there is a hint that two of the women are lesbians—but the romanticized strand of the folk cultural tradition in African American literature basically thrives.

There is also the legacy of intraracial color prejudice that has stretched its long arm from the Harlem Renaissance and still holds sway in black communities. Issues of colorphobia and pigmentocracy informed Hurston's *Color Struck,* which was published in *Fire!!* in 1926. Emma, a very dark-skinned black woman, cannot accept the love of John, a mulatto man, because she believes he really prefers lighter-skinned black women. Emma literally brings about the death of her very fair-skinned daughter because she hesitates overly long in seeking medical assistance for the girl; she is afraid to leave John alone in the same room with her. Although her daughter is comatose and close to death, and although John has repeatedly professed his love for Emma, she cannot bring herself to believe it. Visions of him trying to seduce the fair daughter lead Emma to delay until the child cannot be revived. The absurdity of the mother's actions is matched only by their tragic consequences. Yet the intervening decades since the Harlem Renaissance have not brought about some remarkable resolution to the issue of skin color in black communities, though perhaps the problem is less tragic in recent literary representations.

While the 1960s might have made black beautiful, the late 1980s and the 1990s brought a return to preference for black people with lighter skin and so-called "good hair." It is almost as if Maud Martha did not have her adventures in Brooks's novel from the early 1950s— at least not in the sense of raising consciousness in black communities about *intra*racial prejudice. Instead, darker-skinned black women frequently find themselves in the same devalued position as Maud Martha—purely because of their skin coloring—and black women of all shades frequently find themselves abandoned by black men who take advantage of integrated opportunities to pursue white women.

Yielding to pressures to change their appearance, many black women have gone far beyond the hair straightening that Madame C. J. Walker introduced in the early years of the twentieth century. They alter the color of their hair, and they frequently alter the color of their eyes. These clowns parade around for public appreciation seemingly without the slightest understanding that their cosmetic transformations send messages of deep self-hatred. I was in the Philadelphia airport in 1997 and saw a dark-skinned black woman with close-cropped platinum hair. The woman was beautiful, and she obviously did not need the hair color change, but there it was. Someone had deluded her into thinking it was beautiful, and she walked around proudly advertising her desire to be someone other than who she was. I have seen countless examples of such self-mutilation since then. And what can I say about wigs and braids that would not take a volume or two? Let me just say that when we consider what Halle Berry did to herself to get a role in the movie *Baps,* that says about all there is to say about such representation. Between her blonde wig, her silver—or gold—tooth, and the affected southern dialect she adopted, I need say no more about the living, breathing, Sambo/clown figure in black visual representation.

Black women attempt to achieve a transformative effect with contact lenses as well. Designers of these lenses discovered a new market in the 1980s, and we black women especially are busily keeping them in business. When I was a visiting professor at Ohio State University in 1988, a graduate student came into my office to discuss a literary work. This woman's skin was chocolate, yet she was sporting light blue contact lenses. They were so distracting and incongruous that she felt compelled to comment on them. She explained that her ophthalmologist had given her the lenses—free of charge—in exchange for her promise to wear them as an advertisement for his office. So she did. No thought about serving the clown function to enrich her ophthalmologist. No thought about what that self-mutilation represented. No self-reflection about the image she was presenting. No sense of history that would have warned her about rejecting such an offer.

With these clown figures walking around, and with any number of actors and actresses whooping and hollering from the stages of larger cities in America in shows of the variety of *Mama, I Wanna Sing,* it is hard to see how any progress has been made from the images D. W. Griffith depicted in *Birth of a Nation* or those singing and dancing colored folks Paul Laurence Dunbar gave us in "The Party." How much difference does it make if a black person controls the images as opposed to a white person? The representations still loom large and still control many black people's perceptions of themselves. These folks seem to be trying to reach—in the most absurd way—Jean Toomer's conception of a new American, where race would be erased. Unfortunately, they are merely complicating the issue.

The women with platinum dye in their hair or wearing blonde wigs or blue contact lenses are killing the potential to be put in touch with the very best in themselves. These psychic deaths are no less dramatic than the death of the daughter in Hurston's *Color Struck,* for they sadly comment on a group of people still unsuccessfully confronting issues that were prominent decades ago. But then, Du Bois did predict that the problem of the twentieth century would be the problem of the color line. He could just as easily have predicted that the problem *within* black communities would be the problem of shades of color. That is what Pecola Breedlove suffers in Toni Morrison's *The Bluest Eye* (1970). Morrison rightfully asserted that there were pockets in the country during the height of all that "black is beautiful" rhetoric where black was indeed *not* beautiful and where black people were as guilty of making that judgment as whites. Maureen Peale, the high-yellow dream child against whom Pecola is measured, and against whom she measures herself, has consistently had company throughout the decades of African American literature since Hurston published *Color Struck.* Barbara Neely's Blanche White, a dark-skinned black woman and unlicensed detective, explodes the color scheme of the contemporary black "blue veins" who reside on Martha's Vineyard in *Blanche among the Talented Tenth* (1994). The barely black people she encounters are just as prejudiced against darker-skinned black people as are Chesnutt's blue veins in "The Wife of His Youth" (1900). It was therefore appropriate that Neely revitalize Du Bois's turn of the century concept in developing her novel. Dorothy West's *The Wedding,* which appeared in 1995, revisits some of those same ideas—and in the same location. It seems apparent that here, in the early twenty-first century, this central issue is still unresolved;

the colorphobia legacy from the Harlem Renaissance is still trailing a people who cannot find the psychological strength to love *all* the components, all the *shades,* of themselves.

In addition to reclaiming the folk and focusing on issues of color, black writers during the Harlem Renaissance were concerned with issues of class. What were women of breeding, such as Helga Crane, Clare Kendry, and Irene Redfield, Nella Larsen's heroines in *Quicksand* (1928) and *Passing* (1929), to do in a society that did not have any comfortable place for them? Caught between black and white worlds, they are at home in neither, and they consequently become self-destructive—or merely destructive. In a literature that has seemed more prone to deal with the working class and/or the folk, black middle-class experience has been downplayed in representation as well as in criticism. But there is a legacy. Dorothy West touched upon it in *The Living Is Easy* (1948), Carlene Hatcher Polite explored the ramifications in *The Flagellants* (1974), and Andrea Lee brought the issue almost into contemporary times with *Sarah Phillips* (1984), before West returned to it with *The Wedding* in 1995.

Young African American writers and thinkers who came onto the scene in the 1990s, such as Trey Ellis and Elizabeth Alexander, are confronting color and class issues simultaneously as they demand to be allowed to explore the broadest bases of their cultural heritages. These writers and others who formed "The Dark Room Collective" embrace mixed-race and multicultural heritages and assert their right to depict characters drawn from those sources. They are still confronted with and attempting to work out some of the issues with which Jean Toomer and Georgia Douglass Johnson wrestled. How are class and color related? Does middle-classness short-circuit one from sympathy with the black folk? Is one still black if one elects to depict characters who are not, or *black* characters who have *white* friends and lovers? Crossing boundaries of every kind seems to be the order of the day. And these young writers have their popular counterparts in texts by Terry McMillan, Connie Briscoe, and Paul Beatty.

But the jungle is still here. It is manifested in Ann Allen Shockley's demonizing of black men in her lesbian novel, *Loving Her* (1974), as well as in the autobiographical mode that many writers continue to adopt. Because they thought that was what publishers and readers wanted to hear, or because they thought they could profit from demonizing themselves, Kody Scott in his autobiographical *Monster: The Autobiography of an L.A. Gang Member* (1993) and Ruthie Bolton in *Gal* (1994) rival anything Carl Van Vechten included in the fictional *Nigger Heaven.* Here are black people who relish airing the sickness of their lives for public consumption. They confirm for anyone interested that the jungle is alive and well in black communities, that the primitive drives African American interaction more than any other force. They are stereotypes of violent and depraved individuals exploded into the worst imaginable scenarios. Commercial presses—in these cases Penguin and Harcourt Brace—were immediately drawn to their stories, for these were the happy publishing instances, comparable to Walker's situation with *The Color Purple,* in which black people named their own depravities. And the well-known white American novelist Josephine Humphries helped Bolton ready her personal narrative for publication. Not only did Bolton therefore please the larger public, but she also pleased her own self-appointed plantation mistress in the process.[4]

By any standard of measurement, the issues and concerns of Harlem Renaissance writers have been passed along to and through the almost four generations that have followed them. No problem was solved because more black people published their own work. No problem was solved because more black editors arrived on the scene. No problem was solved because black readership expanded. No issue was resolved because of discrimination—*or* because of integration. The same old problems surround us, whether in literary media or in the popular media. We are still a nation within a nation, one that does not intrinsically value itself. While we may have writers and artists who come along occasionally to allow us to glimpse the best even in tremendously flawed representations, such as Toni Morrison,

Romare Bearden, August Wilson, and Gordon Parks, we seem hesitant to accept those images; instead, we prefer to cling to the uglinesses that defined our existence during slavery in America. Perhaps we can change, but it is obviously not profitable for us to do so.

The jungle is alive and well, especially in the movies. It is supported by the financial plantation owners, both white and black, as well as by the good little slaves on the financial plantation. The financial plantation is direct heir to the one that prevailed in the 1920s and to which African American artists and writers responded in a variety of ways. In 1926, Langston Hughes published the essay "The Negro Artist and the Racial Mountain." It became known as a kind of manifesto for younger black writers of the Harlem Renaissance. In it, Hughes declared in this very familiar quotation: "We younger Negro artists who create now intend to express our individual dark-skinned selves without fear or shame. If white people are pleased we are glad. If they are not, it doesn't matter. We know we are beautiful. And ugly too. The tom-tom cries and the tom-tom laughs. If colored people are pleased we are glad. If they are not, their displeasure doesn't matter either. We build our temples for tomorrow, strong as we know how, and we stand on top of the mountain, free within ourselves" (Mitchell, 59). It could reasonably be argued that it mattered a *great deal* if whites were pleased during the Renaissance, and it sometimes mattered if blacks were pleased, for certainly W. E. B. Du Bois, Charles S. Johnson, and other editors could determine the winners of the *Opportunity* and *Crisis* prizes for literature. It was only with great physical trauma that Langston Hughes was able to deal with his patron's, the white Mrs. Charlotte Osgood Mason's, dislike of his focus on political issues instead of continuing as the little primitive she thought she had purchased with her fellowship support. Similarly, Vanessa L. Williams, Irma P. Hall, Vivica A. Fox, Michael Beach, Mekki Phifer, Brandon Hammond, and their fellow cast members in *Soul Food,* as well as countless other African American actresses and actors, must frequently bow to, acquiesce in, the prevailing popular, commercial notions of how characters they play will be portrayed.

In the past two decades, black actors and actresses seem to be intent more frequently than not upon pleasing their white audiences *exclusively*. The plantation mentality governing the representation of black images in the media reigns supreme. If white people are pleased, shows remain on television. If they are not, those shows are canceled. If white people—and the black people who represent white people and their interests—are pleased, films get made, no matter how they depict black people. If white people are not pleased, the films do not get made. Instead of the late twentieth and early twenty-first centuries reflecting a new kind of freedom of expression in movies, and frequently in arts and literature, they reflect more a reintroduction of voluntary slavery—that is, actresses and actors are enslaved to depraved depictions of black people for financial profit.[5] They pander to popular tastes and, though there might be much more variety in expression than there was in the late-nineteenth-century and early-twentieth-century images of black people, the ultimate effect is one of a relapse. The visual and print legacies of the Harlem Renaissance are reinstatements of positions that blacks held in the late nineteenth century and earlier. Movies such as *Soul Food,* then, are, at best, modern links in chains that enslave African American minds to the dominance of the almighty American dollar and to the insistence that African Americans must accept their own degradation if they want even the paltriest share of that dollar.

(1997, 2001)

Notes

1. Not surprisingly, Irma P. Hall plays the mother/grandmother role in both films.

2. Vanessa L. Williams's character, Terry, is also named in this masculine or transsexual pattern.

3. As one of the readers of this manuscript noted, it is only fair to point to the few actors and actresses who opt *not* to degrade themselves. Cicely Tyson, for example, is well known for refusing roles that she considered degrading to black people. Similarly, John Amos, who played the father fig-

ure on the television show *Good Times,* consistently fought to bring about positive changes in the representation of his character.

4. The African American scholar Carol Marsh-Lockett, of Georgia State University, is currently undertaking a project to examine the complexities of race and representation that are inherent in the Bolton/Humphries collaboration, and I look forward to the results of her work.

5. In terms of audience, however, it must be noted that some of the audiences lauding these despicable performances are almost exclusively black, whether it is television, movie, or stage representation of the *Mama, I Wanna Sing* variety. While I would not venture to offer a psychological explanation for black audiences' acceptance of such self-degradation, it is noteworthy that they join with the white financial backers of some of these shows in turning progress back to minstrelsy.

Works Cited

Bogle, Donald. *Toms, Coons, Mulattoes, Mammies, and Bucks: An Interpretive History of Blacks in American Films.* Rev. ed. New York: Continuum, 1994.

Boskin, Joseph. *Sambo: The Rise and Demise of an American Jester.* New York: Oxford, 1986.

Cullen, Countee. "Heritage." In *Call and Response: The Riverside Anthology of the African American Literary Tradition.* Boston: Houghton Mifflin, 1998, 910–13.

Du Bois, W. E. B., and Alain Locke. "The Younger Literary Movement." *Crisis* 27 (February 1924): 161–62.

Dunbar, Paul Laurence. "The Party." In *Lyrics of Lowly Life.* 1896. Reprint, Salem, N.H.: Ayer Company, Publishers, Inc., 1991, 199–208.

Hughes, Langston. "The Negro Artist and the Racial Mountain (1926)." In *Within the Circle,* Mitchell, ed., 55–59.

Hurston, Zora Neale. "Color Struck." In *Fire!!* 1, no. 1 (November 1926): 7–14.

Locke, Alain. "The New Negro (1925)." In *Within the Circle,* Mitchell, ed., 21–31.

Mitchell, Angelyn, ed. *Within the Circle: An Anthology of African American Literary Criticism from the Harlem Renaissance to the Present.* Durham: Duke University Press, 1994.

Nugent, Bruce. "Smoke, Lilies and Jade." In *Fire!!* 1, no. 1 (November 1926): 33–39.

Soul Food. 20th Century Fox, 1997.

Thurman, Wallace. "Cordelia the Crude." In *Fire!!* 1, no. 1 (November 1926): 5–6.

Index

Abortion, 32, 33

African American folk traditions. *See* Folklore and folk traditions

Aggression. *See* Violence

Alcohol use, 21, 22, 39, 43

Alexander, Elizabeth, 211

Algonquin Press, ix–x, 37

Alliance Theater, 203

American Dream: in Ellison's *Invisible Man,* 36–37; in Petry's *The Street,* 68–71, 72, 77, 89; in Wade's *Company Man,* 37, 39–43, 45, 46, 50

Amos, John, 214–15 (n. 3)

And do remember me (Golden), 34

And This Too Shall Pass (Harris), 205

Andrews, Benny, 118–19 (n. 2)

Andrews, Raymond: compared with other authors, xi, 92, 95; and folklore, x, xi; mythical South in work of, viii, x, 91–118, 149; suicide of, x, 91, 118, 118–19 (n. 2). Works: *Appalachee Red* (see *Appalachee Red* [Andrews]); *Baby Sweet's,* 91; *Jessie and Jesus and Cousin Claire,* 91; *The Last Radio Baby: A Memoir,* 91, 118 (n. 1); "Once upon a Time in Atlanta," 91, 118 (n. 1); *Rosiebelle Lee Wildcat Tennessee,* 91

Anger. *See* Violence

Angola Prison, 122

Animal stories and animal imagery, 60, 64–65, 67 (n. 2), 84–85, 106, 107

Another Country (Baldwin), 19, 20, 24, 33, 49

Appalachee Red (Andrews): animal imagery in, 106, 107; Appalachee Red in, 95–97, 99, 103–18 passim, 119 (n. 8), 120 (n. 10); award for, 92; Baby Sweet Jackson in, 98, 100, 105–17 passim, 119 (nn. 7–8); "bad nigger" syndrome in, 107; biblical references in, 95–96, 99, 101, 119 (n. 4); Big Apple in, 94, 105, 106, 107, 111, 113, 114, 117; Big Man Thompson in, 96–98, 101–2; Blue in, 107, 115, 117–18; Cadillac owned by Red in, 110, 111, 114, 116, 120 (n. 10); Clyde "Boots" White in, 94–117 passim, 119 (nn. 7–8); Dark Town and Light Town in, 93, 100; death of Big Man in, 101–2; death of Boots White in, 116, 117; death of Little Bit in, 115, 117; football in, 92, 94; Hard Labor Holers in, 97–98, 99, 100, 109, 111, 114; heroic nature of Red in, 110–11, 113–15; humor in, 92, 94; injustice versus justice in, 95–96, 99, 102–3; irony in, 106, 117; Jake "Ol' Crip" Turner in, 98–100, 119 (n. 5); John Morgan in, 96, 97, 98, 115, 116; Ku Klux Klan in, 100, 102; lack of narrative closure in, 116–17; language use in, 92, 94; Little Bit Thompson in, 96–98, 101–2, 103, 106, 107, 111, 115, 117; manhood in, 97–98, 107–11; Mist' Ed in, 98, 99–100; mystery surrounding Red in, 97, 103–9, 116–17; mythical South in, 92–118; narrative style in, 92–93, 94; Poor Boy Jackson in, 100, 112; publication date of, 91; race of Red in, 104–5,

Appalachee Red (Andrews) (*continued*)
110; Red's disappearance at end of,
116–18, 120 (n. 10); Roxanne in, 103,
105, 106, 107, 115–16, 118; Sam in,
105–6, 107, 109, 113; Sam's/Red's
Café in, 93, 97, 100, 101, 105–6, 109,
110, 112, 113, 117; satanic figures in,
96, 99, 106, 111; sexuality in, 96–100,
105–9, 112, 116, 117, 119 (n. 8);
Snake in, 111, 113–15; stereotypical
roles of women in, 111–12; violence
in, 96–102, 116; White House in, 94,
96, 97, 98, 106; Yankee Town in, 96,
101
Archangel Gabriel, 162–63, 174 (n. 2)
Architecture: in Morrison's works, 68;
in Petry's *The Street,* 68–89
"Ark of Bones" (Dumas), xii, 141,
142–43
"Ark of Bones" and Other Stories (Dumas),
142, 145–46, 147 (n. 2)
"Aunt Sue's Stories" (Hughes), 198
Autobiography: by Andrews, 91, 118
(n. 1); in Baldwin's *Go Tell It on the
Mountain,* 54; by Bolton, 212; by
Hughes, 51; by Hurston, viii (see also
Dust Tracks on a Road [Hurston]);
by Scott, 212; self-demonizing in
contemporary autobiographies by
African Americans, 212; up-by-
the-bootstraps myth in, 51, 53; in
Wright's *Native Son,* 51
Autobiography of an Ex–Colored Man, The
(Johnson), 191–92
Autobiography of Miss Jane Pittman, The
(Gaines), 178–79

Baby Sweet's (Andrews), 91
"Bad nigger" syndrome, 107
Bailey's Cafe (Naylor), 49
Baldwin, James: attempts of, to escape
from U.S., 29; bisexuality in works
by, 19, 29; on black middle class, 199;
conferences on, vii, ix; cross-dressing,

foppish men ("fairies") in works
by, 19, 20; education of, 54; female
characters of, 32; homosexuality in
works by, 18–29, 33; manhood in
works by, 18–29; race in *Giovanni's
Room,* 24–27, 30 (n. 2), 33; stereotypes
in works by, 28–29. Works: *Another
Country,* 19, 20, 24, 33, 49; *Giovanni's
Room* (see *Giovanni's Room* [Baldwin]);
Go Tell It on the Mountain, 28, 32, 54,
61, 185; "Going to Meet the Man,"
26–27; *If Beale Street Could Talk,* 138
(n. 1); *Just above My Head,* 19, 28;
"Sonny's Blues," 21
Bambara, Toni Cade, xiii, 140, 143
Baps, 209
"Baptism" (McKay), 138 (n. 2)
Beach, Michael, 213
Bearden, Romare, 213
Beatty, Paul, 211
Beavers, Louise, 197
Beloved (Morrison), xii–xiii, 68, 137, 140,
143, 144, 147 (n. 1), 170
Berry, Halle, 209
"Best-foot-forward" literature, 34–35,
198–99
Biblical references: in Andrews's
Appalachee Red, 95–96, 99, 101, 119 (n.
4); in Baldwin's *Giovanni's Room,* 23;
in Dumas's "Ark of Bones," 142–43;
in Ellison's *Juneteenth,* 193–94; in
Hurston's *Dust Tracks on a Road,* 57;
in Kenan's "The Foundations of the
Earth," 166, 170, 172–73; in spirituals,
16; in Wilson's *Joe Turner's Come and
Gone,* 136. *See also* Christianity
Big Mama Stories, The (Youngblood), 207
Birth of a Nation, 209
Black churches. *See* Churches
Black folk traditions. *See* Folklore and
folk traditions
Black Muslims, 123
Blackness: in Baldwin's *Another Country,*
24, 33; "chocklit geography" of

Andrews's *Appalachee Red,* 92–93; in Ellison's *Invisible Man,* 38–39; in Ellison's *Juneteenth,* 177, 183, 190–92; of homosexuality in Baldwin's *Giovanni's Room,* 19–20, 22, 24–29, 30 (n. 2); in Hughes's "The Negro Artist and the Racial Mountain," 213; in Kelley's *A Different Drummer,* 149–59; in movies, 196–203, 209–10, 213; and "niggerishness," 41–43, 50; stereotypes of, in Baldwin's works, 28–29; in television programs and theater productions, 203–5, 214–15 (n. 3), 215 (n. 5); in Wade's *Company Man,* 38, 39, 41–45, 47–50; white-black reversals in Kenan's "The Foundations of the Earth," 171; whites' blindness toward blacks in Kelley's *A Different Drummer,* 157–58. *See also* Colorphobia and pigmentocracy; Race

Blanche among the Talented Tenth (Neely), 210

"Blood Burning Moon" (Toomer), 108

Blues paradigm, 2, 9–10, 14–16, 44, 75, 119 (n. 5), 139 (n. 5)

Bluest Eye, The (Morrison), 14, 32, 33, 34, 41, 146, 183, 210

Body: in Petry's *The Street,* 73, 81–89. *See also* Sexuality

Bogle, Donald, 197

Bolton, Ruthie, 212, 215 (n. 4)

Boskin, Joseph, 158, 204

Brer Rabbit tales, 64–65

Briscoe, Connie, 211

Brooks, Cleanth, xi, 208

Brown, Sterling, 120 (n. 10), 122

Brown, William Wells, 40

Buffalo Soldiers, 44–45

Callahan, John F., 176, 194 (n. 1)

Campbell, Joseph, 53

Cane (Toomer), 32, 191, 206

Carter, Nell, 204

Censorship of black writers, 31–36

Chesnutt, Charles, 24–25, 34–35, 197, 201, 210

Childress, Alice, viii, 6

Christianity: and archangel Gabriel, 162–63, 174 (n. 2); and Baldwin, 29; and black female characters, 31–32; and calling of black ministers, 143–44, 179–80; Dumas on, 144; in Dumas's "Ark of the Bones," 143–44; in Ellison's *Juneteenth,* 180–87; and folk traditions, 16; in Kenan's "The Foundations of the Earth," 161–74; in Morrison's *Beloved,* 137, 144, 170; in Wilson's *Joe Turner's Come and Gone,* 136–37. *See also* Biblical references

Churches, 16, 29, 31–32, 143, 163, 179–80. *See also* Christianity

"Clarence and the Dead" (Kenan), xii, 160

Class issues, 15, 198–202, 211

Cleaver, Eldridge, 45

Cliff, Michelle, 206

Color imagery. *See* Blackness; Whiteness

Color prejudice, 29 (n. 1), 93, 183, 207–11

Color Purple, The (Walker): abuse and brutality against Celie in, 1, 2, 13–14, 16–17, 207, 212; aftershock to humor in, 8–9; Albert and Shug in, 16; Albert's beating of Celie in, 13, 16, 35; Albert's compliments to Nettie in, 9–10; and blues transcendence, 2, 9–10, 14–15; Celie as storyteller in, 6–7, 12–13; Celie's abbreviated humor references in, 2–3; Celie's ability to find humor amid abusive oppression, 2, 13–17; Celie's daughter, 15; Celie's lower-class speech in, 15; and Celie's spitting in water glass, 15, 17 (n. 2); criticism of, by Harris-Lopez, viii–ix; dream house drawing in, 8–9; escape/entertainment function of humor in, 8–9; fights between

Color Purple, The (Walker) (*continued*)
Harpo and Sofia in, 2–8, 13, 15; film version of, 13; folk tradition in, 207; Harpo's eating binges in, 5–8; humor in, vii, ix, 1–17; incest in, 34, 35; joke delivery in, 6, 8; lesbianism in, 15, 33, 35; Nettie in, 9–10; ordering of details and humor in, 6–7; rhythm of Celie's narration in, 7; Shug in, 8–9, 14, 16; signifying in, 3–5; smoking pot in, 12–13; Sofia's advice to Celie, 15; Sofia's response to Miss Eleanor Jane's son in, 10–12; Sofia's treatment by mayor and his wife in, 13; survival strategy of humor in, 9–10; synthesis of seeming dichotomies in, 15–17; women's laughter in, 16
Color Struck (Hurston), 208, 210
Colorphobia and pigmentocracy, 29 (n. 1), 93, 183, 207–11
Company Man (Wade): alcohol use in, 39, 43; American Dream in, 37, 39–43, 46, 50; Billy's identity in, 47–49; Billy's journal writing in, 37, 45–46; Billy's loss of cultural codes in, 44–45; Billy's relationship with Donna in, 45–46; Billy's self-delusion in, 45–46; Billy's suicide attempt in, 37, 45, 49; Billy's "thingafication" in, 45; Billy's wife in, 37, 39, 40–41, 47; compared with Ellison's *Invisible Man,* ix, 31, 37–50; food in, 43; grandmother's voice in, 41, 49; Haviland in, 43, 45, 49; homosexuality in, 31, 46–47, 49, 50; irony in, 46; manhood in, 38, 41, 50; mental instability in, 31, 37, 45, 50; "niggerishness" in, 41–43, 50; Paul in, 45, 46–47; publication of, vii, ix–x; race in, 38–39, 41–45, 47–50; sexuality in, 38, 40–42, 45–47, 50; strike of black machinists in, 43–44
Conner, Bull, 94
Contact lenses, 209, 210
"Cordelia the Crude" (Thurman), 205

"Cornsilk" (Kenan), 34, 161
Cortez, Jane, 146
"Crazy nigger," 32–33, 50. *See also* Mental instability
Criminal justice system. *See* Prisons
Crisis, 206, 213
"Cross" (Hughes), 95
Cullen, Countee, 199

Dance, Daryl Cumber, 120 (n. 10)
"Dark Room Collective, The," 211
Darkness. *See* Blackness; Colorphobia and pigmentocracy
Daughters (Marshall), 33, 34
Davis, Angela, 146
Day of Absence (Ward), xi, 150
De Veaux, Alexis, 206
Def Comedy Jam, 204
Dem (Kelley), xi
Devil, 72, 96, 99, 106, 111, 145
Dichotomies, synthesis of, 15–17
Different Drummer, A (Kelley): African in, xi, 150, 151–53, 155; Bethrah in, 155; Caliban name in, 153–54; disappearance of blacks from, 149–50, 155–57; folkloristic quality of, xi; irony in, 154, 155; killing of land by Tucker Caliban in, 150–51, 154–55; lynching in, 156, 158; Mister Harper in, 152, 155–58; narrative posture in, xi; southern landscape of, 149; Tucker Caliban in, xi, 150–59; whites' blindness toward blacks in, 157–58; Willson family in, 150–57
Dixon, Thomas, 204
Dog imagery, 84–85
Domestic violence: in Petry's *The Street,* 82–86, 88; in Walker's *The Color Purple,* 1, 2–8, 13–17, 35, 207, 212. *See also* Violence
Douglass, Frederick, 99, 119 (n. 6), 207
Dove, Rita, 182
Dozens, 44
Du Bois, W. E. B., 198–99, 206, 210, 213

Dualities, 15–17

Dumas, Henry: biographical information on, 141; on Christianity, 144; death of, xiii, 141, 145–46; and Eastern religion, 141; and folklore, 144–45; as influence on Morrison, xiii, 140–47; writings by and themes of, 141–42, 145–47, 147 (n. 2). Works: "Ark of Bones," xii, 141, 142–43; *"Ark of Bones" and Other Stories,* 142, 145–46, 147 (n. 2); *Goodbye Sweetwater,* 147 (nn. 2–3); *Jonoah and the Green Stone,* 146, 147 (n. 2); *Knees of a Natural Man,* 147 (n. 2); *Play Ebony: Play Ivory,* 145–46, 147 (n. 2); "Rain God," 144–45, 147 (n. 3); *Rope of Wind and Other Stories,* 147 (n. 2)

Dunbar, Paul Laurence, 204, 209

Dust Tracks on a Road (Hurston): backfiring of expectations in, 53–55; Big Sweet in, 61–64, 65; birth of Hurston in, 53–54; chronology and structure of, 52, 55; commercial success of, 66; essayistic digressions in, 52, 55; folklore and folk culture in, 60, 64–66; founding of Eatonville in, 53; humor in, 57, 66; Hurston's resistance to publishing control over, 51–67; literary career of Hurston in, 55; Lucy in, 61–62; mythic dimensions of, 53–55, 66; opinion on imperialism in, 52; publication of, 51; race in, 53–55; revisions of, 51, 52, 60; school experiences of Hurston in, 54–55, 57–58; sexism and racism in, 52; sexuality in, 52; stepmother in, 58–61; violence in, 56–64; voodoo in, 62–63; Walker on, 52; white people in, 53–55

Ellis, Trey, 211

Ellison, Ralph: Callahan as literary executor and editor of, 176; comparison between Wade's *Company Man* and, 31, 32, 33–50; death of, 38; failure of racial calling in *Juneteenth* by, 175–94; female characters of, 32; humor in *Invisible Man,* 14–15; incest in fiction of, 32, 34, 35. See also *Invisible Man* (Ellison); *Juneteenth* (Ellison)

Ervin, Hazel Arnett, x, 69, 70, 89–90 (nn. 1–2)

Evers, Medgar, 179

Evil versus good, 15–17

Eye color, 209, 210

Families. See Fathers; Mothers/grandmothers

Family Matters, 204

Fathers: in Ellison's *Juneteenth,* 176–78, 180–94; in *Good Times,* 215 (n. 3); grandfather's voice in Ellison's *Invisible Man,* 49; in Petry's *The Street,* 71; in Wilson's plays, 125–28, 136, 137. See also Manhood

Faulkner, William, 91, 92, 149

Female characters. See Mothers/grandmothers; Prostitutes; *and entries for specific works*

Fences (Wilson), 124–29, 138 (n. 3), 139 (n. 5), 174 (n. 2)

Ferris, Bill, 143, 180

Fiedler, Leslie A., 27

Fighting. See Violence

Fire!!, 205, 208

Flagellants, The (Polite), 211

Folklore and folk traditions: Andrews's use of, x; Brer Rabbit tales, 64–65; dozens, 44; and Dumas, 144; folk sayings, 44; folk sermonic tradition, 181; and Harlem Renaissance, 206; in Hurston's *Dust Tracks on a Road,* 60; in Kelley's *A Different Drummer,* xi; "The Knee-High Man," 2; Mason on the pastoral, 207; in Morrison's works, 145; nicknames, 44; on saviors for black community, 179; signifying,

Folklore and folk traditions (*continued*)
3–5; "The Signifying Monkey," 39;
spitting in white's water glass, 17 (n.
2); "Stagolee," 39, 65; tar baby story,
145; toast tradition, 39; violence
in African American folktales, 60,
64–65; voodoo and Hurston, 62–63;
in Walker's *The Color Purple,* 207
Food: in Ellison's *Invisible Man,* 43;
Harpo's eating binges in Walker's *The
Color Purple,* 5–8; in Kenan's "The
Foundations of the Earth," 164–65;
soul food, xiv, 198; in Wade's *Company
of Men,* 43
"Foundations of the Earth, The"
(Kenan): Christianity in, 161–74;
Edward in, 161–63, 166, 170, 172,
173; Emma Lewis in, 164–65; food
in, 164–65; Gabriel in, 162–68,
170–73; Henrietta Fuchee in, 163–74;
homosexuality in, 161–63, 166,
170–73; Maggie MacGowan Williams
in, 161–63, 165–74; meanings of
"foundations of the earth" in,
171–74; Minrose Gwin on, xii;
Morton Henry in, 164, 166–71;
Rev. Hezekiah Barden in, 163–74;
reversals in, 171; salt imagery
in, 170; television watching in,
164, 165, 166; themes of, 161,
171–74
Fox, Vivica A., 213
Franklin, Benjamin, 70, 77, 89
Funkiness, 41–42, 50

Gabriel (archangel), 162–63, 174 (n. 2)
Gaines, Ernest, 178–79, 197
Gal (Bolton), 212
Garden of Eden imagery, 23
Garner, Margaret, 140
Gayness. *See* Homosexuality
Gender roles. *See* Fathers; Manhood;
Mothers/grandmothers
Georgia State University, 215 (n. 4)

*Get Your Ass in the Water and Swim Like
Me* (Jackson), 138 (n. 1)
Gimme a Break, 204
Giovanni's Room (Baldwin): alcohol use
in, 21, 22; bisexuality in, 19, 29; as
"coming out" novel, 29; David in,
19–28; death of Giovanni in, 18, 29;
"fairies" in, 20; Garden of Eden
imagery in, 23; Giovanni in, 18, 20,
22–29; Giovanni's room as mirror
image of David's mind in, 22–23;
Hella in, 21, 22, 26, 28; homophobia
in, 28; homosexuality in, 18–29, 33;
"housewife" role of David in, 23, 26;
irony in, 28–29; Jacques in, 26; Joey
in, 19–22, 25, 26, 30 (n. 2); manhood
in, 18–29; power/subjugation in
relationships in, 26–28; race in,
24–27, 30 (n. 2), 33; self-delusion by
David in, 21–24, 29; Sue in, 27, 28
Go Tell It on the Mountain (Baldwin), 28,
32, 54, 61, 185
God's Trombones (Johnson), 162
"Going to Meet the Man" (Baldwin),
26–27
Goldberg, Whoopi, 13
Golden, Marita, 34
Gomez, Jewelle, 206
Gone with the Wind (movie), 197
Good Times, 204, 215 (n. 3)
Good versus evil, 15–17
Goodbye Sweetwater (Dumas), 147 (nn.
2–3)
Grandmothers. *See* Moth-
ers/grandmothers
Griffith, D. W., 209
Grimke, Angelina, 206
Gwin, Minrose, xii

Hair straightening and hair color, 208–9,
210
Hall, Irma P., 213, 214 (n. 1)
Hammond, Brandon, 213
Hansberry, Lorraine, 32, 197, 203

Harcourt Brace, 212

Harlem Renaissance, xiii–xiv, 42, 196, 198, 199, 202–15 passim

Harris, E. Lynn, 205

Hemenway, Robert, 51, 66

Hemingway, Ernest, 91

"Heritage" (Cullen), 199

Hero with a Thousand Faces, The (Campbell), 53

Herron, Carolivia, 206

"Hobo Blues" (Hooker), 15–16

Home to Harlem (McKay), 204

Homophobia, 28, 162. *See also* Homosexuality

Homosexuality: in Baldwin's *Giovanni's Room,* 18–29, 33; in Baldwin's novels generally, 18–19, 33; "blackness" of, in Baldwin's *Giovanni's Room,* 19–20, 22, 24–29; "fairies" in Baldwin's works, 19, 20; in Harris's works, 205; and homophobia of homosexuals, 28; homosexuals as Other, 25; in Kenan's "The Foundations of the Earth," 161–63, 166, 170–73; in Kenan's *A Visitation of Spirits,* 49; and manhood, 18–29; in Nugent's "Smoke Lilies and Jade," 205; as taboo topic for black writers, 33–34; in Wade's *Company Man,* 31, 46–47, 49, 50. *See also* Lesbianism

Hooker, John D., 15–16

Hughes, Langston: in Andrews's *Appalachee Red,* 95; autobiography of, 51; as poet laureate of Harlem, 206; white patron of, 213. Works: "Aunt Sue's Stories," 198; "Cross," 95; "Me and the Mule," 95; "The Negro Artist and the Racial Mountain," 213; "Song for a Dark Girl," 95; "The Weary Blues," 14, 16

Hull, Gloria Akasha, 206

Humor: in Andrews's *Appalachee Red,* 92, 94; in Ellison's *Invisible Man,* 14–15; escape/entertainment function of, 8–9; in Hurston's *Dust Tracks on a Road,* 57, 66; inappropriate humor in television programs and theater productions, 203–5; and signifying, 3–5; and storytelling tradition, 6–7, 12–13; as survival strategy, 9–10; and synthesis of seeming dichotomies, 15–17; in Walker's *The Color Purple,* vii, ix, 1–17

Humphries, Josephine, 212

Huntsville Prison, 122

Hurston, Zora Neale: autobiography of, viii (see also *Dust Tracks on a Road* [Hurston]); birth of, 53–54; conference on, ix; finances of, 52; on founding of Eatonville, 53; literary career of, 55, 66; reading by, 57; on relief from oppression, ix; resistance of, to publishing control over *Dust Tracks on a Road,* 51–67; school experiences of, 54–55, 57–58; themes of, 206–7; and voodoo, 62–63; Walker on, 52; white patron of, 63. Works: *Color Struck,* 208, 210; *Dust Tracks on a Road* (see *Dust Tracks on a Road* [Hurston]); *Jonah's Gourd Vine,* 60; *Mules and Men,* 63; *Their Eyes Were Watching God,* 197

Imperialism, 52

Incest, 34, 35, 161

Insanity. *See* Mental instability

Invisible Life (Harris), 205

Invisible Man (Ellison): American experience in, 35–37; Bledsoe's success in, 40; compared with Wade's *Company Man,* ix, x, 31, 37–50; food in, 43; grandfather's voice in, 49; Harlem riot in, 48; history as boomerang in, 206; humor in, 14–15; incest in, 32, 34, 35; irony in, 46; language in, 192; loss of folk traditions in, 44; manhood in, 36–37; Mary Rambo in, 32, 43; mental

Invisible Man (Ellison) (*continued*)
instability in, 36; race in, 38–39, 48;
scapegoating in, 25; sexuality in,
36–37, 41, 47; socially elite white men
in, 25

Irony: in Andrews's *Appalachee Red,* 106,
117; in Baldwin's *Giovanni's Room,*
28–29; in Ellison's *Invisible Man,* 46;
in Ellison's *Juneteenth,* 184, 188; in
Kelley's *A Different Drummer,* 154,
155; in Wade's *Company Man,* 46

Jackson, Bruce, 122, 138 (n. 1)
Jessie and Jesus and Cousin Claire
(Andrews), 91
Joe Turner's Come and Gone (Wilson), 119
(n. 5), 123, 124, 134–38
Johnson, Charles S., 213
Johnson, Georgia Douglas, 206, 211
Johnson, Jack, 179
Johnson, James Weldon, 162, 191–92,
198–99
Joke delivery, 8
Jonah's Gourd Vine (Hurston), 60
Jonoah and the Green Stone (Dumas), 146,
147 (n. 2)
Juneteenth (Ellison): birth of Bliss
in, 176–77, 193; Bliss as "chosen
one" in, 177, 178, 180–81, 183–89;
Bliss/Senator Adam Sunraider in,
175–94 passim, 194 (n. 1); Bliss's
desire for a mother in, 181–83, 186,
191, 193; Christianity in, 180–87;
coffin scheme in, 180–82, 184–85,
186, 189, 191, 193; criticisms of, xiii;
failure of racial calling in, 175–94;
fatherhood in, 176–78, 180–94;
Hickman in, 176–78, 180–94; identity
issues for Bliss in, 191–92; irony
in, 184, 188; language problem in,
192–94; lynching in, 176; meaning
of title of, 175; movies in, 181, 183,
189–90, 192, 193; naming of Bliss in,
177, 188, 189; posthumous editing

and publication of, 176, 194 (n. 1);
race and racism in, 177, 183, 190–92;
reflections on actions in text in, 178;
sexuality in, 182, 190–91; shooting
of Bliss in, 187, 190; themes of, 176;
violence in, 176, 177, 178
Just above My Head (Baldwin), 19, 28
Just As I Am (Harris), 205

Kelley, William Melvin, xi, 149–59. See
also *Different Drummer, A* (Kelley)
Kenan, Randall: Christianity in works
by, 161–74; compared with Andrews,
92; homosexuality in fiction by, 161–
63, 166, 170–73; southern landscape
of, 149, 160. Works: "Clarence and
the Dead," xii, 160; "Cornsilk," 34,
161; "The Foundations of the Earth"
(*see* "Foundations of the Earth, The"
[Kenan]); *Let the Dead Bury Their
Dead,* 34, 92, 160; "Things of This
World," 160–61; *A Visitation of Spirits,*
49, 92, 160
Kennedy, John F., 117
King, Martin Luther, Jr., 179
"Knee-High Man, The," 2
Knees of a Natural Man (Dumas), 147 (n.
2)
Komunyakaa, Yusef, 119 (n. 8)
Ku Klux Klan, 100, 102

Larsen, Nella, 32, 34, 211
Lash, John S., 30 (n. 2)
Last Radio Baby: A Memoir, The
(Andrews), 91, 118 (n. 1)
Law enforcement. *See* Prisons
Lee, Andrea, 211
Legal system. *See* Prisons
Leon, Kenny, 203
Lesbianism, 15, 33–34, 35, 206, 212
Lesson before Dying, A (Gaines), 197
Let the Dead Bury Their Dead (Kenan),
34, 92, 160
Levine, Lawrence, 65, 67 (n. 2)

Lewis, Cudjo, 55
Like One of the Family (Childress), 6
Lippincott, Bertram, 51, 53, 55, 56
Literature of the American South: A Norton Anthology, xii
Living Is Easy (West), 211
Living Single, 204
Locke, Alain, 63, 203–4, 206
"Long Black Song" (Wright), 133
"Long Gone" (Brown), 120 (n. 10)
Long Gone (Dance), 120 (n. 10)
Louis, Joe, 111, 179
Loving Her (Shockley), 33, 212
Lynching, 156, 158, 176

Ma Rainey's Black Bottom (Wilson), 139 (n. 7)
Male characters. *See* Fathers; Manhood; *and entries for specific works*
Male homosexuality. *See* Homosexuality
Mama Day (Naylor), 92
Mama, I Wanna Sing, 203, 209, 215 (n. 5)
Manhood: in Andrews's *Appalachee Red,* 97–98, 107–11; in Baldwin's *Giovanni's Room,* 18–29; and Cadillac ownership, 110, 111, 114, 116, 120 (n. 10); in Ellison's *Invisible Man,* 36–37; Harpo's fights with Sofia in Walker's *The Color Purple,* 2–8, 13, 15; and homosexuality, 18–29; and power/subjugation in relationships, 26–28; and prison experiences, 121–24, 127, 128, 130–32; in *Soul Food,* 196, 199–202; in Wade's *Company Man,* 38, 41, 50; in Walker's *The Color Purple,* 2–10, 13, 15, 16, 35; and whiteness, 27; in Wilson's plays, 121–24, 127, 128, 130–32, 137. *See also* Fathers
Marley, Bob, 44
Marrow of Tradition, The (Chesnutt), 197
"Mars Jeems's Nightmare" (Chesnutt), 24–25
Marsh-Lockett, Carol, 215 (n. 4)

Marshall, Paule, 33, 34
Martin, 204
Mason, Charlotte Osgood, 63, 213
Mason, Ted, 207
McCorkle, Jill, x
McDaniel, Hattie, 197
McKay, Claude, 138 (n. 2), 204
McMillan, Terry, 34, 211
"Me and the Mule" (Hughes), 95
Media. *See* Movies; Television; Theater productions
Men characters. *See* Fathers; Manhood; *and entries for specific works*
Mental instability, 31, 32–33, 36, 37, 45, 50
Meridian (Walker), 33
Merritt, Theresa, 204
Middle class. *See* Class issues
Minstrel tradition, 158, 215 (n. 5)
Monster: The Autobiography of an L.A. Gang Member (Scott), 212
Montgomery Bus Boycott, 154
Morrison, Toni: architecture in works by, 68; Bambara's influences on, xiii, 140; on characterization, 105; on colorphobia and stereotypes, 29 (n. 1); compared with Andrews, 95; Dumas's influences on, xiii, 140–47; as editor at Random House, 140, 141, 145–47; folklore in works by, 145; on funkiness, 41; honors and awards for, 140, 146; incest in fiction of, 34; insanity in fiction of, 32; on readers' participation with narrative, 2; significance of, 212–13. Works: *Beloved,* xii–xiii, 68, 137, 140, 143, 144, 147 (n. 1), 170; *The Bluest Eye,* 14, 32, 33, 34, 41, 146, 183, 210; *Playing in the Dark,* 29 (n. 1); *Song of Solomon,* 15, 47; *Sula,* 33, 34, 68, 127, 143, 146; *Tar Baby,* 85, 108, 141, 145
Mothers/grandmothers: in Andrews's *Appalachee Red,* 96, 97, 115, 117; in Chesnutt's *The Marrow of Tradition,*

Mothers/grandmothers (*continued*) 197; consequences for family role of, 197–98; in Ellison's *Juneteenth,* 176–77, 181–83, 186, 191, 193; in Gaines's *A Lesson before Dying,* 197; in Hansberry's *A Raisin in the Sun,* 32, 197; in Hughes's works, 198; in Hurston's *Color Struck,* 208, 210; in Hurston's *Dust Tracks on a Road,* 53–54, 58–61; in Hurston's *Their Eyes Were Watching God,* 197; in Kenan's "The Foundations of the Earth," 161–63, 165–74; "masculine" names of, 198, 214 (n. 2); Miss Eleanor Jane's son in Walker's *The Color Purple,* 10–12; in Morrison's *Sula,* 127; in *Nothing to Lose,* 197; in Petry's *The Street,* 70–71, 73; in *Soul Food,* 197–98; on television, 204; in Toomer's works, 198; in Wade's *Company Man,* 41, 49; in Wilson's *Fences,* 125; in Wilson's *Joe Turner's Come and Gone,* 135, 136

Movies: *Baps,* 209; *Birth of a Nation,* 209; in Ellison's *Juneteenth* 181, 183, 189–90, 192, 193; *Gone with the Wind,* 197; images of African Americans in, 196–203, 209–10, 213–14, 215 (n. 5); *Nothing to Lose,* 197; *Soul Food,* xiv, 196–203, 213, 214

Mules and Men (Hurston), 63

Music: blues, 2, 9–10, 14–16, 44, 75, 119 (n. 5), 139 (n. 5); in Petry's *The Street,* 75; in Walker's *The Color Purple,* 14; in Wilson's *Joe Turner's Come and Gone,* 136; work songs, 122

Narrative of the Life of Frederick Douglass (Douglass), 207

Native Son (Wright), 33, 51

Naylor, Gloria, 49, 92, 149

Neely, Barbara, 210

"Negro Artist and the Racial Mountain, The" (Hughes), 213

Nelson, Alice Dunbar, 206

New Negro, The, 63, 203–4

Nicknames, 44

Nigger Heaven (Van Vechten), 204, 212

"Niggerishness," 41–43, 50

Nothing to Lose (movie), 197

Nugent, Bruce, 205

O'Connor, Flannery, 91

"Once upon a Time in Atlanta" (Andrews), 91, 118 (n. 1)

Opportunity, 213

Other, 25, 39

Outsider, The (Wright), 63

Parchman Farm, 122, 130–32

Parks, Gordon, 213

"Party, The" (Dunbar), 204, 209

Passing (Larsen), 34, 211

Patrons. *See* White patrons

Peachtree Publishers, 118 (n. 1)

Penguin, 212

Petry, Ann, viii, x, 32, 68–89. See also *Street, The* (Petry)

Phifer, Mekki, 213

Phillips, Caryl, 142

Physical abuse. *See* Domestic violence; Violence

Piano Lesson, The (Wilson), 121–22, 124, 129–34

Pigmentocracy, 29 (n. 1), 93, 183, 207–11

Plantation mentality in the media, 202–5, 213–14

Play Ebony: Play Ivory (Dumas), 145–46, 147 (n. 2)

Playing in the Dark (Morrison), 29 (n. 1)

Poetry for My People (Dumas), 147 (n. 2)

Polite, Carlene Hatcher, 211

Possessing the Secret of Joy (Walker), 34

Primitivism, 199–202, 204, 205, 212, 213

Prisons: in Andrews's *Appalachee Red,* 96, 100–101; in Baldwin's works, 138 (n. 1); and convict leasing system, 134; and manhood for black men,

121–24, 127, 128, 130–32; in *Soul Food,* 200–201; statistics on incarceration of black men, 123; stigma of prison experience in Wilson's plays, 124, 132–33; talking about, in Wilson's plays, 123–24, 129; violence and brutality in, 122–23; in Wilson's *Fences,* 124–29, 138 (n. 3); in Wilson's *Joe Turner's Come and Gone,* 123, 124, 134–38; in Wilson's *The Piano Lesson,* 124, 129–34; in Wilson's plays, xi–xii, 121–38; work songs of, 122

Prostitutes, 79–81, 119 (n. 8), 185, 205

Publishing world and Hurston, 51–67

Quicksand (Larsen), 32, 211

Race: in Baldwin's *Another Country,* 24, 33; in Baldwin's *Giovanni's Room,* 24–27, 30 (n. 2), 33; and "best-foot-forward" literature by black writers, 34–35, 198–99; "chocklit geography" of Andrews's *Appalachee Red,* 92–93; in Ellison's *Invisible Man,* 38–39, 48; in Ellison's *Juneteenth,* 177, 183, 190–92; Gabriel as Edward's white lover in Kenan's "The Foundations of the Earth," 162–68, 170–73; in Hughes's "The Negro Artist and the Racial Mountain," 213; in Hurston's *Dust Tracks on a Road,* 53–55; in Kelley's *A Different Drummer,* 149–59; Morton Henry as white sharecropper in Kenan's "The Foundations of the Earth," 164, 166–71; in movies, 196–203, 209–10, 213–14; of Red in Andrews's *Appalachee Red,* 104–5, 110; in television programs and theater productions, 203–5, 214, 214–15 (n. 3), 215 (n. 5); in Wade's *Company Man,* 38–39, 41–45, 47–50; white-black reversals in Kenan's "The Foundations of the Earth," 171; whites' blindness toward blacks in Kelley's *A Different Drummer,* 157–58. *See also* Blackness; Whiteness

"Rain God" (Dumas), 144–45, 147 (n. 3)

Raisin in the Sun, A (Hansberry), 32, 197, 203

Rampersad, Arnold, 141

Random House, 140, 141

Rape, 76, 80, 176

Raynaud, Claudine, 52

"Really, Doesn't Crime Pay?" (Walker), 32

Redmond, Eugene B., xii, 141, 144, 146

Religion. *See* Christianity; Churches

Religious versus secular, 15–17

Rolle, Esther, 203, 204

Rope of Wind and Other Stories (Dumas), 147 (n. 2)

Rosiebelle Lee Wildcat Tennessee (Andrews), 91

Rubin, Louis D., Jr., ix

Saints, Sinners, Saviors (Harris-Lopez), 197

Salt Eaters, The (Bambara), 140, 143

Sambo: The Rise and Demise of an American Jester (Boskin), 158, 204

Sambo/clown figure, 158, 204, 209

Same-sex relationships. *See* Homosexuality; Lesbianism

Sarah Phillips (Lee), 211

Satanic figures, 72, 96, 99, 106, 111, 145

Savior role, 177–81, 183–89

Say Jesus and Come to Me (Shockley), 33

Scapegoating, 25

"Scarlet women," 32

Schmeling, Max, 179

Scott, Kody, 212

Secular versus religious, 15–17

Segregation, 118, 154

Self-mutilation, 208–10

Seven Guitars (Wilson), 139 (n. 7)

Sexual abuse. *See* Incest; Rape

Sexuality: in Andrews's *Appalachee Red,*
96, 97, 99–100, 105–9, 112, 116,
117, 119 (n. 8); in Ellison's *Invisible
Man,* 36–37, 41, 47; in Ellison's
Juneteenth, 182, 190–91; in Hurston's
Dust Tracks on a Road, 52; in Kenan's
"Cornsilk," 34, 161; in Kenan's "The
Foundations of the Earth," 161–63,
166, 170–73; in Morrison's *The Bluest
Eye,* 41; in Morrison's *Tar Baby,* 108;
and "niggerishness," 41–43, 50;
in Petry's *The Street,* 73–76, 79–81,
84–88; in *Soul Food,* 199–202, 206; in
Toomer's "Blood Burning Moon,"
108; in Toomer's *Cane,* 206; in Wade's
Company Man, 38, 40–42, 45–47, 50;
in Youngblood's *Soul Kiss,* 205–6. *See
also* Homosexuality; Lesbianism
Shakespeare, William, 153
Shannon, Sandra G., 139 (n. 5)
"Shiny men" legend, 136
Shockley, Ann Allen, 33, 212
Signifying, 3–5
"Signifying Monkey, The," 39
Skin color, 207–9
Slave narratives, 47
Slavery: and African American animal
folktales, 65; convict leasing as, 134;
in Dumas's "Ark of the Bones,"
142–43; in Kelley's *A Different
Drummer,* 151–53; in Morrison's
Beloved, 140, 144; voluntary slavery
of black actors in the media, 214;
wife's role in Wade's *Company Man*
compared with, 40
"Smoke Lilies and Jade" (Nugent), 205
"Song for a Dark Girl" (Hughes), 95
Song of Solomon (Morrison), 15, 47
"Sonny's Blues" (Baldwin), 21
Soul food, xiv, 198
Soul Food (movie): actors in, 213;
"bourgeois realism" in, 198–200;
conference presentation on, xiv;
Kenny and Max in, 198, 202;

Lem/Boo in, 200–202; manhood in,
196, 199–202; mother/grandmother
in, 197, 198; sexuality in, 199–202,
206; Terry and Miles in, 198–200,
202; various reactions to, 196, 214
Soul Kiss (Youngblood), 205–6
"South of tradition," viii
Southern Road (Brown), 122
Spitting in water glass, 15, 17 (n. 2)
"Stagolee," 39, 65
Street, The (Petry): American Dream in,
68–71, 72, 77, 89; body in, 73, 81–89;
Boots Smith in, 32, 73, 74, 75–77, 79;
dog in, 84–85; domestic violence in,
82–86, 88; fire in apartment building
in, 78–79; houses and apartments
in, 68–89; Jones the super in, 72–74,
75, 77, 79, 80, 82–88; Junto Bar and
Grill in, 74, 75, 80; Junto in, 73–76,
78–80; living buildings in, 89; locks
and keys in, 72–73, 76, 85–87; Lutie
Johnson in, 32, 68–77, 80–88 passim;
Lutie's father in, 71; Lutie's killing of
Boots Smith in, 32, 76–77; Min in,
viii, x, 68–70, 80–89 passim, 90 (n. 2);
Mrs. Hedges in, 68–70, 75, 76, 78–81,
83, 88; oppressive spaces in, 74–77,
86–88, 89, 90 (n. 3); Prophet David
in, 80, 83, 85, 86; prostitution in,
79–81; pushcart man in, 88; sexuality
in, 73–76, 79–81, 84–88; whites
in, 70–71, 78; women and survival
strategies in, 68–89
Subservient role of black female
characters, 31–32
Suicide and suicide attempts, 24, 37, 45,
49
Sula (Morrison), 33, 34, 68, 127, 143,
146
Supernatural, 143, 144–45, 160–61
Synthesis of dichotomies, 15–17

Taboo topics for black writers, 31–36
Tar Baby (Morrison), 85, 108, 141, 145

Taylor, Clyde, 142, 144
Television, 164, 165, 166, 204, 214, 214–15 (n. 3), 215 (n. 5)
Tempest, The (Shakespeare), 153
That's My Mama, 204
Theater productions, 203–5, 214, 215 (n. 5)
Their Eyes Were Watching God (Hurston), 197
"Things of This World" (Kenan), 160–61
Thomas and Beulah (Dove), 182
Thurman, Wallace, 205
Toast tradition, 39
Toms, Coons, Mulattoes, Mammies, and Bucks (Bogle), 197
Toomer, Jean, 32, 108, 191, 198, 206, 207, 210, 211
Traylor, Eleanor W., 147 (n. 1)
Trickster tales, 65, 67 (n. 2)
"Tu Do Street" (Komunyakaa), 119 (n. 8)
Turner, Joe, 119 (n. 5), 134, 135–36, 139 (n. 6)
Two Black Churches (Ferris), 143, 180
Tyson, Cicely, 214 (n. 3)

University of Georgia Press, 91
Up-by-the-bootstraps myth, 51, 53

Van Peebles, Melvin, 146
Van Vechten, Carl, 204, 212
Violence: in African American folktales, 60, 64–65; in Andrews's *Appalachee Red,* 96–102, 116; in Bolton's *Gal,* 212; in Ellison's *Juneteenth,* 176, 177, 178; in Gaines's *The Autobiography of Miss Jane Pittman,* 179; in Hurston's *Dust Tracks on a Road,* 56–64; in Kelley's *A Different Drummer,* 156, 158; and Ku Klux Klan, 100, 102; in Petry's *The Street,* 32, 76–77, 82–86, 88; in prisons, 122–23; in Scott's *Monster,* 212; in Walker's *The Color Purple,* 1,

2–8, 13–17, 35, 207, 212; in Wilson's plays, 125, 132, 138, 139 (n. 7). *See also* Domestic violence; Incest; Lynching; Prisons; Rape
Visitation of Spirits, A (Kenan), 49, 92, 160
Voodoo, 62–63

Wade, Brent, vii, ix–x, 31, 37–50. See also *Company Man* (Wade)
Wade-Gayles, Gloria, 69, 90 (nn. 2–3)
Waiting to Exhale (McMillan), 34
Wake Up Dead Men (Jackson), 122, 138 (n. 1)
Walker, Alice: compared with Andrews, 91; humor in *The Color Purple* by, vii, ix, 1–17; on Hurston's *Dust Tracks on a Road,* 52; taboos in fiction of, 15, 32–35. Works: *The Color Purple* (see *Color Purple, The* [Walker]); *Meridian,* 33; *Possessing the Secret of Joy,* 34; "Really, Doesn't Crime Pay?," 32; *You Can't Keep a Good Woman Down,* 33
Walker, Madame C. J., 208
Wallace, George, 175
Ward, Douglas Turner, xi, 150
"Weary Blues, The" (Hughes), 14, 16
Wedding, The (West), 210, 211
Welty, Eudora, 91
West, Dorothy, 210, 211
White patrons, 63, 212, 213, 215 (n. 4)
Whiteness: and African American trickster tales, 65, 67 (n. 2); in Andrews's *Appalachee Red,* 104–5, 110; in Baldwin's *Giovanni's Room,* 24–27; black's spitting in white's water glass, 17 (n. 2); black-white reversals in Kenan's "The Foundations of the Earth," 171; Clyde "Boots" White in Andrews's *Appalachee Red,* 94–104, 106–10, 112, 114–17, 119 (nn. 7–8); in Ellison's *Invisible Man,* 38; in Ellison's *Juneteenth,* 176–77, 183, 190–92; Gabriel as Edward's white lover in

Whiteness (*continued*)

Kenan's "The Foundations of the Earth," 162–68, 170–73; in Hurston's *Dust Tracks on a Road,* 53–55, 63, 65; in Kelley's *A Different Drummer,* 149–59; and manhood, 27; Miss Eleanor Jane's son in Walker's *The Color Purple,* 10–12; Morrison on, 29 (n. 1); Morton Henry as white sharecropper in Kenan's "The Foundations of the Earth," 164, 166–71; in Petry's *The Street,* 70–71, 78; of Red in Andrews's *Appalachee Red,* 104–5, 110; in Wade's *Company Man,* 38; whites' blindness toward blacks in Kelley's *A Different Drummer,* 157–58. *See also* Race

Wife beating. *See* Domestic violence

"Wife of His Youth, The," (Chesnutt), 210

Williams, Bert, 204

Williams, John A., 146

Williams, Vanessa L., 198–99, 213, 214 (n. 2)

Wilson, August: appreciation of works by, 203; Christianity in plays by, 136–37; fatherhood in plays by, 125–28, 136, 137; manhood in plays by, 121–24, 127, 128, 130–32, 137; prison experiences in works by, xi–xii, 121–38; and "shiny men" legend, 136; significance of, 213; stigma of prison experience in plays by, 124, 132–33; and ten-cycle play about African Americans in twentieth century, 138. Works: *Fences,* 124–29, 138 (n. 3), 139 (n. 5), 174 (n. 2); *Joe Turner's Come and Gone,* 119 (n. 5), 123, 124, 134–38; *Ma Rainey's Black Bottom,* 139 (n. 7); *The Piano Lesson,* 121–22, 124, 129–34; *Seven Guitars,* 139 (n. 7)

Wolfe, Bernard, 65

Women characters. *See* Mothers/grandmothers; Prostitutes; *and entries for specific works*

Work songs, 122

Working class. *See* Class issues

Wright, Richard: on "ethics of living Jim Crow," 131; insanity in fiction of, 32. Works: "Long Black Song," 133; *Native Son,* 33, 51; *The Outsider,* 63

You Can't Keep a Good Woman Down (Walker), 33

Youngblood, Shay, 205–6, 207

PS 153 .N5 H295 2002

Harris-Lopez, Trudier.

South of tradition